Advanced Chinese

Edited by
Erin Quirk and Tanying Dong

Content in this program has been modified and enhanced from *Starting Out in Chinese* and *Complete Course Chinese: The Basics*, both published in 2008.

Published in the United States by Living Language, an imprint of Random House, Inc.

www.livinglanguage.com

Editor: Erin Quirk
Production Editor: Ciara Robinson
Production Manager: Tom Marshall
Interior Design: Sophie Chin
Illustrations: Sophie Chin

First Edition

Library of Congress Cataloging-in-Publication Data

Advanced Chinese / edited by Erin Quirk and Tanying Dong. — 1st ed.
p. cm.
ISBN 978-0-307-97167-8
1. Chinese language—Textbooks for foreign speakers—English. 2. Chinese language—Grammar.
3. Chinese language—Spoken Chinese. I. Quirk, Erin. II. Dong, Tanying.
PL1129.E5A38 2011
495.1'82421—dc23

2011021872

PRINTED IN THE UNITED STATES OF AMERICA

10 9 8 7 6 5 4 3 2 1

Acknowledgments

Thanks to the Living Language team: Amanda D'Acierno, Christopher Warnasch, Suzanne McQuade, Laura Riggio, Erin Quirk, Amanda Munoz, Fabrizio LaRocca, Siobhan O'Hare, Sophie Chin, Sue Daulton, Alison Skrabek, Carolyn Roth, Ciara Robinson, and Tom Marshall.

How to Use This Course **9**

UNIT 1: Asking Directions **14**

LESSON 1
Words
14

LESSON 2
Phrases
28

LESSON 3
Sentences
39

LESSON 4
Conversations
50

Zhèlǐ 这里 (here) and nàli 那里 (there)
16

Yǒu duō yuǎn? 有多远？(how far?)
30

Using lǐ 里 and zài 在 in location expressions
41

Cóng 从 ... dào 到 (from ... to ...)
54

Other location expressions
20

Expressing direction or motion with location phrases
34

Yǒu 有 (there is/there are)
46

Shì 是 (to be)
60

C O U R S E

UNIT 2: At a Restaurant 74

LESSON 5	LESSON 6	LESSON 7	LESSON 8
Words	Phrases	Sentences	Conversations
74	**85**	**97**	**106**

Making suggestions: hǎo ma? 好吗？

76

More commands and requests

80

Modal verbs

87

Negative questions

92

Polite requests

99

Adverbial expressions with de 得

102

Huòzhě/Háishi 或者/还是 (or)

109

Expressing quantities

114

OUTLINE

UNIT 3: Work and School **130**

LESSON 9
Words
130

LESSON 10
Phrases
143

LESSON 11
Sentences
151

LESSON 12
Conversations
165

Yīnggāi 应该
(*should, ought to*)
132

Making comparisons
137

The Double
Conjunction yòu ...
yòu 又 ... 又
145

Ordinal numbers
148

Functions of huì 会
153

Making equal
comparisons
157

The interrogative
wèishénme 为什么
(*why*)
168

The conjunctions
yīnwèi 因为
(*because*) and suǒyǐ
所以 (*therefore*)
the number two
(èr 二 and liǎng 两)
174

C O U R S E

UNIT 4: Doctors and Health **190**

LESSON 13
Words
190

LESSON 14
Phrases
202

LESSON 15
Sentences
211

LESSON 16
Conversations
224

The verb dǎ qiú 打球
(*to play ball*)
192

Uses of bǎ 把
196

Expressing
frequency with cì 次
or biàn 遍
204

Expressing duration
207

Indefinite pronouns

213

Expressing
conditions with rúguǒ
如果 (*if*)
218

Making comparisons
with gèng 更 (*even*)
227

Intensifying
comparisons
232

Pronunciation and Pīnyīn Guide **246**
Grammar Summary **251**
Glossary **277**

OUTLINE

How to Use This Course

Huānyíng! 欢迎! Welcome to *Living Language Advanced Chinese*!

Before we begin, let's take a quick look at what you'll see in this course.

CONTENT

Advanced Chinese is a continuation of *Intermediate Chinese*.

Now that you've mastered the basics with *Essential* and *Intermediate Chinese*, you'll take your Chinese even further with a comprehensive look at irregular verbs, advanced verb tenses, and complex sentences.

UNITS

There are four units in this course. Each unit has four lessons arranged in a "building block" structure: the first lesson will present essential *words*, the second will introduce longer *phrases*, the third will teach *sentences*, and the fourth will show how everything works together in everyday *conversations*.

At the beginning of each unit is an introduction highlighting what you will learn in that unit. At the end of each unit you'll find the Unit Essentials, which review the key information from that unit, and a self-graded Unit Quiz, which tests what you've learned.

LESSONS

There are four lessons per unit for a total of 16 lessons in the course. Each lesson has the following components:

- **Introduction** outlining what you will cover in the lesson.

- **Word Builder 1** (first lesson of the unit) presenting key words and phrases.

- **Phrase Builder 1** (second lesson of the unit) introducing longer phrases and expressions.

- **Sentence Builder 1** (third lesson of the unit) teaching sentences.

- **Conversation 1** (fourth lesson of the unit) for a natural dialogue that brings together important vocabulary and grammar from the unit.

- **Take It Further** providing extra information about the new vocabulary you just saw, expanding on certain grammar points, or introducing additional words and phrases.

- **Word/Phrase/Sentence/Conversation Practice 1** practicing what you learned in Word Builder 1, Phrase Builder 1, Sentence Builder 1, or Conversation 1.

- **Word Recall** reviewing important vocabulary and grammar from any of the previous lessons in *Essential*, *Intermediate*, or *Advanced Chinese*.

- **Grammar Builder 1** guiding you through important Chinese grammar that you need to know.

- **Work Out 1** for a comprehensive practice of what you saw in Grammar Builder 1.

- **Word Builder 2/Phrase Builder 2/Sentence Builder 2/Conversation 2** for more key words, phrases, or sentences, or a second dialogue.

- **Take It Further** for expansion on what you've seen so far and additional vocabulary.

- **Word/Phrase/Sentence/Conversation Practice 2** practicing what you learned in Word Builder 2, Phrase Builder 2, Sentence Builder 2, or Conversation 2.

- **Word Recall** reviewing important vocabulary and grammar from any of the previous lessons in *Essential*, *Intermediate*, or *Advanced Chinese*.

- **Grammar Builder 2** for more information on Chinese grammar.

- **Work Out 2** for a comprehensive practice of what you saw in Grammar Builder 2.

- **Drive It Home** ingraining an important point of Chinese grammar for the long term.

- **Culture Note** for useful cultural information related to the lesson or unit.

UNIT ESSENTIALS

You will see the **Unit Essentials** at the end of every unit. This section summarizes and reviews key grammar from the unit, and tests your knowledge of vocabulary by allowing you to fill in your very own "cheat sheet," with hints directing you back to the vocabulary in the lessons. Once you complete the blanks with the missing vocabulary, the Unit Essentials will serve as your very own reference for the most essential vocabulary and grammar from each unit.

UNIT QUIZ

After each Unit Essentials, you'll see a **Unit Quiz** testing your progress. Your quiz results will allow you to see which sections, if any, you need to review before moving on to the next unit.

PROGRESS BAR

You will see a **Progress Bar** on each page that has course material. It indicates your current position within each unit and lets you know how much progress you're making. Each line in the bar represents a Grammar Builder section.

AUDIO

Look for this symbol ⊙ to help guide you through the audio as you're reading the book. It will tell you which track to listen to for each section that has audio. When

Zhèlǐ 这里 (here) and
nàli 那里 (there)

Yǒu duō yuǎn? 有多远?
(how far?)

Other Location Expressions

Expressing Direction or Motion
with Location Phrases

ANSWER KEY
1. d; 2. a; 3. e; 4. b; 5. c

Grammar Builder 1
ZHÈLǏ 这里 (*HERE*) AND NÀLI 那里 (*THERE*)

▶ 1B Grammar Builder 1 (CD 7, Track 2)

You've already seen how the demonstrative pronouns zhè 这 (*this*) and nà 那 (*that*) combine with nouns with the help of measure words:

Zhè zhī bǐ shì wǒ de.
这支笔是我的。
This pen is mine.

Nàge fángzi hěn dà.
那个房子很大。
That house is very big.

When these demonstrative pronouns are combined with lǐ 里, which literally means *place*, they become location expressions: zhèlǐ 这里 (*here*) and nàli 那里 (*there*).

Keep in mind that nàli 那里 (*there*) is different from nǎli 哪里 (*where*), which you learned in *Intermediate Chinese*. Notice the difference in tones. Nàli 那里 comes from nà 那 (*that*) while nǎli 哪里 comes from nǎ 哪 (*which*).

In formal speech, the full forms zhèlǐ 这里 and nàli 那里 are used to indicate location:

Wǒ zài zhèlǐ.
我在这里。
I'm here. (lit., I'm at this place.)

Yǒu 有 (there is/there are)   Shì 是 (to be)

Tā de péngyou zài nàli.
他的朋友在那里。
His friend is over there (lit., His friend is at that place.)

Nàli shì tā de jiā.
那里是他的家。
That's his home. (lit., That place is his home.)

In colloquial Chinese, these forms are usually expressed as zhèr 这儿 and nàr 那儿 respectively:

Wǒ zhù zài zhèr.
我住在这儿。
I live here.

Tā de péngyou zài nàr.
他的朋友在那儿。
His friend is over there.

(II)

✎ Work Out 1

Translate the following sentences from Chinese into English.

1. Nǐ shénme shíhou lái? 你什么时候来? _____

   _____

2. Wǒ lái zhèlǐ, nǐ qù nàli. 我来这里, 你去那里。 _____

   _____

| | Other Location Expressions | Expressing Direction or Motion with Location Phrases |

3. Wǒ de shū zài nàli. 我的书在那里。_____

   _____

4. Zhèlǐ shì wǒ de jiā. 这里是我的家。_____

   _____

5. Tā zài nàli chīfàn. 他/她在那里吃饭。_____

   _____

6. Wǒ qù nàli kàn diànyǐng. 我去那里看电影。_____

   _____

ANSWER KEY

1. *When will you come here?* 2. *I'll come here. You go there.* 3. *My book is over there.* 4. *This is my home. (lit., Here is my home.)* 5. *He/She is eating over there.* 6. *I am going there to watch a movie.*

Word Builder 2

▶ 1C Word Builder 2 (CD 7, Track 3)

jiē	街	street
lùkǒu	路口	corner
hónglǜdēng	红绿灯	traffic light
shízì lùkǒu	十字路口	intersection
rénxíngdào	人行道	sidewalk
rénxíng dìdào	人行地道	underpass
lìjiāoqiáo	立交桥	overpass
chūzūchē	出租车	taxi
gōngchē	公车	bus
gōngchē zhàn	公车站	bus stop
chē/qìchē	车/汽车	car
mótuōchē	摩托车	motorcycle

Using **lǐ** 里 and **zài** 在
in Location Expressions

Cóng 从 ... **dào** 到
(*from ... to ...*)

Yǒu 有 (*there is/there are*)

Shì 是 (*to be*)

zìxíngchē	自行车	*bicycle*
huǒchē	火车	*train*
huǒchē zhàn	火车站	*train station*
dìtiě	地铁	*subway*
dìtiě zhàn	地铁站	*subway station*
chuán	船	*ship*
fēijī	飞机	*airplane*
cóng	从	*from*

(II)

✎ Word Practice 2

Fill in the blanks of the pīnyīn phrases. The Chinese characters are given for additional help and practice.

1. _____ chē zhàn

   火车站 (*train station*)

2. dì _____ zhàn

   地铁站 (*subway station*)

3. shízì _____ kǒu

   十字路口 (*intersection*)

4. rén _____ dào

   人行道 (*sidewalk*)

5. _____ chē

   公车 (*bus*)

Other Location Expressions

Tā de māo xǐhuan zài shāfā shàng shuìjiào.

她的猫喜欢在沙发上睡觉。

Her cat likes to sleep on the sofa.

Wǒ de fángzi zài shāngdiàn yòubian.

我的房子在商店右边。

My house is on the right side of the shop.

Diànhuàjiān zài cānguǎn wàibian.

电话间在餐馆外边。

The telephone booth is outside the restaurant.

Cèsuǒ zài wòshì lǐbian/lǐ.

厕所在卧室里边/里。

The toilet is inside/in the bedroom.

Wǒ de chē zài qiáo shàngbian/shàng huàile.

我的车在桥上边/上坏了。

My car broke down on the bridge.

Wǒ māma de bàngōngshì zài jǐngchájú pángbiān.

我妈妈的办公室在警察局旁边。

My mother's office is next to the police station.

Dìtiězhàn zài yóujú hé yínháng zhōngjiān.

地铁站在邮局和银行中间。

The subway station is between the post office and the bank.

Note that, in the last example, zhōngjiān 中间 links two nouns, yóujú 邮局
(*post office*) and yínháng 银行 (*bank*). Whenever something is spatially located
between two other things, their relationship is described in Chinese using the
grammatical structure zài 在 A hé 和 B zhōngjiān 中间 (*lit., at* A *and* B *between*).

When location and time expressions are both used in a sentence, the time
expression usually comes first, then the location word, and finally the main verb.
For example:

Wǒ měitiān qù gōngyuán pángbiān de xuéxiào shàngxué.
我每天去公园旁边的学校上学。
I go to school next to the park every day.

Nàge xiǎo péngyou měitiān zài wǒmen fángzi qiánbiān wán.
那个小朋友每天在我们房子前边玩。
That child (lit., little friend) plays in front of our house every day.

When a location word is used with a personal pronoun, the pronoun is
traditionally followed by the particle de: Tā de māma zài tā de qiánbian. 他的
妈妈在他的前边。 (*His mother is in front of him.*) The resulting word order
assumes the following pattern: zài 在 + pronoun + de 的 + location word.

In this case, de 的 turns tā 他 into a possessive pronoun and the location word
qiánbian 前边 acts as a noun (lit., [his] front) rather than as a preposition (*in
front*). In colloquial conversation, however, de 的 is usually dropped and the
pronoun is used on its own:

Tā de māma zài tā qiánbiān.
他的妈妈在他前边。
(*His mother is in front of him.*)

Here are some additional sentences that highlight how location words are used in
combination with personal pronouns in Chinese:

Wǒ de péngyoǔ zài wǒ (de) pángbiān.
我的朋友在我(的)旁边。
My friend is next to me.

Zhèlǐ 这里 (*here*) and
nàlǐ 那里 (*there*)

Yǒu duō yuǎn? 有多远？
(*how far?*)

Other Location Expressions

Expressing Direction or Motion
with Location Phrases

Lǎoshī zhàn zài tāmen (de) hòubian.

老师站在他们(的)后边。

The teacher is standing behind them.

✎ Work Out 2

Take a look at the following diagram, which shows eight people zuò 坐 (*sitting*) in two rows at a movie theater. Choose the appropriate location word in each of the following sentences.

MOVIE SCREEN			
Xiǎo Měi 小美	Guó Zhōng 国忠	Měi Lì 美丽	Xīn Míng 新名
Hóng Huā 红花	Zhèng Dōng 郑东	Xiù Chūn 秀春	Xué Míng 学明

1. Xiǎo Měi (小美) *is sitting* _____ (qiánbian 前边/hòubian 后边/
   zuǒbian 左边) *of Hong Hua.*

2. Hóng Huā (红花) *is sitting* _____ (qiánbian 前边/hòubian 后边/
   zuǒbian 左边) *of Zheng Dong.*

3. Zhèng Dōng (郑东) *is sitting* _____ (zhōngjiān 中间/hòubian 后边/
   zuǒbian 左边) *Hong Hua and Xiu Chun.*

4. Měi Lì (美丽) *is sitting* _____ (yòubian 右边/zhōngjiān 中间/
   zuǒbian 左边) *of Guo Zhong.*

5. Xīn Míng (新名) *is sitting* _____ (yòubian 右边/zhōngjiān 中间/
   zuǒbian 左边) *of Mei Li.*

6. Xiù Chūn (秀春) *is sitting* _____ (pángbiān 旁边/zhōngjiān 中间/ qiánbian 前边) *to Zheng Dong.*

7. Xué Míng (学明) *is sitting* _____ (qiánbian 前边/hòubian 后边/ zuǒbian 左边) *Xin Ming.*

8. Guó Zhōng (国忠) *is sitting* _____ (yòubian 右边/zhōngjiān 中间/ zuǒbian 左边) *of Xiao Mei.*

ANSWER KEY
1. qiánbian 前边; 2. zuǒbian 左边; 3. zhōngjiān 中间; 4. yòubian 右边; 5. yòubian 右边; 6. pángbiān 旁边; 7. hòubian 后边; 8. yòubian 右边

Take It Further

The verb *to take (a form of transportation)* can be translated as dā 搭 or zuò 坐 in Chinese. Here are several examples of how these words are used to convey a sense of travel:

Wǒ měitiān zuò gōngchē shàngxué.
我每天做公车上学。
I take the bus to school everyday.

Tā zuótiān zuò fēijī lái.
他昨天坐飞机来。
He came here by plane yesterday.

Wǒmen dā huǒchē shàngbān.
我们搭火车上班。
We go to work by train.

Zhèlǐ 这里 (*here*) and
nàlǐ 那里 (*there*)

Yǒu duō yuǎn? 有多远?
(*how far?*)

Other Location Expressions

Expressing Direction or Motion
with Location Phrases

Lǎoshī bù xǐhuan dā dìtiě.
老师不喜欢搭地铁。
The teacher doesn't like to take the subway.

There is a subtle difference between dā 搭 and zuò 坐. Dā 搭 is usually used when one takes public transportation, while zuò 坐 is used for both public and private transportation. To illustrate, if you take your friend's car to work, you would say: Wǒ zuò tā de chē shàngbān. 我坐他的车上班。 (*I take his car to work.*) But, if you take the subway, you would say Wǒ dā dìtiě shàngbān. 我搭地铁上班。 (*I take the subway to work.*)

Please note that in cases where someone is going somewhere by bicycle, motorcycle, or horse, the verb qí 骑 (*to ride*) is used rather than dā 搭 or zuò 坐.

Wǒ qí zìxíngchē shàngbān.
我骑自行车上班。
I ride a bike to work./I go to work by bicycle.

Tā qí mǎ shàngxué.
他骑马上学。
He rides a horse to school.

✎ Drive It Home

For each pair of people or things, write out sentences describing their relative location to each other using the location expressions provided in parentheses. For example, with shū 书 – zhuōzi 桌子 (shàngbian, xiàbian, pángbian) you would write: Shū zài zhuōzi shàngbian. 书在桌子上边。 (*The book is on the table.*) Shū zài zhuōzi xiàbian. 书在桌子下边。 (*The book is under the table.*) Shū zài zhuōzi pángbian. 书在桌子旁边。 (*The book is next to the table.*)

Using lǐ 里 and zài 在
in Location Expressions

Cóng 从 ... dào 到
(from ... to ...)

Yǒu 有 (there is/there are)

Shì 是 (to be)

1. chē 车 – fángzi 房子 (zuǒbian 左边, hòubian 后边, pángbiān 旁边) _____

_____

2. wàzi 袜子 – xiézi 鞋子 (lǐbian 里边 , yòubian 右边, shàngbian 上边) _____

_____

3. dìtiě zhàn 地铁站 – gōngyuán 公园 (wàibian 外边, hòubian 后边, qiánbian 前
边) _____

_____

ANSWER KEY

1. Chē zài fángzi zuǒbian. 车在房子左边。 (*The car is on the left side of the house.*) Chē zài fángzi hòubian. 车在房子后边。 (*The car is behind the house.*) Chē zài fángzi pángbiān. 车在房子旁边。 (*The car is beside the house.*) 2. Wàzi zài xiézi lǐbian. 袜子在鞋子里边。 (*The socks are inside the shoes.*) Wàzi zài xiézi yòubian. 袜子在鞋子右边。 (*The socks are to the right of the shoes.*) Wàzi zài xiézi shàngbian. 袜子在鞋子上边。 (*The socks are above the shoes.*) 3. Dìtiě zhàn zài gōngyuán wàibian. 地铁站在公园外边。 (*The subway station is outside the park.*) Dìtiě zhàn zài gōngyuán hòubian. 地铁站在公园后边。 (*The subway station is behind the park.*) Dìtiě zhàn zài gōngyuán qiánbian. 地铁站在公园前边。 (*The subway station is in front of the park.*)

✏ Word Recall

Match the English word in the column on the left with its appropriate translation in the column on the right.

1. *ship*

a. chūzūchē 出租车

2. *intersection*

b. mótuōchē 摩托车

3. *shop/store*

c. diànyǐngyuàn 电影院

4. *corner*

d. hónglǜdēng 红绿灯

5. *taxi*

e. dìtiě 地铁

6. *train station*

f. shāngdiàn 商店

7. *airport*

g. shízì lùkǒu 十字路口

8. *train*

h. lùkǒu 路口

9. *cinema, movie theater*

i. huǒchēzhàn 火车站

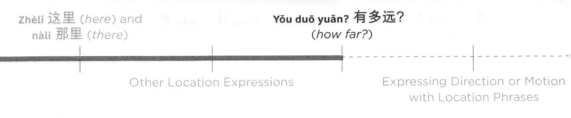

A: Xièxie!

谢谢! (*Thank you!*)

ANSWER KEY
A. nǎli 哪里
B. jìn 近, páng 旁
A. duō 多
B. lùkǒu 路

Grammar Builder 1
YǑU DUŌ YUĂN? 有多远？ (*HOW FAR?*)

▶ 2B Grammar Builder 1 (CD 7, Track 6)

You've already learned a few question words with duō 多 (*how*), for example duōshǎo 多少 (*how many/how much*) and duōjiǔ 多久 (*how long*). When talking about location and distance, a very useful question phrase using duō 多 is yǒu duō yuǎn 有多远 (*how far*). In Chinese, this phrase is preceded by cóng 从 … dào 到 … (*from … to …*), which indicates the two locations that determine the distance being measured. So the formula is: Cóng 从 A dào 到 B yǒu duō yuǎn? 有多远？ (lit., *From A to B, how far is it?*)

For example:

Cóng zhèlǐ dào huǒchē zhàn yǒu duō yuǎn?
从这里到火车站有多远？
How far is it from here to the train station?

Cóng yínháng dào fànguǎn yǒu duō yuǎn?
从银行到饭馆有多远？
How far is it from the bank to the restaurant?

Using **lǐ** 里 and **zài** 在
in Location Expressions

Cóng 从 ... **dào** 到
(*from* ... *to* ...)

Yǒu 有 (*there is/there are*)

Shì 是 (*to be*)

Cóng zhèlǐ kāichē dào yīyuàn yǒu duō yuǎn?

从这里开车到医院有多远？

How far is it from here to the hospital by car?

Cóng zhèlǐ zǒulù dào xuéxiào yǒu duō yuǎn?

从这里走路到学校有多远？

How far is it from here to the school on foot?

Cóng zhèlǐ dào nà dào qiáng yǒu duō yuǎn?

从这里到那道墙有多远？

How far is it from here to that wall?

To answer, simply replace duō yuǎn 多远 with a specified distance, measured in mǐ 米 (*meters*) or gōnglǐ 公里 (*kilometers*), or with a specific period of time:

Cóng zhèlǐ kāichē dào yīyuàn yǒu duō yuǎn?

从这里开车到医院有多远？

How far is it from here to the hospital by car?

Cóng zhèlǐ kāichē dào yīyuàn yǒu liǎng gōnglǐ.

从这里开车到医院有两公里。

It's two kilometers from here to the hospital by car.

Cóng yínháng dào fànguǎn yǒu duō yuǎn?

从银行到饭馆有多远？

How far is it from the bank to the restaurant?

Cóng yínháng dào fànguǎn dàgài zǒu shí wǔ fēnzhōng.

从银行到饭馆大概走十五分钟。

It takes about fifteen minutes to walk from the bank to the restaurant.

�

Zhèlǐ 这里 (here) and
nàli 那里 (there)

Yǒu duō yuǎn? 有多远?
(how far?)

Other Location Expressions

Expressing Direction or Motion
with Location Phrases

✎ Work Out 1

Translate the following questions into Chinese.

1. *How far is it from the park to the bank?* _____

_____

2. *How far is it from here to the post office?* _____

_____

3. *How far is it from your home to the school?* _____

_____

4. *How far is it from his school to the museum* (bówùguǎn 博物馆)*?* _____

_____

5. *How far is it from the hotel to the train station?* _____

_____

6. *How far is it from here to the food market?* _____

_____

7. *How far is it from here to the airport by car?* _____

_____

8. *How far is it from your home to the bus stop?* _____

_____

ANSWER KEY
1. Cóng gōngyuán dào yínháng yǒu duō yuǎn? 从公园到银行有多远？ 2. Cóng zhèlǐ dào yóujú yǒu
duō yuǎn? 从这里到邮局有多远？ 3. Cóng nǐ (de) jiā dào xuéxiào yǒu duō yuǎn? 从你(的) 家到
学校有多远？ 4. Cóng tā de xuéxiào dào bówùguǎn yǒu duō yuǎn? 从他的学校到博物馆有多
远？ 5. Cóng jiǔdiàn dào huǒchē zhàn yǒu duō yuǎn? 从酒店到火车站有多远？ 6. Cóng zhèlǐ dào
càishìchǎng yǒu duō yuǎn? 从这里到菜市场有多远？ 7. Cóng zhèlǐ kāichē dào jīchǎng yǒu duō

yuǎn? 从这里开车到机场有多远? 8. Cóng nǐ (de) jiā dào gōngchē zhàn yǒu duō yuǎn? 从你(的)家到公车站有多远?

Phrase Builder 2

▶ 2C Phrase Builder 2 (CD 7, Track 7)

yìzhí wǎng qián zǒu	一直往前走	go straight ahead
wǎng zuǒ zhuǎn	往左转	turn left
wǎng yòu zhuǎn	往右转	turn right
guǎi ge wān	拐个弯	(turn) around the corner
zài zuǒbian	在左边	to/on the left
zài yòubian	在右边	to/on the right
zhè biān	这边	this way
duìmiàn	对面	across the street/on the other side of the street
zài dàlóu qiánbian	在大楼前边	in front of the building
zài dàlóu hòubian	在大楼后边	behind the building
zài fùjìn	在附近	(it's) nearby
zài yínháng hé yóujú zhōngjiān	在银行和邮局中间	between the bank and the post office
zài qiáo shàngbian/shàng	在桥上边/上	on the bridge

⏸

✎ Phrase Practice 2

Translate the following phrases into English.

1. Yínháng zài dàlóu qiánbian. 银行在大楼前边。 _____

_____

Zhèlǐ 这里 (here) and
nàli 那里 (there)

Yǒu duō yuǎn? 有多远?
(how far?)

Other Location Expressions

Expressing Direction or Motion
with Location Phrases

2. Shāngdiàn zài fùjìn. 商店在附近。 _____

_____

3. Nàge Měiguórén zài qiáo shàngbian. 那个美国人在桥上边。 _____

_____

4. Wǒ de jiā zài yóujú duìmiàn. 我的家在邮局对面。 _____

_____

5. Diànyǐngyuàn zài dìtiě zhàn hé fàndiàn zhōngjiān. 电影院在地铁站和饭店中间。 _____

_____

ANSWER KEY
1. *The bank is in front of the building. 2. The store is nearby. 3. That American is on the bridge. 4. My home is across from the post office. 5. The movie theater is between the subway station and the restaurant.*

Grammar Builder 2
EXPRESSING DIRECTION OR MOTION WITH LOCATION PHRASES

▶ 2D Grammar Builder 2 (CD 7, Track 8)

You've already learned a lot of ways of expressing location in Chinese: qiánbian 前边 (*in front of*), hòubian 后边 (*behind*), zuǒbian 左边 (*left side*), yòubian 右边 (*right side*), wàibian 外边 (*outside*), lǐbian 里边 (*inside*), shàngbian 上边 (*over or on*), pángbiān 旁边 (*next to*), and zhōngjiān 中间 (*between*).

Don't forget that these location expressions are usually used along with zài 在 (*in, at, on*), and they're placed immediately after the object noun, rather than before it as in English. In other words, the English phrase *in front of the bus stop* would be translated literally as *the bus stop in front of* in Chinese, or zài gōngchēzhàn qiánbian 在公车站前边.

Here are some examples to show you how this word pattern (zài 在 + noun/pronoun + location word) is typically used in Chinese:

Tā zài yínháng qiánbian děng nǐ.
他在银行前边等你。
He's waiting for you in front of the bank.

Huǒchēzhàn zài yínháng hòubian.
火车站在银行后边。
The train station is behind the bank.

You can also express direction or motion with location phrases. To do so, you must use them in sentences containing dynamic verbs that indicate an activity is taking place in or around the location.

For example, the phrase zài yínháng hòubian 在银行后边 (*behind the bank*) can be used in Chinese to describe a state of being or static sense of location: Tā zài yínháng hòubian. 他在银行后边。 (*He's behind the bank.*) But it can also describe direction or motion when immediately followed by a verb that denotes movement: Tā zài yínháng hòubian zǒu. 他在银行后边走。 (*He's walking behind the bank.*) As you can see, direction or motion is expressed by placing the location phrase in a sentence whose word pattern is subject + zài 在 + (noun) + location word + verb.

Here are some additional examples that show how this works.

Tā zài (mǎlù) duìmiàn zǒu.
他在(马路)对面走。
He's walking on the opposite side of the street.

Unit 1 Lesson 2: Phrases

Tāmen zài gōngyuán pángbiān kāichē.

他们在公园旁边开车。

They're driving next to/alongside the park.

Tā zài jiàoshì lǐ shuìjiào.

她在教室里睡觉。

She is sleeping in the classroom.

Nà tiáo gǒu zài fángzi wàibian pǎo.

那条狗在房子外边跑。

The dog ran outside of the house.

Wǒ zài xuéxiào pángbiān děng nǐ.

我在学校旁边等你。

I'll wait for you next to the school.

Nǐ fàng yǐzi zài zhuōzi hé diànshì zhōngjiān.

你放椅子在桌子和电视中间。

You put the chair between the table and the television.

(‖)

✎ Work Out 2

Translate the words in parentheses and fill in the blanks to describe the location of each person in the following sentences. Then, translate the sentence into English.

1. Huáng xiānsheng zài Huáng tàitai _____ (*next to*) tiàowǔ.

   黄先生在黄太太 _____ 跳舞。

Using **lǐ** 里 and **zài** 在
in Location Expressions

Cóng 从 ... **dào** 到
(from ... to ...)

Yǒu 有 (there is/there are)

Shì 是 (to be)

2. Měilì zhàn zài wǒ de _____ (in front of).

美丽站在我的 _____ 。

3. Tā de jiā _____ (behind) méiyǒu gōngyuán.

他的家 _____ 没有公园。

4. _____ (left side) shì wèishēngjiān.

_____ 是卫生间。

5. Yínháng zài fànguǎn _____ diànyǐngyuàn _____

(between).

银行在饭馆 _____ 电影院 _____.

6. Wǒ de péngyou zài xuéxiào _____ (inside) yóuyǒng.

我的朋友在学校 _____ 游泳。

7. Lǎoshī zài _____ (outside) děng zhe wǒmen.

老师在 __ _____ 等着我们。

8. Nà tiáo gǒu zài zhuōzi _____ _____ (under) shuìjiào.

那条狗在桌子 _____ 睡觉。

ANSWER KEY
1. pángbiān 旁边 (*Mr. Huang is dancing next to Mrs. Huang.*) 2. qiánbian 前边 (*Meili is standing in front of me.*) 3. hòubian 后边 (*There is no park behind his house.*) 4. Zuǒbian 左边 (*There is a toilet on the left side.*) 5. hé, zhōngjiān 和, 中间 (*The bank is between the restaurant and the cinema.*) 6. lǐ 里 (*My friend is swimming in the school.*) 7. wàibian 外边 (*The teacher is waiting for us outside.*) 8. xiàbian 下边 (*The dog is sleeping under the table.*)

✎ Drive It Home

Let's practice expressing direction or motion with location phrases. Modify each simple phrase using the location phrases provided in parentheses. For example, with Wǒ shàngxué 我上学 (yóujú pángbiān 邮局旁边), you would write wǒ zài

Other Location Expressions

Expressing Direction or Motion with Location Phrases

yóujú pángbiān shàngxué 我在邮局旁边上学 (*I go to school next to the post office*).

1. Tāmen kàn shū 他们看书 (shāngdiàn wàibian 商店外边, gōngyuán lǐbian 公园里边, chē pángbiān 车旁边) _____

    _____

2. Nǐ qí zìxíngchē 你骑自行车 (qiáo shàng 桥上, lùkou 路口, bǎihuò gōngsī lǐbian 百货公司里边) _____

    _____

3. Wǒmen dǎ qiú 我们打球 (jiàotáng hòubian 教堂后边, diànyǐngyuàn qiánbian 电影院前边, fàndiàn yòubian 饭店右边) _____

    _____

ANSWER KEY
1. Tāmen zài shāngdiàn wàibian kàn shū. 他们在商店外边看书。(*They are reading outside the store.*) Tāmen zài gōngyuán lǐbian kàn shū. 他们在公园里边看书。(*They are reading inside the park.*) Tāmen zài chē pángbiān kàn shū. 他们在车旁边看书。(*They are reading next to the car.*) 2. Nǐ zài qiáo shàng qí zìxíngchē. 你在桥上骑自行车。(*You are riding a bicycle on the bridge.*) Nǐ zài lùkou qí zìxíngchē. 你在路口骑自行车。(*You are riding a bicycle on the corner.*) Nǐ zài bǎihuò gōngsī lǐbian qí zìxíngchē. 你在百货公司里边骑自行车。(*You are riding a bicycle inside the department store.*) 3. Wǒmen zài jiàotáng hòubian dǎ qiú. 我们在教堂后边打球。(*We are playing ball behind the church.*) Wǒmen zài diànyǐngyuàn qiánbian dǎ qiú. 我们在电影院前边打球。(*We are playing ball in front of the movie theater.*) Wǒmen zài fàndiàn yòubian dǎ qiú. 我们在饭店右边打球。(*We are playing ball to the right of the hotel.*)

✎ Phrase Recall

Match the English phrase in the column on the left with its appropriate translation in the column on the right.

1. *how far?*   a. shàng chē 上车

2. *very far*   b. guǎi ge wān 拐个弯

Using **lǐ** 里 and **zài** 在
in Location Expressions

Cóng 从 ... **dào** 到
(from ... to ...)

Yǒu 有 (there is/there are)

Shì 是 (to be)

3. *turn right*	c. zài lùkǒu 在路口
4. *to get off (a vehicle)*	d. zǒu lù 走路
5. *(it's) nearby*	e. hěn yuǎn 很远
6. *on the corner*	f. wǎng yòu zhuǎn 往右转
7. *to read a map*	g. zài fùjìn 在附近
8. *very near*	h. yǒu duō yuǎn? 有多远？
9. *(turn) around the corner*	i. yǒu diǎn yuǎn 有点远
10. *on foot*	j. duìmiàn 对面
11. *to get on (a vehicle)*	k. hěn jìn 很近
12. *a bit far*	l. guò mǎlù 过马路
13. *across the street/on the other side of the street*	m. yīzhí wǎng qián zǒu 一直往前走
14. *to cross the street*	n. xià chē 下车
15. *go straight ahead*	o. kàn dìtú 看地图

ANSWER KEY
1. h; 2. e; 3. f; 4. n; 5. g; 6. c; 7. o; 8. k; 9. b; 10. d; 11. a; 12. i; 13. j; 14. l; 15. m

Lesson 3: Sentences

By the end of this lesson, you'll learn:

☐ How to ask for directions to various locations.

☐ How to use lǐ 里 and zài 在 in location expressions.

☐ Yǒu 有 (there is/there are).

Zhèlǐ 这里 (*here*) and
nàlǐ 那里 (*there*)

Yǒu duō yuǎn? 有多远?
(*how far?*)

Other Location Expressions

Expressing Direction or Motion
with Location Phrases

Wǒ xiànzài zài Měiguó.

我现在在美国。

I'm in the U.S. now.

Tāmen de dàxué zài Hā'ěrbīn.

他们的大学在哈尔滨。

Their university is in Harbin.

However, if you want to emphasize that something is contained within a given
space, you can add lǐ 里 (which also means *in*) to zài 在。 This is similar to the
English distinction between *in* and *inside* or *within*. Note that the word order is zài
在 + noun + lǐ 里。

Tā zài fángjiān lǐ.

他在房间里。

He is inside the room.

Yàoshi zài hézi lǐ.

钥匙在盒子里。

The keys are inside the box.

Háizimen zài chē lǐ./Háizimen zài chē shàng.

孩子们在车里。/ 孩子们在车上。

*The children are inside the car./The children are in the car. (lit., The children are on
the car.)*

(II)

Using **lǐ** 里 and **zài** 在
in Location Expressions

Cóng 从 ... **dào** 到
(from ... to ...)

Yǒu 有 *(there is/there are)*

Shì 是 *(to be)*

✎ Work Out 1

Let's review basic location expressions. Re-arrange the following words and phrases so that they form meaningful sentences in Chinese.

1. shàngkè/wǒ de lǎoshī/zài bówùguǎn 上课/我的老师/在博物馆 _____

_____

2. měitiān/nàge rén/chīfàn/zài zhèlǐ 每天/那个人/吃饭/在这里 _____

_____

3. měige lǐbài sān/tā hé péngyou/tiàowǔ/zài nàli 每个礼拜三/他和朋友/跳舞/
在那里

_____

4. shuìjiào/zài zhèlǐ/shéi/? 睡觉/在这里/谁/? _____

_____

ANSWER KEY

1. Wǒ de lǎoshī zài bówùguǎn shàngkè. 我的老师在博物馆上课。 (*My teacher attends class at the museum.*) 2. Nàge rén měitiān zài zhèlǐ chīfàn. 那个人每天在这里吃饭。 (*That person eats here every day.*) 3. Tā hé péngyou měige lǐbài sān zài nàli tiàowǔ. 他和朋友每个礼拜三在那里跳舞。 (*He and his friends dance there every Wednesday.*) 4. Shéi zài zhèlǐ shuìjiào? 谁在这里睡觉？ (*Who sleeps here?*)

Sentence Builder 2

▶ 3C Sentence Builder 2 (CD 7, Track 11)

Shāngdiàn pángbiān yǒu liǎng jiā yínháng.
商店旁边有两家银行。
There are two banks next to the shop.

Yǒu méiyǒu piányi de lǚguǎn?
有没有便宜的旅馆？
Is there an inexpensive hotel?

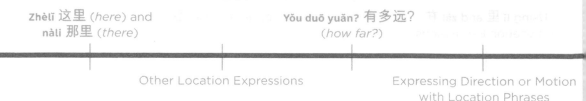

Zhèlǐ 这里 (here) and
nàlǐ 那里 (there)

Yǒu duō yuǎn? 有多远?
(how far?)

Other Location Expressions

Expressing Direction or Motion
with Location Phrases

Grammar Builder 2
YǑU 有 (*THERE IS/THERE ARE*)

▶ 3D Grammar Builder 2 (CD 7, Track 12)

You already know that yǒu 有 (*to have*) can indicate possession in Chinese. But as several of the examples above demonstrate, yǒu 有 can also mean *there is* or *there are*. In other words, yǒu 有 can also indicate the existence of something.

There's a difference in usage to keep in mind, though. When the subject of yǒu 有 is a personal pronoun or a living object, then yǒu 有 is being used to indicate possession and can be translated as *to have*. But if the subject is a place or a location phrase, then yǒu 有 is being used to indicate existence and can be translated as *there is* or *there are*. Take a look at this contrast:

Wǒ yǒu liǎng zhī māo.
我有两只猫。
I have two cats.

Zhuōzi shàng yǒu liǎng zhī māo.
桌子上有两只猫。
There are two cats on the table.

Here are some more examples of the existential yǒu 有。 Don't forget that the negative of yǒu 有, both as a possessive and an existential, is méiyǒu 没有。

Zhèlǐ yǒu yì jiā fēicháng hǎo de cānguǎn.
这里有一家非常好的餐馆。
There's a great restaurant here.

Yǒu 有 (there is/there are)   Shì 是 (to be)

Zhèlǐ méiyǒu Zhōngguórén.

这里没有中国人。

There are no Chinese people here.

Zhège chéngshì méiyǒu hǎo de bówùguǎn.

这个城市没有好的博物馆。

There's no good museum in this city.

Zhōngguó yǒu lǎohǔ ma?

中国有老虎吗?

Are there any tigers in China?

Yínháng lǐ yǒu tíkuǎnjī ma?

银行里有提款机吗?

Is there an ATM at the bank?

Two quantity phrases that you may want to use with the existential yǒu 有 are: hěn duō 很多 (*a lot, many, much*) and yì diǎndiǎn 一点点 (*a few, a little*), which literally means *very few*.

Nǐ de shūjià shàng yǒu hěn duō CD.

你的书架上有很多CD.

There are a lot of CDs on your shelf.

Bēizi lǐ zhǐ yǒu yì diǎndiǎn shuǐ.

杯子里只有一点点水。

There is only a little water in the glass.

Ⓘ

Zhèlǐ 这里 *(here)* and
nàlǐ 那里 *(there)*

从

Yǒu duō yuǎn? 有多远?
(how far?)

Other Location Expressions

Expressing Direction or Motion
with Location Phrases

✎ Word Recall

Match the English word in the column on the left with its appropriate translation
in the column on the right.

1. *where is ... ?*	a. xǐshǒujiān 洗手间
2. *to buy tickets*	b. huǒchēzhàn 火车站
3. *which station*	c. zài nǎli? 在哪里?
4. *inexpensive*	d. zuì hǎo de 最好的
5. *road*	e. nǎge zhàn 哪个站
6. *restroom*	f. bówùguǎn 博物馆
7. *to live in*	g. mǎi piào 买票
8. *the best*	h. huàn chē 换车
9. *someone*	i. lù 路
10. *museum*	j. zhù zài 住在
11. *to look for, to find*	k. piányi 便宜
12. *train station*	l. lǚguǎn 旅馆
13. *telephone booth*	m. yǒu rén 有人
14. *to change trains/subways/buses*	n. zhǎo 找
15. *hotel*	o. diànhuàtíng 电话亭

ANSWER KEY
1. c; 2. g; 3. e; 4. k; 5. i; 6. a; 7. j; 8. d; 9. m; 10. f; 11. n; 12. b; 13. o; 14. h; 15. l

Lesson 4: Conversations

In this lesson, you'll learn:

☐ More about asking for directions.

☐ Cóng 从 ... dào 到 ... *(from ... to ...).*

☐ Shì 是 *(to be)* to express existence.

Using **lǐ** 里 and **zài** 在
in Location Expressions

Cóng 从 ... **dào** 到
(*from ... to ...*)

Yǒu 有 (*there is/there are*)

Shì 是 (*to be*)

Conversation 1

▶ 4A Conversation 1 (CD 7, Track 13-Chinese, Track 14-Chinese and English)

Listen as Jess asks for directions.

Jiéxī:
Láojià, qǐngwèn Guāngmíng Lù zěnme zǒu?

洁希:
劳驾, 请问光明路怎么走?

Lùrén:
Nín yìzhí wǎng qián zǒu, zài dì sì ge lùkǒu wǎng zuǒ zhuǎn, zǒu sān ge lùkǒu. Guāngmíng Lù jiù zài nínde yòubian.

路人:
您一直往前走, 在第四个路口往左转, 走三个路口。光明路就在您的右边。

Jiéxī:
Xièxie!

洁希:
谢谢!

Lùrén:
Bú kèqi.

路人:
不客气。

(Jiéxī zhōngyú zhǎo dào le Guāngmíng lù.)

(洁希终于找到了光明路。)

Jiéxī:
Láojià, qǐngwèn yī lù gōngchē zhàn zài nǎli?

洁希:
劳驾, 请问一路公车站在哪里?

Lùrén:
Nín kànjiàn qiánbian nà zuò bái sè de dàlóu ma? Gōngchē zhàn jiù zài nà zuò dàlóu de qiánbian.

路人:
您看见前边那座白色的大楼吗? 公车站就在那座大楼的前边。

Jiéxī:
Xièxie!

洁希:
谢谢!

(Jiéxī zhōngyú zhǎo dào le gōngchē zhàn.)

(洁希终于找到了公车站。)

Jiéxī:
Láojià, wǒ yào qù zhège dìzhǐ, qǐngwèn wǒ zài nǎ yí zhàn xiàchē?

洁希:
劳驾, 我要去这个地址, 请问我在哪一站下车?

Zhèlǐ 这里 (here) and
nàli 那里 (there)

Yǒu duō yuǎn? 有多远?
(how far?)

Other Location Expressions

Expressing Direction or Motion
with Location Phrases

Grammar Builder 1
CÓNG 从 ... DÀO 到 (FROM ... TO ...)

▶ 4B Grammar Builder 1 (CD 7, Track 15)

In Lesson 2, you learned how to use cóng 从 ... dào 到 ... (from ... to ...) with
the question phrase yǒu duō yuǎn 有多远 (how far) and in answers indicating a
specific distance or time.

However, cóng 从 ... dào 到 ... can also be used on its own and without a
reference to a specified time or distance.

Simply combine cóng 从 (from) with the word dào 到 (to) to form the expression
cóng A dào 到 B (from A to B).

Cóng zhèlǐ dào huǒchēzhàn zěnme zǒu?
从这里到火车站怎么走?
*How do I get to the train station from here? (lit., From here to the train station how
(to) go?)*

Cóng fēijīchǎng dào jiǔdiàn zěnme zǒu?
从飞机场到酒店怎么走?
How do I get to the hotel from the airport?

Tāmen cóng Chéngdū bān dào Chóngqìng.
他们从成都搬到重庆。
They moved from Chengdu to Chongqing.

⑪

✎ Work Out 1

Translate the following sentences into English.

1. Cóng huǒchēzhàn dào nǐ de jiā yǒu duō yuǎn? 从火车站到你的家有多远? __

   _____

2. Cóng xuéxiào dào dìtiězhàn zěnme zǒu? 从学校到地铁站怎么走? _____

   _____

3. Cóng zhèlǐ dào yīyuàn yǒu duō yuǎn? 从这里到医院有多远? _____

   _____

4. Cóng wǒ de jiā dào xuéxiào yǒu sān gōnglǐ. 从我的家到学校有三公里。 ____

   _____

5. Cóng fàndiàn dào yínháng yǒu duō yuǎn? 从饭店到银行有多远? _____

   _____

6. Cóng yóujú dào càishìchǎng zěnme zǒu? 从邮局到菜市场怎么走? _____

   _____

7. Cóng zhèlǐ wǎng yòu zhuǎn. 从这里往右。 _____

   _____

ANSWER KEY

1. How far is it from the train station to your home? 2. How can I get to the subway station from the school? 3. How far is it from here to the hospital? 4. It's three kilometers from my home to the school. 5. How far is it from the restaurant to the bank? 6. How can I get to the food market from the post office? 7. From here, turn right.

Zhèlǐ 这里 *(here)* and
nàlǐ 那里 *(there)*

Yǒu duō yuǎn? 有多远?
(how far?)

Other Location Expressions

Expressing Direction or Motion
with Location Phrases

◄◄ Conversation 2

▶ 4C Conversation 2 (CD 7, Track 16-Chinese, Track 17-Chinese and English)

Jess asks Wang Hai how to get to Jingshan Park. She also wants his
recommendation for a good Chinese restaurant.

Jiéxī:	Wáng Hǎi, nǐ zài zhèlǐ zhùle duō jiǔ? 王海，你在这里住了多久？
Hai:	Wǒ cóng sān suì kāishǐ zhù zài zhèlǐ, xiànzài chàbùduō yǒu shíbā nián le. 我从三岁开始住在这里，现在差不多有十八年了。
Jiéxī:	Nǐ duì zhèlǐ hěn shúxi ma? 你对这里很熟悉吗？
Hai:	Dāngrán. 当然。
Jiéxī:	Wǒ míngtiān qù Jǐngshān Gōngyuán jiàn yí ge péngyou, nǐ zhīdao zěnme qù ma? 我明天去景山公园见一个朋友，你知道怎么去吗？
Hai:	Nǐ cóng zhèlǐ zuò sān lù gōngchē, dào Rénmín Dàshà ménkǒu xiàchē, ránhòu huàn dìtiě, zài Jǐngshān Yīyuàn xiàchē. Jǐngshān Gōngyuán jiù zài yīyuàn de pángbiān. 你从这里坐三路公车，到人民大厦门口下车，然后换地 铁，在景山医院下车。景山公园就在医院的旁边。
Jiéxī:	Cóng zhèlǐ zuò gōngchē dào Jǐngshān Gōngyuán yǒu duō yuǎn? 从这里坐公车到景山公园有多远？
Hai:	Dàgài èrshí fēnzhōng. Nǐ bú huì kàn bú jiàn. 大概二十分钟。你不会看不见。
Jiéxī:	Jǐngshān Gōngyuán fùjìn yǒu cānguǎn ma? Wǒ xiǎng gēn péngyou zài nàlǐ chī wǔfàn. 景山公园附近有餐馆吗？我想跟朋友在那里吃午饭。

Yǒu 有 (*there is/there are*)   **Shì** 是 (*to be*)

Hai:	Cóng gōngyuán wǎng zuǒ zǒu, guòle qiáo, mǎlù duìmiàn shì yí zuò báisè de dàlóu. Nǐ huì kànjiàn Jǐngshān Cānguǎn. Tāmen de cài bú cuò, érqiě jiàqian bú guì.

从公园往左走, 过了桥, 马路对面是一座白色的大楼。
你会看见景山餐馆。他们的菜不错, 而且价钱不贵。

Jess: *Wang Hai, how long have you been living here?*

Hai: *I've been living here since I was three. It's almost been 18 years now.*

Jess: *Are you very familiar with this place?*

Hai: *Of course.*

Jess: *I'm going to see a friend in Jingshan Park tomorrow. Do you know how to get there?*

Hai: *You take the number three bus from here and get off in front of the Renmin Building. Then you transfer to the subway and get off at Jingshan Hospital. Jingshan Park is next to the hospital.*

Jess: *How long does it take to get to Jingshan Park from here?*

Hai: *About twenty minutes. You can't miss it.*

Jess: *Is there a restaurant near the park? I want to have lunch there with my friend.*

Hai: *From the park, walk left and cross over a bridge; across the street, there is a white building. You will see Jingshan Restaurant. The food there is very good, and (what's more) it's not expensive.*

✎ Conversation Practice 2

Fill in the blanks with the missing words in pīnyīn based upon the conversation between Jess and Wang Hai.

1. Wáng Hǎi zài zhèlǐ zhùle _____ nián le.

王海在这里住了十八年。

Other Location Expressions

Expressing Direction or Motion
with Location Phrases

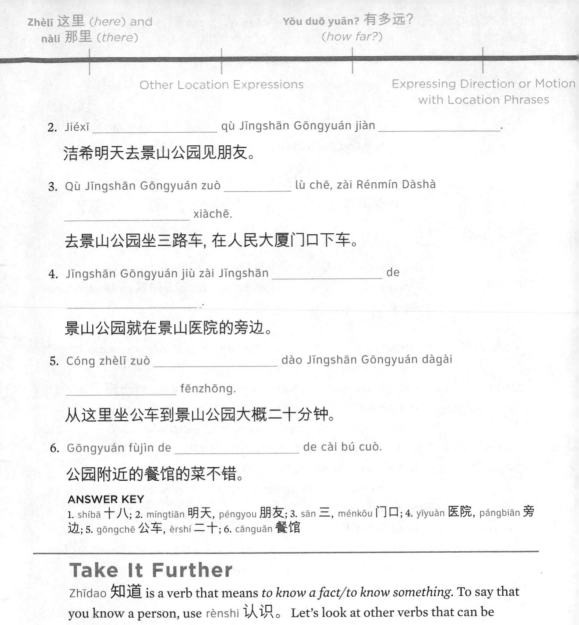

2. Jiéxī _____ qù Jǐngshān Gōngyuán jiàn _____.

洁希明天去景山公园见朋友。

3. Qù Jǐngshān Gōngyuán zuò _____ lù chē, zài Rénmín Dàshà

_____ xiàchē.

去景山公园坐三路车, 在人民大厦门口下车。

4. Jǐngshān Gōngyuán jiù zài Jǐngshān _____ de

_____.

景山公园就在景山医院的旁边。

5. Cóng zhèlǐ zuò _____ dào Jǐngshān Gōngyuán dàgài

_____ fēnzhōng.

从这里坐公车到景山公园大概二十分钟。

6. Gōngyuán fùjìn de _____ de cài bú cuò.

公园附近的餐馆的菜不错。

ANSWER KEY
1. shíbā 十八; 2. míngtiān 明天, péngyou 朋友; 3. sān 三, ménkǒu 门口; 4. yīyuàn 医院, pángbiān 旁边; 5. gōngchē 公车, èrshí 二十; 6. cānguǎn 餐馆

Take It Further

Zhīdao 知道 is a verb that means *to know a fact/to know something*. To say that you know a person, use rènshi 认识。 Let's look at other verbs that can be translated as *to know* in English.

Wǒ zhīdao zěnme qù nàli.
我知道怎么去那里。
I know how to get there.

Using **lǐ** 里 and **zài** 在
in Location Expressions

Cóng 从 ... **dào** 到
(*from ... to ...*)

Yǒu 有 (*there is/there are*)

Shì 是 (*to be*)

Wǒ hěn shúxī zhèlǐ./Wǒ hěn shúxī zhège qū.

我很熟悉这里。 我很熟悉这个区。

I know this neighborhood very well. (lit., I'm very familiar with it.)

Wǒ huì shuō yì diǎndiǎn Zhōngwén.

我会说一点点中文。

I know how to speak a little Chinese.

Kāishǐ 开始 is a verb meaning *to start*. You can use it along with another verb.

Tāmen kāishǐ jiǎng le.

他们开始讲了。

They began speaking.

Kāishǐ xiàyǔ le

开始下雨了。

It started to rain.

Chàbuduō 差不多 is an adverb that means *almost*. When combined with yǒu 有, it means *approximately* or *about,* as in the phrase chàbuduō yǒu liù suì 差不多有 六岁 (*approximately/about six years old*).

Huàn 换 means *to exchange*. Placed before a form of transportation such as a car, bus, train, etc., it means to transfer from one vehicle to another. For example:

Wǒ zài zhèlǐ huàn gōngchē.

我在这里换公车。

I transfer to the bus here.

Érqiě 而且 is a conjunction that means *moreover* or *what's more* ... You can use it when you're adding information to something that you've just said.

Zhèlǐ 这里 (here) and   Yǒu duō yuǎn? 有多远?
nàli 那里 (there)   (how far?)

Other Location Expressions   Expressing Direction or Motion
                              with Location Phrases

2. Gōngyuán qiánbian yǒu sān kē shù. 公园前边有三棵树。 _____

_____

3. Qiáo xiàbian yǒu yì tiáo hé. 桥下边有一条河。 _____

_____

4. Fàndiàn zuǒbian yǒu yì tiáo hěn cháng de jiē. 饭店左边有一条很长的街。 ____

_____

5. Huǒchē shàng yǒu hěn duō rén. 火车上有很多人。 _____

_____

6. Zhōngguó yǒu hěn duō rén. 中国有很多人。 _____

_____

ANSWER KEY
1. Fángzi qiánbian shì yí ge gōngyuán. 房子前边是一个公园。 2. N 3. Qiáo xiàbian shì yì tiáo hé. 桥下边是一条河。 4. Fàndiàn zuǒbian shì yì tiáo hěn cháng de jiē. 饭店左边是一条很长的街。 5. N 6. N

✎ Drive It Home

Practice writing sentences with shì 是 and yǒu 有. With the subject and location provided, form sentences with the phrases in parentheses and the existential shì 是 or yǒu 有. Be aware of when only yǒu 有 can be used.

1. Dàlóu hòubian 大楼后边 (sān kē shù 三颗树, yì tiáo gǒu 一条狗, yí liàng chē 一辆车) _____

_____

2. Wòfáng lǐbian 卧房里边 (yì zhāng chuáng 一张床, liǎng bǎ yǐzi 两把椅子, yì zhāng zhuōzi 一张桌子) _____

_____

Using **lǐ** 里 and **zài** 在
in Location Expressions

Cóng 从 ... **dào** 到
(*from ... to ...*)

Yǒu 有 (*there is/there are*)

Shì 是 (*to be*)

3. Càishìchǎng hé dìtiě zhàn zhōngjiān 菜市场和地铁站中间 (yí ge shāngdiàn 一
个商店, yì tiáo lù 一条路, wǔ liàng zìxíngchē 五辆自行车) _____

_____

ANSWER KEY
1. Dàlóu hòubian yǒu sān kē shù. 大楼后边有三棵树。 (*There are three trees behind the bulding.*)
Dàlóu hòubian shì/yǒu yì tiáo gǒu. 大楼后边是/有一条狗。 (*There is a dog behind the building.*)
Dàlóu hòubian shì/yǒu yí liàng chē. 大楼后边是/有一辆车。 (*There is a car behind the building.*) 2.
Wòfáng lǐbian shì/yǒu yì zhāng chuáng. 卧房里边是/有一张床。 (*There is a bed in the bedroom.*)
Wòfáng lǐbian yǒu liǎng bǎ yǐzi. 卧房里边有两把椅子。 (*There are two chairs in the bedroom.*)
Wòfáng lǐbian shì/yǒu yì zhāng zhuōzi. 卧房里边是/有一张桌子。 (*There is a table in the bedroom.*)
3. Càishìchǎng hé dìtiě zhàn zhōngjiān shì/yǒu yí ge shāngdiàn. 菜市场和地铁站中间是/有一个商
店。 (*There is a store between the vegetable market and the subway station.*) Càishìchǎng hé dìtiě zhàn
zhōngjiān shì/yǒu yì tiáo lù. 菜市场和地铁站中间是/有一条路。 (*There is a road between the
vegetable market and the subway station.*) Càishìchǎng hé dìtiě zhàn zhōngjiān yǒu wǔ liàng zìxíngchē.
菜市场和地铁站中间有五辆自行车。 (*There are five bicycles between the vegetable market and
the subway station.*)

✎ Word Recall

Match the English word in the column on the left with its appropriate translation
in the column on the right.

1. *almost*	a. zěnme zǒu 怎么走
2. *to go ahead*	b. láojià 劳驾
3. *finally*	c. yìzhí 一直
4. *to see*	d. wǎng qián 往前
5. *address*	e. wǎng zuǒ zhuǎn 往左转
6. *how to get to ...?*	f. bú kèqi 不客气
7. *to start*	g. zhōngyú 终于
8. *straight*	h. kànjiàn 看见
9. *Excuse me*	i. dìzhǐ 地址
10. *to turn left*	j. kāishǐ 开始
11. *in front of (lit., at the door)*	k. chàbùduō 差不多
12. *you're welcome*	l. dāngrán 当然

Zhèlǐ 这里 (here) and
nàli 那里 (there)

Yǒu duō yuǎn? 有多远?
(how far?)

Other Location Expressions

Expressing Direction or Motion
with Location Phrases

13. *to exchange*

14. *moreover*

15. *of course*

m. ménkǒu 门口

n. huàn 换

o. érqiě 而且

ANSWER KEY
1. k; 2. d; 3. g; 4. h; 5. i; 6. a; 7. j; 8. c; 9. b; 10. e; 11. m; 12. f; 13. n; 14. o; 15. l

◉ Culture Note

When speaking to people outside your family, it is impolite to approach or interrupt them without using certain polite forms of speech in Chinese. For example, if you're asking for directions or for help, it is customary to start your request with the words láojià 劳驾 (*excuse me*) and qǐng wèn 请问 (*may I ask*): Láojià, qǐng wèn nín huǒchēzhàn zài nǎli? 劳驾, 请问您火车站在哪里? (*Excuse me, may I ask where the train station is?*) Likewise, if you don't understand or didn't hear what someone said and want them to repeat it, you need to begin your request with the word duìbuqǐ 对不起, which means *I'm sorry*: Duìbuqǐ, qǐng zài shuō yí cì. 对不起, 请再说一次。 (*I'm sorry, please say it again.*) Generally, these words are considered too formal or too polite to be used among family members and close friends, so they are usually reserved only for addressing strangers or people with whom you do not have a close relationship.

Don't forget to practice and reinforce what you've learned by visiting **www.livinglanguage.com/ languagelab** for flashcards, games, and quizzes.

Unit 1 Essentials

Vocabulary Essentials

Test your knowledge of the key material in this unit by filling in the blanks in the following charts. Once you've completed these pages, you'll have tested your retention, and you'll have your own reference for the most essential vocabulary. This is also a great time to practice a few Chinese characters. Fill in the middle column with the characters that you remember. Or, if you only remember the pīnyīn, go back through the unit to find the character.

LOCATIONS

PĪNYĪN	CHARACTER	
		food market
		cinema, movie theater
		department store
		clothing store
		book store
		electronics store (lit., home appliances store)
		shoe store
		shop/store
		restaurant
		hotel
		train station
		airport
		here
		there

DIRECTIONS

PĪNYĪN	CHARACTER	
		go straight ahead
		turn left
		turn right
		to/on the left
		to/on the right
		this way
		across the street/on the other side of the street
		in front of the building
		behind the building
		(it's) nearby
		between the bank and the post office
		outside the shop
		on the corner
		in the restaurant
		over there
		(it's) nearby
		how far?
		very near
		very far
		a little further
		two blocks
		next to the hotel

MORE VOCABULARY FOR LOCATIONS

PĪNYĪN	CHARACTER	
		street
		corner
		traffic light
		intersection
		sidewalk
		taxi
		bus
		bus stop
		car
		motorcycle
		bicycle
		train
		train station
		subway
		subway station
		airplane
		from

If you're having a hard time remembering this vocabulary, don't forget to check out the flashcards, games and quizzes for this unit online. Go to **www.livinglanguage.com/languagelab** for a great way to help you practice what you've learned.

Grammar Essentials

Here is a reference for the key grammar that was covered in Unit 1. Make sure you understand the summary and can use all of the grammar it covers.

LOCATION EXPRESSIONS

nǎli 哪里	*where*
nàli 那里	*there*
zhèlǐ 这里	*here*
qiánbian 前边	*in front of*
hòubian 后边	*behind*
pángbiān 旁边	*next to*
shàngbian/shàng 上边/上	*on*
lǐ/lǐbian 里/里边	*in, inside*
wàibian 外边	*outside*
xiàbian/xià 下边/下	*under*
zuǒbian 左边	*on the left side of*
yòubian 右边	*on the right side of*
zhōngjiān 中间	*between*

ASKING HOW FAR?

To ask how far a place B is from your location A: Cóng 从 A dào 到 B yǒu duō yuǎn? 有多远？ (lit., *From A to B, how far is it?*)

Cóng zhèlǐ dào huǒchē zhàn yǒu duō yuǎn?	从这里到火车站有多远？	*How far is it from here to the train station?*
Cóng yínháng dào fànguǎn yǒu duō yuǎn?	从银行到饭馆有多远？	*How far is it from the bank to the restaurant?*
Cóng zhèlǐ kāichē dào yīyuàn yǒu duō yuǎn?	从这里开车到医院有多远？	*How far is it from here to the hospital by car?*
Cóng zhèlǐ kāichē dào yīyuàn yǒu shí fēnzhōng.	从这里开车到医院有十分钟。	*It's ten minutes from here to the hospital by car.*

EXPRESSING EXISTENCE WITH YOU 有 AND SHI 是

Both yǒu 有 and shì 是 can be used to express existence. When the subject of yǒu 有 is a place or a location phrase, then yǒu 有 is being used to indicate existence. Use shì 是 to assert the existence of one thing. Use yǒu 有 to assert the existence of one or more things.

Nàge fángzi hòubian shì yì tiáo hé.	那个房子后边是一条河。	*There is a/one river behind the house.*
Nàge fángzi hòubian yǒu yì tiáo hé.	那个房子后边有一条河。	*There is a/one river behind the house.*
Nàge fángzi hòubian yǒu sān tiáo hé.	那个房子后边有三条河。	*There are three rivers behind the house.*

Unit 1 Quiz

A. Translate the following sentences from Chinese into English.

1. Wǒ lái zhèlǐ, tāmen qù nàli. 我来这里, 他们去那里。 _____

   _____

2. Wǒ de xuésheng zài nàli. 我的学生在那里。 _____

   _____

3. Wǒ de yéye zài wǒ de nǎinai yòubian. 我的爷爷在我的奶奶右边。 _____

   _____

4. Māo zài Wáng xiānsheng hé Wáng tàitai de zhōngjiān. 猫在王先生和王太太的
   中间。 _____

   _____

B. Translate the words in parentheses and fill in the blanks to describe the
   location of each person in the following sentences.

1. Tā de jiā _____ (behind) méiyǒu huǒchēzhàn.
   他的家 _____ 没有火车站。

2. Zhāng lǎoshī zài Wáng lǎoshī _____ (next to) kàn dìtú.
   张老师在王老师 _____ 看地图。

3. Měilì zuò zài wǒ de _____ (in front of).
   美丽坐在我的 _____ 。

4. Yínháng zài fànguǎn _____ diànyǐngyuàn _____ (between).

银行在饭馆 _____ 电影院 _____ 。

5. _____ (right side) shì wǒ de fángzi.

_____ 是我的房子。

6. Tā de tàitai zài shāngdiàn _____ (inside) mǎi ěrhuán.

他的太太在商店 _____ 买耳环。

C. Re-arrange the following words and phrases so that they form meaningful sentences in Chinese.

1. tīng yīnyuè/wǒ de péngyou/zài bówùguǎn 听音乐/我的朋友/在博物馆 _____

_____

2. měige xīngqī tiān/yīsheng hé hùshi/tiàowǔ/zài nàli 每个星期天/医生和护士/

跳舞/在那里 _____

_____

3. qiánbian/xuéxiào/gōngchēzhàn/yǒu 前边/学校/公车站/有 _____

_____

4. méiyǒu/jiàoshì/lǐbian/xuésheng 没有/教室/里边/学生 _____

_____

5. hěn duō/lù shàng/chē/yǒu 很多/路上/车/有 _____

_____

D. Translate the following sentences into English.

1. Cóng càishìchǎng dào nǐ de jiā yǒu duō yuǎn? 从菜市场到你的家有多远? _____

_____

2. Cóng bǎihuò gōngsī dào gōngchēzhàn zěnme zǒu? 从百货公司到公车站怎么走? _____

_____

3. Cóng gōngyuán dào cānguǎn yǒu sān gōnglǐ. 从公园到餐馆有三公里。 _____

_____

4. Cóng zhèlǐ wǎng yòu zhuǎn. 从这里往右转。 _____

_____

5. Cóng nàli guǎi ge wān, ránhòu yì zhí wǎng qián zǒu. 从那里拐个弯, 然后一直往前走。 _____

_____

ANSWER KEY

A. 1. *I'll come here, they will go there.* 2. *My student is over there.* 3. *My grandfather is to the right of my grandmother.* 4. *The cat is between Mr. and Mrs. Wang.*

B. 1. hòubian 后边 2. pángbiān 旁边 3. qiánbian 前边 4. hé, zhōngjiān 和,中间 5. Yòubian 右边 6. lǐbian 里边

C. 1. Wǒ de péngyou zài bówùguǎn tīng yīnyuè. 我的朋友在博物馆听音乐。 (*My friend is listening to music in the museum.*) 2. Yīshēng hé hùshi měige xīng qī tiān zài nàli tiàowǔ. 医生和护士每个星期天在那里跳舞。 (*Doctors and nurses dance there every Sunday.*) 3. Xuéxiào qiánbian yǒu gōngchēzhàn. 学校前边有公车站。 (*There is a bus stop in front of the school.*) 4. Jiàoshì lǐbian méiyǒu xuésheng. 教室里边没有学生。 (*There are no students inside the classroom.*) 5. Lù shàng yǒu hěn duō chē. 路上有很多车。 (*There are many cars on the road.*)

D. 1. *How far is it from the vegetable market to your home?* 2. *How to get from the department store to the bus stop?* 3. *It's three kilometers from the park to the restaurant.* 4. *Turn right from here.* 5. *Turn around the corner from there, then keep going straight ahead.*

How Did You Do?

Give yourself a point for every correct answer, then use the following key to tell whether you're ready to move on:

0-7 points: It's probably a good idea to go back through the lesson again. You may be moving too quickly, or there may be too much "down time" between your contact with Chinese. Remember that it's better to spend 30 minutes with

Chinese three or four times a week than it is to spend two or three hours just once a week. Find a pace that's comfortable for you, and spread your contact hours out as much as you can.

8-12 points: You would benefit from a review before moving on. Go back and spend a little more time on the specific points that gave you trouble. Re-read the Grammar Builder sections that were difficult, and do the Work Outs one more time. Don't forget to check out the flashcards, games and quizzes for this unit online. Go to **www.livinglanguage.com/languagelab** for a great way to help you practice what you've learned.

13-17 points: Good job! There are just a few points that you might consider reviewing before moving on. If you haven't worked with the games and quizzes on **www.livinglanguage.com/languagelab**, please give them a try.

18-20 points: Great! You're ready to move on to the next unit.

 **points**

Making Suggestions:
hǎo ma? 好吗?

Modal verbs

More Commands and
Requests

Negative Questions

Unit 2: At a Restaurant

Zài cānguǎn lǐ
在餐馆里

In this unit, you'll learn vocabulary words and expressions that will come in handy when you want to order food in a restaurant. You'll also add to your knowledge of Chinese grammar by learning how to make suggestions, give commands, and form requests. Plus, you'll learn how to express what you want, and how to ask negative questions.

So, let's get started!

Lesson 5: Words

In this lesson, you'll learn:

☐ Vocabulary related to dining and food.

☐ Making suggestions: hǎo ma? 好吗?

☐ More commands and requests.

Word Builder 1

▶ 5A Word Builder 1 (CD 7, Track 19)

zǎocān	早餐	*breakfast*
wǔcān	午餐	*lunch*
wǎncān	晚餐	*dinner, supper*

Polite Requests

huòzhě/háishi
或者/还是 *(or)*

Adverbial Expressions
with **de** 得

Expressing Quantities

yèxiāo/xiāoyè	夜宵/消夜	*late night snack*
tiándiǎn	甜点	*dessert*
kāfēi	咖啡	*coffee*
chá	茶	*tea*
sūdǎshuǐ	苏打水	*soda*
niúnǎi	牛奶	*milk*
táng	糖	*sugar*
shíwù	食物	*food*
guǒzhī	果汁	*juice*
píjiǔ	啤酒	*beer*
jiǔ	酒	*wine, alcohol*
hújiāo	胡椒	*pepper*
yán	盐	*salt*
jiàngyóu	酱油	*soy sauce*
jièmo	芥末	*mustard*
là	辣	*hot, spicy*
lěng	冷	*cold*
hǎochī	好吃	*delicious*

(II)

✎ Word Practice 1

Match the English word in the column on the left with its appropriate translation in the column on the right.

1. *milk*

2. *juice*

3. *soy sauce*

4. *delicious*

a. jiàngyóu 酱油

b. kāfēi 咖啡

c. niúnǎi 牛奶

d. guǒzhī 果汁

Making Suggestions:
hǎo ma? 好吗？

Modal verbs

More Commands and
Requests

Negative Questions

3. *Let's take the bus, okay?* _____

_____

4. *Let's go to a movie tomorrow, okay?* _____

_____

5. *Let's go over there, shall we?* _____

_____

6. *Let's go swimming next Monday. Is that okay with you?* _____

_____

7. *Let's watch TV together, okay?* _____

_____

ANSWER KEY
1. Zánmen jīntiān wǎnshang chī Zhōngguó cài, hǎo ma? 咱们今天晚上吃中国菜，好吗？ 2. Zánmen tiàowǔ, hǎo ma? 咱们跳舞，好吗？ 3. Zánmen zuò gōngchē, hǎo ma? 咱们坐公车，好吗？ 4. Zánmen míngtiān (qù) kàn diànyǐng, hǎo ma? 咱们明天(去)看电影，好吗？ 5. Zánmen qù nàli, hǎo ma? 咱们去那里，好吗？ 6. Zánmen xià ge lǐbài yī qù yóuyǒng, hǎo ma? 咱们下个礼拜一去游泳，好吗？ 7. Zánmen yìqǐ kàn diànshì, hǎo ma? 咱们一起看电视，好吗？

Word Builder 2

▶ 5C Word Builder 2 (CD 7, Track 21)

tāng	汤	soup
ròu	肉	meat
niúpái	牛排	steak
niúròu	牛肉	beef
zhūpái	猪排	pork chop(s)
jī	鸡	chicken
jīròu	鸡肉	chicken meat (boneless)
huǒtuǐ	火腿	ham

Polite Requests

huòzhě/háishi
或者/还是 (*or*)

Adverbial Expressions
with **de** 得

Expressing Quantities

yú	鱼	*fish*
xiā	虾	*shrimp*
lóngxiā	龙虾	*lobster*
dàn	蛋	*egg(s)*
shūcài	蔬菜	*vegetables*
bāoxīncài	包心菜	*cabbage*
húluóbo	红萝卜	*carrot*
qíncài	芹菜	*celery*
huánggua	黄瓜	*cucumber*
tǔdòu	马铃薯/土豆	*potatoes*
shāla	沙拉	*salad*
miàntiáo	面条	*noodles*
diǎnxīn	点心	*dim sum*
shuǐguǒ	水果	*fruit*
miànbāo	面包	*bread*
huángyóu	黄油	*butter*

(II)

✎ Word Practice 2

Fill in the blanks of the following conversation with the words from the list above.

A: Nǐ xǐhuan chī shénme _____?

你喜欢吃什么 _____？

(*What kind of meat do you like to eat?*)

Making Suggestions:
hǎo ma? 好吗?

Modal verbs

More Commands and
Requests

Negative Questions

B: Wǒ xǐhuan _____ hé _____.

我喜欢 _____ 和 _____。

(*I like ham and lobster.*)

A: Nǐ yào chī _____ ma?

你要吃沙 _____ 吗?

(*Do you want to eat salad?*)

B: Wǒ chī yì diǎn _____.

我吃一点 _____。

(*I'll have some carrots.*)

A: Hǎo. Wǒmen zài diǎn liǎng wǎn _____.

好。 我们再点两碗 _____。

(*Ok. We will also order two bowls of soup.*)

ANSWER KEY
A. ròu 肉; B. huǒtuǐ 火腿, lóngxiā 龙虾; A. shāla 沙拉; B. húluóbo 红萝卜; A. tāng 汤

Grammar Builder 2
MORE COMMANDS AND REQUESTS

▶ 5D Grammar Builder 2 (CD 7, Track 22)

You learned in *Intermediate Chinese* that a command can be formed in Chinese simply by using a verb without any subject in a sentence. You can soften the tone of a command by using the particle ba 吧 after the verb.

Zǒu!
走!
Leave!

Polite Requests

huòzhě/háishi
或者/还是 (*or*)

Adverbial Expressions
with **de** 得

Expressing Quantities

Zǒu ba.

走吧。

Leave. Go ahead and leave.

Shuì!

睡!

Sleep!

Shuì ba.

睡吧。

Go to sleep.

As you know, negative commands are formed by adding bié 别 (or búyào 不要) in front of the verb.

Bié shuì ba.

别睡吧。

Don't sleep.

Bié zǒu!

别走!

Do not leave!

Bié děngle. Nǐ xiān chī ba.

别等了。你先吃吧。

Don't wait. You eat first.

You can also form a third-person command in Chinese by putting ràng 让 ... ba 吧 around a declarative sentence. This phrase can be translated into English as *Let* ...

Making Suggestions:
hǎo ma? 好吗?

Modal verbs

More Commands and
Requests

Negative Questions

Ràng tā kàn nǐ de shū ba.

让他看你的书吧。

Let him see/read your book.

Ràng tāmen xiān zǒu ba.

让他们先走吧。

Let them go first.

Ràng nǐ de nǚ'ér xiān chī ba.

让你的女儿先吃吧。

Let your daughter eat first.

Ⓘ

✎ Work Out 2

Translate the following commands into Chinese.

1. *Let's dance.* _____

   _____

2. *Let your daughter and her friend go to that restaurant this Sunday.* _____

   _____

3. *You eat first. (soft tone)* _____

   _____

4. *Let them go to school to study Chinese.* _____

   _____

5. *Give him two yuan. (soft tone)* _____

   _____

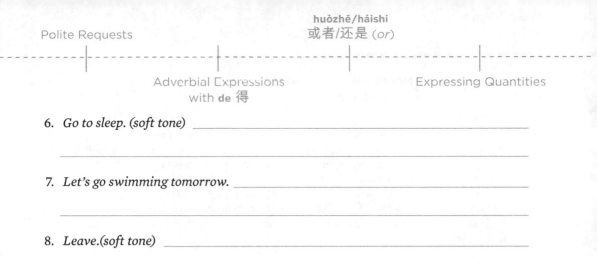

6. *Go to sleep. (soft tone)* _____

_____

7. *Let's go swimming tomorrow.* _____

_____

8. *Leave.(soft tone)* _____

_____

ANSWER KEY
1. Zánmen tiàowǔ. 咱们跳舞。 2. Ràng nǐ de nǚ'ér hé tā de péngyou zhège xīngqī rì qù nà jiā cānguǎn. 让你的女儿和他的朋友这个星期日去那家餐馆。 3. Nǐ xiān chī ba. 你先吃吧。 4. Ràng tāmen qù xuéxiào xué Zhōngwén ba. 让他们去学校学中文吧。 5. Gěi tā liǎng kuài qián ba. 给他两块钱吧。 6. Shuì ba. 睡吧。 7. Zánmen míngtiān qù yóuyǒng ba. 咱们明天去游泳吧。 8. Zǒu ba. 走吧。

✎ Drive It Home

Practice writing command sentences using ba 吧. For each pronoun, write three command sentences using the phrases provided in parentheses, being aware of when to use the ràng 让 . . . ba 吧 construction.

1. Zánmen 咱们 (kàn diànshì 看电视, zuò zài zhèlǐ 坐在这里, qù nàge niúpái cānguǎn chī wǎnfàn 去那个牛排餐馆吃晚饭) _____

_____

2. Tā 他 (kàn shū 看书, qù jiàn tā de péngyou 去见他的朋友, bú yào qí tā de xīn zìxíngchē 不要骑他的新自行车) _____

_____

3. Nǐ 你 (jīntiān bié shàngxué 今天别上学, hē yì diǎn jiǔ 喝一点酒, zuò huǒchē qù Niǔyuē 坐火车去纽约) _____

_____

Making Suggestions:
hǎo ma? 好吗？

Modal verbs

More Commands and
Requests

Negative Questions

ANSWER KEY

1. Zánmen kàn diànshì ba. 咱们看电视吧。 (*Let's watch TV.*) Zánmen zuò zài zhèlǐ ba. 咱们坐在这里吧。 (*Let's sit here.*) Zánmen qù nàge niúpái cānguǎn chī wǎnfàn ba. 咱们去那个牛排餐馆吃晚饭吧。 (*Let's go to that steak restaurant to have dinner.*) 2. Ràng tā kàn shū ba. 让他看书吧 (*Let him read.*) Ràng tā qù jiàn tā de péngyou ba. 让他去见他的朋友吧。 (*Let him go see his friend.*) Ràng tā bú yào qí tā de xīn zìxíngchē ba. 让他不要骑他的新自行车吧。 (*Don't let him ride his new bicycle.*) 3. Nǐ bié jīntiān shàngxué ba. 你别今天上学吧。 (*Don't go to school today.*) Nǐ hē yì diǎn jiǔ ba. 你喝一点酒吧。 (*Have a little wine.*) Nǐ zuò huǒchē qù Niǔyuē ba. 你坐火车去纽约吧。 (*Take the train to New York.*)

✎ Word Recall

Match the English word in the column on the left with its appropriate translation in the column on the right.

1. *fruit*   a. tiándiǎn 甜点

2. *shrimp*   b. wǎncān 晚餐

3. *vegetables*   c. sūdǎshuǐ 苏打水

4. *dinner*   d. shuǐguǒ 水果

5. *chicken meat (boneless)*   e. shíwù 食物

6. *mustard*   f. ròu 肉

7. *cold*   g. miànbāo 面包

8. *soda*   h. táng 糖

9. *noodles*   i. xiā 虾

10. *dessert*   j. lěng 冷

11. *meat*   k. dàn 蛋

12. *food*   l. jièmo 芥末

13. *bread*   m. miàntiáo 面条

14. *egg(s)*   n. jīròu 鸡肉

15. *sugar*   o. shūcài 蔬菜

ANSWER KEY

1. d; 2. i; 3. o; 4. b; 5. n; 6. l; 7. j; 8. c; 9. m; 10. a; 11. f; 12. e; 13. g; 14. k; 15. h

Polite Requests

huòzhě/háishi
或者/还是 (or)

Adverbial Expressions
with de 得

Expressing Quantities

Lesson 6: Phrases

In this lesson, you'll learn:

☐ Vocabulary and measure words used to talk about food and dining.

☐ Modal verbs.

☐ Negative questions.

Phrase Builder 1

6A Phrase Builder 1 (CD 7, Track 23)

yì bǎ dāo	一把刀	*a knife*
yì zhī tāngchí/sháozi	一只汤匙/勺子	*a spoon*
yì zhī chāzi	一只叉子	*a fork*
yì bēi kāfēi	一杯咖啡	*a cup of coffee*
yì bēi chá	一杯茶	*a cup of tea*
yì bēi nǎichá	一杯奶茶	*a cup of milk tea (tea with milk)*
yì tiáo cānjīn	一条餐巾	*a napkin*
yí ge pánzi	一个盘子	*a plate*
yí zhī bēizi	一只杯子	*a cup/glass*
yì shuāng kuàizi	一双筷子	*a pair of chopsticks*
yì wǎn tāng	一碗汤	*a bowl of soup*
yí kuài miànbāo	一块面包	*a piece of bread*
yì píng jiǔ	一瓶酒	*a bottle of wine*
yì píng hóngjiǔ	一瓶红酒	*a bottle of red wine*
yì píng báijiǔ	一瓶白酒	*a bottle of white spirits*

Making Suggestions:
hǎo ma? 好吗?

Modal verbs

More Commands and
Requests

Negative Questions

yì bēi jiǔ	一杯酒	*a glass of wine*
yì wǎn mǐfàn	一碗米饭	*a bowl of rice*
yì hé niúnǎi	一盒牛奶	*a carton of milk*
yí guàn mógu	一罐蘑菇	*a can of mushrooms*
yì bāo mǐ	一包米	*a bag of rice*
yì bāo miàn	一包面	*a bag of noodles*
yì xiāng fāngbiànmiàn	一箱方便面	*a box of instant noodles*

✎ Phrase Practice 1

Select the appropriate measure word for each blank.

1. yì _____ kuàizi (一____筷子)

   bēi 杯

   shuāng 双

   hé 盒

2. yì _____ hóngjiǔ (一____红酒)

   píng 瓶

   zhī 只

   bǎ 把

3. yì _____ kāfēi (一____咖啡)

   tiáo 条

   wǎn 碗

   bēi 杯

Polite Requests

huòzhě/háishi
或者/还是 *(or)*

Adverbial Expressions
with **de** 得

Expressing Quantities

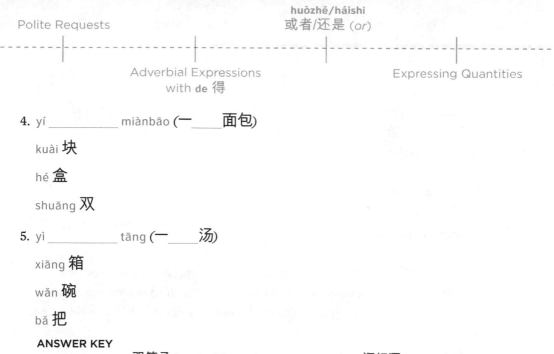

4. yí _____ miànbāo (一____面包)

   kuài **块**

   hé **盒**

   shuāng **双**

5. yì _____ tāng (一____汤)

   xiāng **箱**

   wǎn **碗**

   bǎ **把**

ANSWER KEY
1. yì shuāng kuàizi 一双筷子 (*a pair of chopsticks*); 2. yì píng hóngjiǔ 一瓶红酒 (*a bottle of red wine*);
3. yì bēi kāfēi 一杯咖啡 (*a cup of coffee*); 4. yí kuài miànbāo 一块面包 (*a piece of bread*); 5. yì wǎn tāng
一碗汤 (*a bowl of soup*)

Grammar Builder 1
MODAL VERBS

▶ 6B Grammar Builder 1 (CD 8, Track 1)

A modal verb is a verb that you can use along with another verb, as in *want to eat* or *must learn*. Yào 要 (*to want*) and xiǎng 想 (*to want/would like*) can both be used as modal verbs in Chinese to express a willingness to do something or a wish for something to happen. As the following examples demonstrate, the verb yào 要 indicates a stronger sense of desire:

Wǒ yào zhù zài xuéxiào fùjìn.
我要住在学校附近。
I (really) want to live near school.

Making Suggestions:
hǎo ma? 好吗？
Modal verbs

More Commands and
Requests
Negative Questions

Wǒ xiǎng hē yì bēi kāfēi.

我想喝一杯咖啡。

I'd like to drink a cup of coffee.

Tā xiǎng yào yì bēi chá.

他想要一杯茶。

He wants to have a cup of tea.

Note that yào 要 can be used as both a main verb (meaning *to have* or *to need*) or as a modal verb (meaning *to want*) in Chinese. In the third example above, yào 要 is the main verb, and xiǎng 想 is the modal verb. Combined, they mean *wants to have*.

Another common modal verb is kěyǐ 可以, which means can, may or to be able to in the sense of being permitted or allowed to do something. The modal verb néng(gòu) 能(够), on the other hand, is used to mean can or to be able to when referring to one's ability or proficiency in performing an action.

Here are some examples that illustrate how these modal verbs are used in Chinese:

Wǒmen xiànzài kěyǐ chīle. Dàjiā dōu láile.

我们现在可以吃了。大家都来了。

We can eat now. Everyone has arrived.

Wǒ nénggòu zài wǔ fēnzhōng zhīnèi chī wán liǎng wǎn miàntiáo.

我能够在五分钟之内吃完两碗面条。

I can eat two bowls of noodles in five minutes.

Tā jīntiān wǎnshang bù néng láile.

他今天晚上不能来了。

He can't come tonight. (He won't be able to come tonight.)

Polite Requests

huòzhě/háishi
或者/还是 (or)

Adverbial Expressions
with de 得

Expressing Quantities

Wǒ kěyǐ cháng dào zhège cài lǐbiān yǒu jiāng.

我可以尝到这个菜里边有姜。

I can taste ginger in this dish.

Nǐ huì shāo Zhōngguó cài ma?

你会烧中国菜吗？

Can you cook Chinese food? (lit., Do you know how to cook Chinese food?)

Wǒ huì kāichē. Dànshì, yīnwèi wǒ méiyǒu jiàzhào, suǒyǐ wǒ bù kěyǐ kāichē.

我会开车。但是，因为我没有驾照，所以我不可以开车。

I can drive. But, since I don't have a license, I can't drive.

Note that in the last two examples, *can* is translated as huì 会 in Chinese when it means *know how to*. Also note that when néng(gòu) 能(够) is negated by adding the negative particle bù 不, the resulting verb form bù néng(gòu) 能(够) is always shortened to bù néng 不能。

Bìxū 必须 is another commonly used modal verb in Chinese. It is translated as *have to* or *must* and is used to indicate necessity or an obligation to do something.

Wǒ xiànzài bìxū kāishǐ zuòfàn le.

我现在必须开始做饭了。

I have to start cooking now.

Wǒmen bìxū duō mǎi yìxiē zhūròu zuò wǎnfàn. Wǒmen jiā lǐ de ròu bú gòu le.

我们必须多买一些猪肉做晚饭。我们家里的肉不够了。

We have to buy more pork for dinner. We don't have enough meat at home. (lit., Our home doesn't have enough meat.)

Ⅱ

Making Suggestions:
hǎo ma? 好吗?

Modal verbs

More Commands and
Requests

Negative Questions

✎ Work Out 1

Translate the following sentences into Chinese.

1. *I would like to have a glass of wine.* _____

_____

2. *I don't feel well. I can't drink coffee.* _____

_____

3. *I want to go to China next year.* _____

_____

4. *I'd like to have a knife.* _____

_____

5. *I would like to drink soup.* _____

_____

6. *Can you give me some tea?* _____

_____

7. *He wants to go to a movie tomorrow night.* _____

_____

8. *We must buy more beef today.* _____

_____

ANSWER KEY
1. Wǒ xiǎng yào yì bēi jiǔ. 我想要一杯酒。 2. Wǒ bù shūfu. Wǒ bù néng hē kāfēi. 我不舒服。我不能喝咖啡。 3. Wǒ míngnián yào qù Zhōngguó. 我明年要去中国。 4. Wǒ xiǎng yào yì bǎ dāo. 我想要一把刀。 5. Wǒ xiǎng hē tāng. 我想喝汤。 6. Nǐ kěyǐ gěi wǒ yìxiē chá ma? 你可以给我一些茶吗？ 7. Tā míngtiān wǎnshang yào kàn diànyǐng. 他明天晚上要看电影。 8. Wǒmen jīntiān bìxū duō mǎi yìxiē niúròu. 我们今天必须多买一些牛肉。

Polite Requests

huòzhě/háishi
或者/还是 (or)

Adverbial Expressions
with **de** 得

Expressing Quantities

Phrase Builder 2

▶ 6C Phrase Builder 2 (CD 8, Track 2)

Gěi wǒ …	给我 …	*Bring me … /Give me …*
Wǒ xiǎng yào …	我想要 …	*I would like to have …*
Nǐ kěyǐ gěi wǒ … ma?	你可以给我 … 吗?	*May I have … ? (lit., Could you give me … ?)*
yìxiē shuǐguǒ	一些水果	*some fruit*
Zài gěi wǒ yì tiáo cānjīn.	再给我一条餐巾。	*(Give me) another napkin. (lit., Give me a napkin again.)*
Zài gěi wǒ yí zhī chāzi hé yì bǎ dāo.	再给我一只叉子和一把刀。	*(Give me) another fork and knife. (lit., Give me a fork and a knife again.)*
zài lái yì píng jiǔ	再来一瓶酒	*another bottle of wine*
zài lái yìdiǎn nàge	再来一点那个	*a little more of that*
zài lái yìdiǎn miànbāo	再来一点面包	*a little more bread*
zài lái yìdiǎn ròu	再来一点肉	*a little more meat*
Nǐmen yǒu … ma?	你们有 … 吗?	*Do you have … ?*
Wǒ yào …	我要 …	*I need …*
Nǐ yào … ?	你要 … ?	*Do you want … ?*
Máfan nǐ gěi wǒmen …	麻烦你给我们 …	*Could I trouble you for …*
Qǐng nǐ jiézhàng!	请你结帐!	*Check please!*

⏸

Making Suggestions:
hǎo ma? 好吗?

Modal verbs

More Commands and
Requests

Negative Questions

✎ Phrase Practice 2

Translate the following sentences into English.

1. Wǒ yào yì xiē shuǐguǒ. 我要一些水果。 _____

   _____

2. Nǐmen yǒu niúnǎi ma? 你们有牛奶吗? _____

   _____

3. Nǐ kěyǐ gěi wǒ yì bēi shuǐ ma? 你可以给我一杯水吗? _____

   _____

4. Zài lái yì wǎn mǐfàn. 再来一碗米饭。 _____

   _____

5. Máfan nǐ gěi wǒmen liǎng bēi kāfēi. 麻烦你给我们两杯咖啡。 _____

   _____

ANSWER KEY

1. *I want some fruit.* 2. *Do you have any milk?* 3. *May I have a glass of water?* 4. *Another bowl of rice.* 5. *Could you give us two cups of coffee?*

Grammar Builder 2
NEGATIVE QUESTIONS

▶ 6D Grammar Builder 2 (CD 8, Track 3)

As in English, Chinese questions can be posed both in the affirmative and in the negative forms:

Nǐ xǐhuan yú ma?
你喜欢鱼吗?
Do you like fish?

Polite Requests

huòzhě/háishi
或者/还是 (or)

Adverbial Expressions
with de 得

Expressing Quantities

Nǐ bù xǐhuan yú ma?

你不喜欢鱼吗?

Don't you like fish?

To answer a negative question in English, you have a choice between showing agreement (*No, I don't*) and disagreement (*Yes, I do!*). In Chinese, however, these answers take on a different form. To show agreement, start with the positive word shì 是 (*yes*), and then repeat the (negative content of the) question, so that you literally reply: *Yes, I don't like fish.* To show disagreement, start with the negative phrase bú shì 不是 (*no*), and follow it with a sentence that rephrases the question in a positive way, so literally: *No, I like fish.* You may find this pattern confusing, because it's quite the opposite of English. But if you think about it, it's really very logical!

Nǐ bù xǐhuan yú ma?

你不喜欢鱼吗?

Don't you like fish?

Shì. Wǒ bù xǐhuan yú.

是。我不喜欢鱼。

No, I don't like fish. (lit., Yes. I don't like fish.)

Bú shì. Wǒ xǐhuan yú.

不是。我喜欢鱼。

Yes, I like fish. (lit., No. I like fish.)

Ⅱ

Making Suggestions:
hǎo ma? 好吗？

More Commands and
Requests

Modal verbs

Negative Questions

✎ Work Out 2

Translate the answers in parentheses into Chinese:

1. Nǐ bù chī zǎocān ma? 你不吃早餐吗? *(No, I don't eat breakfast.)* _____

    _____

2. Nǐ bù chī zǎocān ma? 你不吃早餐吗? *(Yes, I do eat breakfast.)* _____

    _____

3. Tāmen bù qù xuéxiào ma? 他们不去学校吗? *(No, they don't go to school.)* _____

    _____

4. Tāmen bù qù xuéxiào ma? 他们不去学校吗? *(Yes, they do go to school.)* _____

    _____

5. Nǐ de māma méiyǒu zuòfàn ma? 你的妈妈没有做饭吗? *(Yes, she did cook.)* _____

    _____

6. Nǐ de māma méiyǒu zuòfàn ma? 你的妈妈没有做饭吗? *(No, she didn't cook.)* _____

    _____

7. Nàge Měiguórén bú huì shuō Zhōngwén ma? 那个美国人不会说中文吗? *(Yes,*

    he does know how to speak Chinese.) _____

    _____

8. Nàge Měiguórén bú huì shuō Zhōngwén ma? 那个美国人不会说中文吗? *(No,*

    he doesn't know how to speak Chinese.) _____

ANSWER KEY

1. Shì. Wǒ bù chī zǎocān. 是。我不吃早餐。 2. Bú shì. Wǒ chī zǎocān. 不是。我吃早餐。 3. Shì.
Tāmen qù le xuéxiào. 是。他们去了学校。 4. Bú shì. Tāmen (huì) qù xuéxiào. 不是。他们(会)去

Polite Requests

huòzhě/háishi
或者/还是 (or)

Adverbial Expressions
with de 得

Expressing Quantities

学校。5. Bú shì. Wǒ de māma zuòle fàn. 不是。我的妈妈做了饭。6. Shì. Wǒ de māma méiyǒu zuòfàn. 是。我的妈妈没有做饭。7. Bú shì. Nàge Měiguórén huì shuō Zhōngwén. 不是。那个美国人会说中文。8. Shì. Nàge Měiguórén bú huì shuō Zhōngwén. 是。那个美国人不会说中文。

✏️ Drive It Home

Answer each negative question with an agreeing and disagreeing response.

1. Nǐ bù mǎi shūcài ma? 你不买蔬菜吗? *(Don't you buy vegetables?)* _____

    _____

2. Nǐ bù xǐhuan Měiguó diànyǐng ma? 你不喜欢美国电影吗? *(Don't you like American movies?)* _____

    _____

3. Nǐ bù zǎo shuìjiào ma? 你不早睡觉吗? *(Don't you go to sleep early?)* _____

    _____

4. Nǐ bú rènshi nàge rén ma? 你不认识那个人吗? *(Don't you know that person?)* _____

    _____

5. Nǐ bù míngbai jīntiān de kè ma? 你不明白今天的课吗? *(Don't you understand today's class?)* _____

    _____

ANSWER KEY

1. Shì. Wǒ bù mǎi shūcài. 是。我不买蔬菜。 Bú shì. Wǒ mǎi shūcài. 不是。我买蔬菜。 2. Shì. Wǒ bù xǐhuan Měiguó diànyǐng. 是。我不喜欢美国电影; Bú shì. Wǒ xǐhuan Měiguó diànyǐng. 不是。我喜欢美国电影。 3. Shì. Wǒ bù zǎo shuìjiào. 是。我不早睡觉。 Bú shì. Wǒ zǎo shuìjiào. 不是。我早睡觉。 4. Shì. Wǒ bú rènshi nàge rén. 是。我不认识那个人。 Bú shì. Wǒ rènshi nàge rén. 不是。我认识那个人。 5. Shì. Wǒ bù míngbai jīntiān de kè. 是。我不明白今天的课; Bú shì. Wǒ míngbai jīntiān de kè. 不是。我明白今天的课。

Making Suggestions:
hǎo ma? 好吗?

Modal verbs

More Commands and
Requests

Negative Questions

✎ Phrase Recall

Match the English word in the column on the left with its appropriate translation in the column on the right.

1. *Do you have … ?*

a. yì tiáo cānjīn 一条餐巾

2. *a plate*

b. gěi wǒ … 给我 …

3. *a glass of wine*

c. yì bēi nǎichá 一杯奶茶

4. *(Give me) another napkin. (lit., Give me a napkin again.)*

d. yì wǎn tāng 一碗汤

5. *check please!*

e. Wǒ xiǎng yào … 我想要 …

6. *a napkin*

f. Zài gěi wǒ yì tiáo cānjīn. 再给我一条餐巾.

7. *a bowl of rice*

g. yì zhī chāzi 一只叉子

8. *a pair of chopsticks*

h. Nǐmen yǒu … ma? 你们有 … 吗?

9. *Bring me … /Give me …*

i. Qǐng nǐ jiézhàng! 请你结帐!

10. *a fork*

j. yí ge pánzi 一个盘子

11. *May I have … ? (lit., Could you give me … ?)*

k. zài lái yìdiǎn nàge 再来一点那个

12. *a bowl of soup*

l. yì bēi jiǔ 一杯酒

13. *I would like to have …*

m. Nǐ kěyǐ gěi wǒ … ma? 你可以给我 … 吗?

14. *a little more of that*

n. yì shuāng kuàizi 一双筷子

15. *a cup of milk tea (tea with milk)*

o. yì wǎn mǐfàn 一碗米饭

ANSWER KEY
1. h; 2. j; 3. l; 4. f; 5. i; 6. a; 7. o; 8. n; 9. b; 10. g; 11. m; 12. d; 13. e; 14. k; 15. c

Polite Requests

huòzhě/háishi
或者/还是 (or)

Adverbial Expressions
with de 得

Expressing Quantities

Lesson 7: Sentences

In this lesson, you'll learn:

☐ How to ask for things in a restaurant.

☐ How to make polite requests.

☐ Adverbial expressions with de 得.

Sentence Builder 1

▶ 7A Sentence Builder 1 (CD 8, Track 4)

Gěi wǒ yì bēi chá hé yìxiē chūnjuǎn.	给我一杯茶和一些春卷。	*Bring me a cup of tea and some spring rolls.*
Qǐng nǐ gěi wǒ liǎng fèn zǎocān.	请你给我两份早餐。	*May I have breakfast for two?/Please give me breakfast for two.*
Qǐng nǐ gěi wǒ càidān.	请你给我菜单。	*May I have a menu?/ Please give me a menu.*
Máfan nǐ gěi wǒ yìxiē hújiāo.	麻烦你给我一些胡椒。	*Could I trouble you for some black pepper (please)?*
Nǐmen yǒu shénme hē de?	你们有什么喝的？	*What do you have to drink?*
Qǐng nǐ ná yí ge chāzi gěi wǒ.	请你拿一个叉子给我。	*May I have a fork? (lit., Please give me a fork.)*
Nǐ zěnme shāo zhège ròu?	你怎么烧这个肉？	*How do you cook the meat?*
Nǐ kěyǐ jiāo wǒ zěnme yòng kuàizi ma?	你可以教我怎么用筷子吗？	*Can you teach me how to use chopsticks?*

Making Suggestions:
hǎo ma? 好吗?

Modal verbs

More Commands and
Requests

Negative Questions

Wǒ xiǎng zài yào yì wǎn mǐfàn.	我想再要一碗米饭。	*I would like to have another bowl of rice.*
Qǐng bú yào fàng tài duō yóu.	请不要放太多油。	*Please don't put too much oil (in it).*
Wǒ shì chīsù de.	我是吃素的。	*I'm a vegetarian.*
Qǐng nǐ jiézhàng.	请你结帐。	*May I have the check?*
Wǒ kěyǐ shuākǎ ma?	我可以刷卡吗？	*Can I pay by credit card?*

⏸

✎ Sentence Practice 1

Fill in the blanks of the following conversation.

A: Nǐmen yǒu _____ hē de?

你们有什么喝的？

(*What do you have to drink?*)

B: Wǒmen _____ sūdǎshuǐ , guǒzhī, chá, hé píjiǔ.

我们有苏打水, 果汁, 茶, 和啤酒。

(*We have soda, juice, tea, and beer.*)

A: _____ wǒ yì _____ chá hé yìxiē chūnjuǎn.

给我一杯茶和一些春卷。

(*Give me a cup of tea and some spring rolls.*)

B: Nín _____ zhūpái ma?

您喜欢猪排吗？

(*Do you like pork spare ribs?*)

Polite Requests

huòzhě/háishi
或者/还是 (or)

Adverbial Expressions
with de 得

Expressing Quantities

A: Wǒ shì _____ de. Nǐmen yǒu shénme _____?

我是吃素的。你们有什么蔬菜？

(*I'm a vegetarian. What kind of vegetables do you have?*)

B: Wǒmen de kǎo mógū _____.

我们的烤蘑菇不错。

(*Our roasted mushrooms are pretty good.*)

A: Hǎo. Nǐ _____ jiāo wǒ zěnme _____ _____ kuàizi ma?

好。你可以教我怎么用筷子吗？

(*Ok. Can you teach me how to use chopsticks?*)

ANSWER KEY
A. shénme 什么; B. yǒu 有; A. gěi 给, bēi 杯; B. xǐhuan 喜欢; A. chīsù 吃素, shūcai 蔬菜; B. búcuò 不错; A. kěyǐ 可以, yòng 用

Grammar Builder 1
POLITE REQUESTS

▶ 7B Grammar Builder 1 (CD 8, Track 5)

As you know, it is polite to add the word qǐng 请 (*please*) before a request or command. You can also add qǐng nǐ/nín 请你/您 to the beginning of a sentence in order to say *Please ...* or *May I ...*

Qǐng nín gěi wǒ nín de míngpiàn.
请您给我您的名片。
May I have your business card?/Please give me your business card.

Qǐng nǐ gěi wǒ yì bēi rè kāishuǐ.
请你给我一杯热开水。
May I have a glass of hot water?/Please give me a glass of hot water.

Making Suggestions:
hǎo ma? 好吗?

Modal verbs

More Commands and
Requests

Negative Questions

✎ **Sentence Practice 2**

Translate the following sentences into English.

1. Niú ròu shāo de tài lǎo le. 牛肉烧得太老了。 _____

   _____

2. Tā měi dùn fàn dōu chī de tài kuài. 他每顿饭都吃得太快。 _____

   _____

3. Zhège cānguǎn de chúshī shāocài shāo de bù hǎo. 这个餐馆的厨师烧菜烧得
   不好。 _____

   _____

4. Nǐ ná kuàizi ná de búcuò. 你拿筷子拿得不错。 _____

   _____

5. Wǒ de māma shāocài shāo de hěn hǎo. 我的妈妈烧菜烧得很好。 _____

   _____

ANSWER KEY
1. *The beef is too tough. (lit., The beef is cooked too tough.)* 2. *He eats too fast at every meal.* 3. *The chef in this restaurant doesn't cook well.* 4. *You handle chopsticks very well.* 5. *My mother cooks very well.*

Grammar Builder 2
ADVERBIAL EXPRESSIONS WITH DE 得

▶ 7D Grammar Builder 2 (CD 8, Track 7)

So far, you have learned the use of the particle de 的 with possessives and adjectives. There's also an adverbial particle de 得, which is used between a

Polite Requests

huòzhě/háishi
或者/还是 (or)

Adverbial Expressions
with **de** 得

Expressing Quantities

verb and an adjective to form an adverbial expression that describes how an action is performed. De 得 is always placed immediately after the verb in this construction. In colloquial Chinese, the adverbs hěn 很 (*very*) or tài 太 (*too*) are commonly added before the adjective in this type of sentence. Here are some examples:

Tā chī de hěn kuài.
他吃得很快。
He eats very quickly.

Nǐ shuō de hěn hǎo.
你说得很好。
You speak very well.

Nǐ de māma shuō de tài kuài.
你的妈妈说得太快。
Your mother speaks too fast.

If an object follows the verb, then the verb needs to be repeated, and the object must be placed between the duplicated verbs in the following manner: verb + object + duplicated verb + de 得.

Wǒ shuō Zhōngwén shuō de hěn bù hǎo.
我说中文说得很不好。
I don't speak Chinese very well. (lit., I speak Chinese not very well.)

Tā chī tiándiǎn chī de hěn kuài.
他吃甜点吃得很快。
He eats dessert very quickly.

With verb-object verbs, this means that just the verb (tiào 跳) is repeated, not the full two syllable verb-object verb (tiàowǔ 跳舞).

Making Suggestions:
hǎo ma? 好吗？

Modal verbs

More Commands and
Requests

Negative Questions

3. *measure word for meal*

c. shāocài 烧菜

4. *menu*

d. chūnjuǎn 春卷

5. *to be careful*

e. chīsù 吃素

6. *black pepper*

f. càidān 菜单

7. *happy*

g. dùn 顿

8. *spring rolls*

h. jiāo 教

9. *something to drink*

i. hēihújiāo 黑胡椒

10. *hot, scalding*

j. fēicháng 非常

11. *to teach*

k. tàng 烫

12. *to put*

l. kuàilè 快乐

13. *very*

m. xiǎng 想

14. *to think, to want*

n. nèn 嫩

15. *tender*

o. fàng 放

ANSWER KEY
1. c; 2. e; 3. g; 4. f; 5. b; 6. i; 7. l; 8. d; 9. a; 10. k; 11. h; 12. o; 13. j; 14. m; 15. n

Lesson 8: Conversations

In this lesson, you'll learn:

☐ More about language used at a restaurant.

☐ Huòzhě/háishi 或者/还是 (*or*).

☐ How to express quantities.

Polite Requests

huòzhě/háishi
或者/还是 (or)

Adverbial Expressions
with **de** 得

Expressing Quantities

◖◗ Conversation 1

▶ 8A Conversation 1 (CD 8, Track 8-Chinese, Track 9-Chinese and English)

Jess and her friend Hai are going to a Chinese restaurant to have lunch.

Jiéxī:	Wǒ yǒu diǎn è le. Wǒmen qù nǎli chīfàn?
洁希:	我有点饿了。我们去哪里吃饭？
Hai:	Nǐ xǐhuan chī Zhōngcài háishi xī cài?
海:	你喜欢吃中菜还是西菜？
Jiéxī:	Wǒ xǐhuan chī Zhōngcài. Nà jiā cānguǎn kàn qǐlái búcuò. Wǒmen jiù zài nàli chīfàn ba.
洁希:	我喜欢吃中菜。那家餐馆看起来不错。我们就在那里吃饭吧。
Hai:	Hǎo ba.
海:	好吧。

(Tāmen zài cānguǎn lǐbian zuò xiàlái.)
(他们在餐馆里边坐下来。)

Hai:	Nǐ xǐhuan diǎn shénme dōngxi? Jīròu háishì niúròu?
海:	你喜欢点什么东西？ 鸡肉还是牛肉？
Jiéxī:	Wǒ ài chī sùcài hé jīròu huòzhě yú. Tāmen yǒu shāla ma?
洁希:	我爱吃素菜和鸡肉或者鱼。他们有沙拉吗？
Hai:	Zhōng cānguǎn shì méiyǒu shāla de. Rúguǒ nǐ xǐhuan cài de huà, wǒmen kěyǐ diǎn yì dié chǎocài, zěnme yàng?
海:	中餐馆是没有沙拉的。如果你喜欢菜的话，我们可以点一碟炒菜，怎么样？
Jiéxī:	Hǎo. Méi wèntí.
洁希:	好。没问题。

Jess:	*I'm hungry. Where should we go to eat?*
Hai:	*Do you want Chinese or Western food?*

Making Suggestions:
hǎo ma? 好吗?

Modal verbs

More Commands and
Requests

Negative Questions

When huòzhě 或者 is used in questions, the implication is that there is no preference between one choice and the other, or that there is no control over the choice. For example, you could ask about items on a menu using huòzhě 或者。 You would also use huòzhě 或者 to ask about states of being over which there is no control:

Càidān yǒu mǐfàn huòzhě miàntiáo ma?
菜单有米饭或者面条吗?
Is there rice or noodles on the menu?

Nǐ juéde lěng huòzhě rè ma?
你觉得冷或者热吗?
Do you feel cold or hot?

✎ Work Out 1

Translate the following sentences into Chinese.

1. *Do you want chicken (meat) or beef?* _____

_____

2. *I'll go to China in January or March.* _____

_____

3. *Are you British or American?* _____

_____

4. *Do you want to eat noodles or bread?* _____

_____

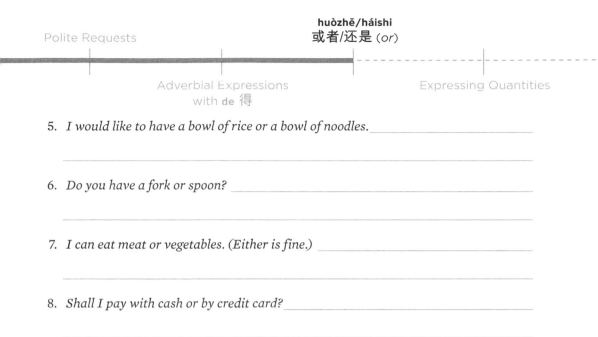

huòzhě/háishi
或者/还是 (or)

Polite Requests

Adverbial Expressions
with de 得

Expressing Quantities

5. *I would like to have a bowl of rice or a bowl of noodles.* _____

_____

6. *Do you have a fork or spoon?* _____

_____

7. *I can eat meat or vegetables. (Either is fine.)* _____

_____

8. *Shall I pay with cash or by credit card?* _____

_____

ANSWER KEY

1. Nǐ yào jīròu háishi niúròu? 你要鸡肉还是牛肉？ 2. Wǒ huì zài yī yuè huòzhě sān yuè qù Zhōngguó. 我会在一月或者三月去中国。 3. Nǐ shì Yīngguórén háishi Měiguórén? 你是英国人还是美国人？ 4. Nǐ yào chī miàntiáo háishi miànbāo? 你要吃面条还是面包？ 5. Wǒ xiǎng yào yì wǎn mǐfàn huòzhě yì wǎn miàntiáo. 我想要一碗米饭或者一碗面条。 6. Nǐ yǒu chāzi huòzhě tāngshí/sháozi ma? 你有叉子或者汤匙/勺子吗？ 7. Wǒ kěyǐ chī ròu huòzhě shūcài. 我可以吃肉或者蔬菜。 8. Wǒ fù xiànjīn háishi shuākǎ? 我付现金还是刷卡？

🔊 Conversation 2

▶ 8C Conversation 2 (CD 8, Track 11-Chinese, Track 12-Chinese and English)

Hai and Jess go to a restaurant. Listen to this conversation between Hai and their waiter.

Fúwùyuán: 服务员：	Qǐngwèn nǐmen yào diǎn shénme cài? 请问你们要点什么菜？
Hai: 海：	Nǐmen jīntiān de wǔcān yǒu shénme cài? 你们今天的午餐有什么菜？
Fúwùyuán: 服务员：	Wǒmen jīntiān yǒu hěnduō bùtóng de cài, bǐrú hóng shāo ròu, gōng bào jīdīng, mápó dòufu, huíguōròu hé sìjìdòu. 我们今天有很多不同的菜, 比如红烧肉、宫爆鸡丁、麻婆豆腐、回锅肉和四季豆。

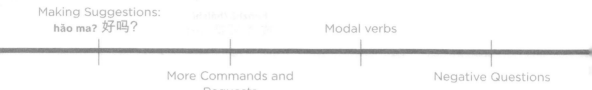

Making Suggestions:
hǎo ma? 好吗?

Modal verbs

More Commands and
Requests

Negative Questions

Grammar Builder 2
EXPRESSING QUANTITIES

▶ 8D Grammar Builder 2 (CD 8, Track 13)

The phrases hěnduō 很多 and bùshǎo 不少 can be used to express *many, a lot* or *quite a few*. The phrases yìxiē 一些 and hěnshǎo 很少 are used in Chinese to express *some* and *very few* respectively. As you can see from the following examples, they always precede the noun they modify, and no measure word is necessary.

Wǒ yǒu bù shǎo gǒu.
我有不少狗。
I have many dogs.

Wǒmen zài yànhuì shàng chīle hěn duō dōngxi.
我们在宴会上吃了很多东西。
We ate a lot of food at the banquet. (lit., We ate a lot of things at the banquet.)

Zhōngguó yǒu hěn duō rén.
中国有很多人。
There are a lot of people in China.

Tā yǒu yìxiē wèntí.
他有一些问题。
He has some questions.

Hěn shǎo kèrén lái wǔhuì.
很少客人来舞会。
Very few guests came to the dance party.

�643⑪

Polite Requests

huòzhě/háishi
或者/还是 (or)

Adverbial Expressions
with de 得

Expressing Quantities

Work Out 2

Fill in the blanks in the following sentences by translating the words in parentheses, and then give the English translation for the entire sentence.

1. Wǒ xiǎng yào _____ (some) miànbāo.

   我想要 _____ 面包。

2. Qǐng nǐ gěi wǒ _____ (some) huángyóu.

   请你给我 _____ 黄油。

3. Shànghǎi yǒu _____ (many) hěn hǎo de

   cānguǎn.

   上海有 _____ 很好的餐馆。

4. Nàge dàxué yǒu _____ (many) Zhōngguórén.

   那个大学有 _____ 中国人。

5. _____ (Very few) rén qù nà jiā cānguǎn chīfàn.

   _____ 人去那家餐馆吃饭。

ANSWER KEY

1. yìxiē 一些 *I would like (to have) some bread.* 2. yìxiē 一些 *Please give me some butter.* 3. hěn duō/bù shǎo 很多/不少 *There are many very good restaurants in Shanghai.* 4. hěn duō/bù shǎo 很多/不少 *There are many Chinese (students) at that university.* 5. Hěn shǎo 很少 *Very few people go eat at that restaurant.*

Culture Note

When the waiter in a Chinese restaurant asks you what kind of drink you would like, he expects you to request soda, beer, juice or wine. Of course, you could ask only for chá 茶 (tea), which is always served hot rather than cold and always without sugar in China.

Making Suggestions:
hǎo ma? 好吗?

Modal verbs

More Commands and
Requests

Negative Questions

猫在这里。Hěnshǎo māo zài zhèlǐ. 很少猫在这里。 3. Tā gěile wǒ hěnduō shū. 他给了我很多书。Tā gěile wǒ yìxiē shū. 他给了我一些书。 Tā gěile wǒ hěnshǎo shū. 他给了我很少书。 4. Dàlóu hòubian yǒu hěnduō chē. 大楼后边有很多车。Dàlóu hòubian yǒu yìxiē chē. 大楼后边有一些车。 Dàlóu hòubian yǒu hěnshǎo chē. 大楼后边有很少车。

✎ Word Recall

Match the English word in the column on the left with its appropriate translation in the column on the right.

1. either … or …	a. kàn qǐlái 看起来
2. stir-fried dish	b. rúguǒ 如果
3. Chinese cuisine	c. huòzhě 或者
4. carp	d. è 饿
5. looks to be, appears to be	e. lǐyú 鲤鱼
6. twice-cooked pork	f. bǐrú 比如
7. hungry	g. sìjìdòu 四季豆
8. such as, for example	h. Zhōngcài 中菜
9. or (suggesting a preference)	i. cháng 尝
10. Western cuisine	j. chǎocài 炒菜
11. if	k. ài 爱
12. different	l. háishi 还是
13. to love, to like	m. xī cài 西菜
14. string beans	n. huíguōròu 回锅肉
15. to taste	o. bùtóng 不同

ANSWER KEY
1. c; 2. j; 3. h; 4. e; 5. a; 6. n; 7. d; 8. f; 9. l; 10. m; 11. b; 12. o; 13. k; 14. g; 15. i

Don't forget to practice and reinforce what you've learned by visiting **www.livinglanguage.com/languagelab** for flashcards, games, and quizzes.

Unit 2 Essentials

Vocabulary Essentials

Test your knowledge of the key material in this unit by filling in the blanks in the following charts. Once you've completed these pages, you'll have tested your retention, and you'll have your own reference for the most essential vocabulary. This is also a great time to practice a few Chinese characters. Fill in the middle column with the characters that you remember. Or, if you only remember the pīnyīn, go back through the unit to find the character.

RESTAURANT VOCABULARY

PĪNYĪN	CHARACTER	
		breakfast
		lunch
		dinner, supper
		dessert
		coffee
		tea
		soda
		milk
		sugar
		food
		juice
		beer
		wine, alcohol
		soup
		meat
		steak

PĪNYĪN	CHARACTER	
		beef
		pork chop(s)
		chicken meat (boneless)
		ham
		fish
		shrimp
		lobster
		egg(s)
		vegetables
		potatoes
		salad
		noodles
		fruit
		bread

MEASURE WORDS WITH RESTAURANT VOCABULARY

PĪNYĪN	CHARACTER	
		a knife
		a spoon
		a fork
		a cup of coffee
		a cup of tea
		a napkin
		a plate
		a cup/glass
		a pair of chopsticks
		a bowl of soup
		a piece of bread

PĪNYĪN	CHARACTER	
		a bottle of wine
		a bowl of rice
		a carton of milk
		a can of mushrooms
		a bag of rice

USEFUL PHRASES FOR RESTAURANTS

PĪNYĪN	CHARACTER	
		Bring me … /Give me …
		I would like to have …
		May I have … ? (lit., Could you give me … ?)
		(Give me) another napkin. (lit., Give me a napkin again.)
		another bottle of wine
		a little more of that
		Do you have … ?
		I need …
		Do you want … ?
		Could I trouble you for …
		Check please!
		May I have a menu?/ Please give me a menu.
		What do you have to drink?
		How do you cook the meat?

PĪNYĪN	CHARACTER	
		I would like to have another bowl of rice.
		I'm a vegetarian.

If you're having a hard time remembering this vocabulary, don't forget to check out the flashcards, games and quizzes for this unit online. Go to **www.livinglanguage.com/languagelab** for a great way to help you practice what you've learned.

Grammar Essentials

Here is a reference for the key grammar that was covered in Unit 2. Make sure you understand the summary and can use all of the grammar it covers.

SUGGESTIONS AND COMMANDS

Zánmen qù nà jiā xīn cānguǎn, hǎo ma?	咱们去那家新餐馆，好吗？	*Let's go to the new restaurant, okay?*
—Hǎo ba.	好吧。	*Yes, let's go.*
—Wǒ bù xiǎng qù nà jiā xīn cānguǎn.	我不想去那家新餐馆。	*No, I don't want to/I'd rather not go to the new restaurant.*
Zǒu!	走!	*Leave! Let's go!*
Zǒu ba.	走吧。	*Leave. Go ahead.*
Ràng tā kàn nǐ de shū ba.	让他看你的书吧。	*Let him see/read your book.*

EXPRESSING WISHES WITH MODAL VERBS

| Wǒ yào zhù zài xuéxiào fùjìn. | 我要住在学校附近。 | *I (really) want to live near school.* |

Wǒ xiǎng hē yì bēi kāfēi.	我想喝一杯咖啡。	*I'd like to drink a cup of coffee.*
Tā xiǎng yào yì bēi chá.	他想要一杯茶。	*He wants to have a cup of tea.*

EXPRESSING PERMISSION, ABILITY, AND NECESSITY

Wǒmen xiànzài kěyǐ chīle. Dàjiā dōu láile.	我们现在可以吃了。大家都来了。	*We can eat now. Everyone has arrived.*
Wǒ nénggòu zài wǔ fēnzhōng zhīnèi chī wán liǎng wǎn miàntiáo.	我能够在五分钟之内吃完两碗面条。	*I can eat two bowls of noodles in five minutes.*
Tā jīntiān wǎnshang bù néng láile.	他今天晚上不能来了。	*He can't come tonight. (He won't be able to come tonight.)*
Wǒ kěyǐ cháng dào zhège cài lǐbiān yǒu jiāng.	我可以尝到这个菜里边有姜。	*I can taste ginger in this dish.*
Nǐ huì shāo Zhōngguó cài ma?	你会烧中国菜吗？	*Can you cook Chinese food? (lit., Do you know how to cook Chinese food?)*
Wǒ xiànzài bìxū kāishǐ zuòfàn le.	我现在必须开始做饭了。	*I have to start cooking now.*

POLITE REQUESTS

The equivalent of using the conditional *could* for polite requests in Chinese is máfan nǐ 麻烦你, which literally means *to bother you*.

Máfan nǐ gěi wǒ yì bēi chá hé yìxiē chūnjuǎn.	麻烦你给我一杯茶和一些春卷。	*Could you bring me a cup of tea and some spring rolls (please)?*
Máfan nǐ gěi wǒ yìxiē hújiāo.	麻烦你给我一些胡椒。	*Could you give me some pepper (please)?*

ADVERBIAL EXPRESSIONS

- Use verb + adverbial particle de 得 + adjective to form an adverbial expression that describes how an action is performed.

- With objects: verb + object + duplicated verb + de 得

Tā chī de hěn kuài.	他吃得很快。	*He eats very quickly.*
Nǐ shuō de hěn hǎo.	你说得很好。	*You speak very well.*
Nǐ de māma shuō de tài kuài.	你的妈妈说得太快。	*Your mother speaks too fast.*
Wǒ shuō Zhōngwén shuō de hěn bù hǎo.	我说中文说得很不好。	*I don't speak Chinese very well. (lit., I speak Chinese not very well.)*
Tā chī tiándiǎn chī de hěn kuài.	他吃甜点吃得很快。	*He eats dessert very quickly.*

EXPRESSING OR

Huòzhě 或者 (*or*) is usually used to form statements, linking two nouns or larger phrases. Háishi 还是 is used in questions that suggest a preference for one choice or the other.

When huòzhě 或者 is used in questions, the implication is that there is no preference or no control over a choice.

Nǐ xǐhuan wǒ háishì tā?	你喜欢我还是他?	*Do you like me or him?*
Nǐ jīntiān qù háishì míngtiān qù?	你今天去还是明天去?	*Do you go today or tomorrow?*
Nǐ xǐhuan píngguǒ háishì júzi?	你喜欢苹果还是橘子?	*Do you like apples or oranges?*
Càidān yǒu mǐfàn huòzhě miàntiáo ma?	菜单有米饭或者面条吗?	*Is there rice or noodles on the menu?*
Nǐ juéde lěng huòzhě rè ma?	你觉得冷或者热吗?	*Do you feel cold or hot?*

Unit 2 Quiz

A. Translate the following commands into Chinese using ba 吧.

1. *Let's have tea.* _____

2. *Give him that book.* _____

3. *Let her go see this movie.* _____

4. *Let's go play ball next week.* _____

B. Translate the following sentences featuring modal verbs into English.

1. Wǒ bù néng hē tàiduō kāfēi. 我不能喝太多咖啡。 _____

_____

2. Nǐ kěyǐ ràng wǒ kàn nà jiàn wàitào ma? 你可以让我看那件外套吗？ _____

_____

3. Wǒmen míngtiān bìxū duō jiàn yìxiē péngyou. 我们明天必须多见一些朋友。 ___

_____

4. Wǒ xiǎng yào yì bēi jiǔ. 我想要一杯酒。 _____

_____

5. Wǒ míngnián yào qù Zhōngguó. 我明年要去中国。 _____

_____

C. Make adverbial sentences using de 得 and the phrase and adjective provided.

1. Tā chīfàn, màn 他吃饭, 慢 _____

_____

2. Wǒmen kàn diánshi, kuàilè 我们看电视, 快乐 _____

_____

3. Nǐ xué Zhōngwén, hěn hǎo 你学中文, 很好 _____

_____

4. Tā de lǎoshī zǒulù, hěn kuài 她的老师走路, 很快 _____

_____

5. Wǒ tiàowǔ, bù hǎo 我跳舞, 不好 _____

_____

D. Fill in the blank with either háishi 还是 or huòzhě 或。

1. Nǐ yào jīròu _____ niúròu?

你要鸡肉 _____ 牛肉?

(*Do you want chicken or beef?*)

2. Nǐ shì Yīngguórén _____ Měiguórén?

你是英国人 _____ 美国人?

(*Are you British or American?*)

3. Wǒ xiǎng yào yì wǎn mǐfàn _____ yì wǎn miàntiáo.

我想要一碗米饭 _____ 一碗面条。

(*I would like to have a bowl of rice or a bowl of noodles.*)

4. Wǒ kěyǐ chī ròu _____ shūcài.

我可以吃肉 _____ 蔬菜。

(*I can either eat meat or vegetables.*)

Yīnggāi 应该
(should, ought to)

The Double Conjunction
yòu ... yòu 又 ... 又

Making Comparisons

Ordinal Numbers

Unit 3: Work and School

Gōngzuò he xuéxiào
工作和学校

This unit focuses on work and school, so you'll learn a lot of useful vocabulary and expressions for talking about your studies or your job. In addition, you'll learn how to talk about the future and make comparisons, and how to express suggestions similar to *ought to* or *should* in English. Unit 3 also teaches ordinal numbers like *first*, *second*, and so on, as well as some important conjunctions, or linking words, that you can use to form more complex sentences. Are you ready?

Lesson 9: Words

In this lesson, you'll learn:

☐ Vocabulary related to work and school.

☐ How to use the modal yīnggāi 应该 (*should, ought to*).

☐ How to make comparisons.

Word Builder 1

▶ 9A Word Builder 1 (CD 8, Track 14)

Let's start with some vocabulary that will come in handy around the office.

diànhuà	电话	*telephone*
chuánzhēnjī	传真机	*fax machine*
diànnǎo	电脑	*computer*

Functions of **huì** 会

The Interrogative
wèishénme 为什么 (*why*)

Making Equal Comparisons

The Conjunctions **yīnwèi** 因为
(*because*) and **suǒyǐ** 所以 (*therefore*)

bàngōngshì	办公室	office
dǎyìnjī/yìnbiǎojī	打印机/印表机	printer
shūjià	书架	bookshelf
wénjiàn	文件	document, file
dǎngàn	档案	file
dǎngàn guì	档案柜	filing cabinet
gōngsī	公司	company
huìyì	会议	meeting
xīnshuǐ	薪水	salary
lǎobǎn	老板	boss
tóngshì	同事	colleague
gùyuán	雇员	employee
gōngzuò rényuán/ yuángōng	工作人员/员工	staff
jiàqī	假期	holiday, vacation
jiānzhí	兼职	part-time job

(II)

✎ Word Practice 1

Match the English word in the column on the left with its appropriate translation in the column on the right.

1. *company*   a. gùyuán 雇员

2. *salary*   b. gōngsī 公司

3. *employee*   c. bàngōngshì 办公室

4. *holiday, vacation*   d. xīnshuǐ 薪水

5. *office*   e. jiàqī 假期

Yīnggāi 应该
(should, ought to)

The Double Conjunction
yòu . . . yòu 又 . . . 又

Making Comparisons

Ordinal Numbers

ANSWER KEY
1. b; 2. d; 3. a; 4. e; 5. c

Grammar Builder 1
YĪNGGĀI 应该 (*SHOULD, OUGHT TO*)

▶ 9B Grammar Builder 1 (CD 8, Track 15)

The word yīnggāi 应该 is placed before a main verb in Chinese to make a suggestion or give advice, like the English *should* or *ought to*. As the following sentences illustrate, this construction is used to tell someone that it is their duty to do something because of obligation or correctness. It is typically used when criticizing someone's actions.

Nǐ yīnggāi zuò gōngkè.
你应该做功课。
You should do your homework.

Tā yīnggāi tīng māma de huà.
他应该听妈妈的话。
He should listen to his mother.

Tāmen yīnggāi xiǎoxīn diǎn.
他们应该小心点。
They ought to be more careful.

Yīnggāi 应该 can also be separated from the main verb by an adverb that indicates, for example, when or how something should be done:

Nǐ yīnggāi mǎshàng zuò fēijī qù Běijīng.
你应该马上坐飞机去北京。
You should take a plane to (go to) Beijing immediately.

Functions of **huì** 会

The Interrogative
wèishénme 为什么 (*why*)

Making Equal Comparisons

The Conjunctions **yīnwèi** 因为
(*because*) and **suǒyǐ** 所以 (*therefore*)

Xuésheng yīnggāi měitiān zhǔnshí shàngxué.

学生应该每天准时上学。

Students should get to school on time everyday.

Nǐ yīnggāi gèng nǔlì gōngzuò.

你应该更努力工作。

You should work harder.

If you want to negate a sentence with yīnggāi 应该, add the negative particle bù 不 immediately before yīnggāi 应该 rather than before the main verb.

Nǐ bù yīnggāi chídào.

你不应该迟到。

You shouldn't be late.

Nǐ bù yīnggāi zài wǎncān qián chī qiǎokèlì.

你不应该在晚餐前吃巧克力。

You shouldn't eat chocolate before dinner.

Rúguǒ tāmen méiyǒu qián, jiù bù yīnggāi qù lǚxíng.

如果他们没有钱, 就不应该去旅行。

They shouldn't travel if they don't have money.

Nàge rén zuì le, tā bù yīnggāi kāichē.

那个人醉了, 他不应该开车。

That person is drunk. He shouldn't drive.

Note the punctuation and translation of the last example. In Chinese, it's perfectly grammatical to join two full sentences and separate them only with a comma. This would be a run-on sentence in English, so translations of this and similar sentences often separate the two sentences or add *and* in between the two.

Yīnggāi 应该
(should, ought to)

The Double Conjunction
yòu ... yòu 又 ... 又

Making Comparisons

Ordinal Numbers

(II)

✎ Work Out 1

Rewrite the following sentences using yīnggāi 应该 (*should*) or bù yīnggāi 不应该 (*shouldn't*) as indicated.

1. Wǒ chídào. 我迟到。(*shouldn't*) _____

2. Tā de péngyou qù xuéxiào xué Zhōngwén. 他的朋友去学校学中文。(*should*) __

3. Tā jīntiān dǎ diànhuà gěi nǐ. 他今天打电话给你。(*should*) _____

4. Tā yǒu sān tiān de jiàqī. 他有三天的假期。(*should*) _____

5. Gōngsī mǎi liǎng tái dǎyìnjī. 公司买两台打印机。(*should*) _____

ANSWER KEY
1. Wǒ bù yīnggāi chídào. 我不应该迟到。 (*I shouldn't be late.*) 2. Tā de péngyou yīnggāi qù xuéxiào xué Zhōngwén. 他的朋友应该去学校学中文。 (*His friend should go to a school to study Chinese.*)
3. Tā jīntiān yīnggāi dǎ diànhuà gěi nǐ. 他今天应该打电话给你。 (*He should give you a call today.*)
4. Tā yīnggāi yǒu sān tiān de jiàqī. 他应该有三天的假期。 (*He should have three vacation days.*)
5. Gōngsī yīnggāi mǎi liǎng tái dǎyìnjī. 公司应该买两台打印机。 (*The company should buy two printers.*)

Functions of **huì** 会

The Interrogative
wèishénme 为什么 (*why*)

Making Equal Comparisons

The Conjunctions **yīnwèi** 因为
(*because*) and **suǒyǐ** 所以 (*therefore*)

Word Builder 2

▶ 9C Word Builder 2 (CD 8, Track 16)

Now let's look at some vocabulary for school.

jiàoshì	教室	*classroom*
xiàozhǎng	校长	*principal*
dàxué	大学	*university*
yánjiūyuàn/yánjiūsuǒ	研究院/研究所	*graduate school*
yánjiūshēng	研究生	*graduate student*
bìyè	毕业	*to graduate*
xì	系	*department (college level)*
zhuānyè/zhǔxiū	专业/主修	*major*
zhéxué	哲学	*philosophy*
wàiyǔ	外语	*foreign language*
shēngwù	生物	*biology*
wùlǐ	物理	*physics*
huàxué	化学	*chemistry*
lìshǐ	历史	*history*
cānkǎo shū	参考书	*reference book*
kèběn	课本	*textbook*
túshūzhèng	图书证	*library card*
xiàoyuán	校园	*campus*
shūdiàn	书店	*bookstore*
shíyànshì	实验室	*laboratory*
kèwài huódòng	课外活动	*extracurricular activities*
chéngjì	成绩	*academic performance*
kǎoshì	考试	*examination, test; to take a test*

�

Yīnggāi 应该
(should, ought to)

The Double Conjunction
yòu … yòu 又 … 又

Making Comparisons

Ordinal Numbers

✎ Word Practice 2

Fill in the blanks of the following conversation. The Chinese characters are given for additional help and practice.

A: Nǐ shàng _____ ma?

你上大学吗?

(*Do you go to university?*)

B: Wǒ shì _____.

我是研究生。

(*I'm a graduate student.*)

A: Nǎge _____ ?

哪个系?

(*Which department?*)

B: Wǒ xué _____.

我学物理。

(*I study physics.*)

A: Nǐmen yǒu hěnduō _____ ma?

你们有很多考试吗?

(*Do you have a lot of exams?*)

B: Shì de. Wǒmen méiyǒu hěnduō ___.

是的。我们没有很多课外活动。

(*Yes. We don't have a lot of extracurricular activities.*)

Functions of **huì** 会

The Interrogative
wèishénme 为什么 (*why*)

Making Equal Comparisons

The Conjunctions **yīnwèi** 因为
(*because*) and **suǒyǐ** 所以 (*therefore*)

ANSWER KEY
A. dàxué 大学; B. yánjiūshēng 研究生; A. xì 系; B. wùlǐ 物理; A. kǎoshì 考试; B. kèwài huódòng 课外
活动

Grammar Builder 2
MAKING COMPARISONS

▶ 9D Grammar Builder 2 (CD 8, Track 17)

To express differences in size, age, quantity, distance, and so on, you can use the
following construction: A **bǐ** 比 B + adjective.

This construction is the equivalent of the English comparative that uses *more*
or the ending *-er*. So, *she is older than he is* would literally be *she* **bǐ** 比 *he old* in
Chinese. Notice that the verb *to be* is not used in this construction.

Ta bǐ wǒ dà.
他比我大。
He is older/bigger than I (am).

Wǒ bǐ nǐ gāo.
我比你高。
I am taller than you.

Zhè běn shū bǐ nà běn shū guì.
这本书比那本书贵。
This book is more expensive than that one.

Yīngtáo bǐ píngguǒ xiǎo.
樱桃比苹果小。
Cherries are smaller than apples.

Yīnggāi 应该
(should, ought to)

The Double Conjunction
yòu ... yòu 又 ... 又

Making Comparisons

Ordinal Numbers

Tāmen bǐ wǒmen niánqīng.
他们比我们年轻。
They are younger than we are.

Běijīng bǐ Shànghǎi yuǎn.
北京比上海远。
Beijing is farther than Shanghai.

Tāmen de cǎodì bǐ nǐmen de lǜ.
他们的草地比你们的绿。
Their lawn is greener than yours.

To express the exact degree of difference between two nouns, words specifying age or amount are placed immediately after the adjective:

Wǒ bǐ nǐ dà sān suì.
我比你大三岁。
I am three years older than you.

Nàge nánhái bǐ tā de jiějie qīng shí bàng.
那个男孩比他的姐姐轻十磅。
The boy is ten pounds lighter than his older sister.

Chéngdū bǐ Guǎngzhōu jìn jǐ bǎi gōnglǐ.
成都比广州近几百公里。
Chengdu is several hundred kilometers closer than Guangzhou.

The degree of difference can also be described in broader terms by using the adverb hěn duō 很多, which is translated as *much*.

Functions of **huì** 会

The Interrogative
wèishénme 为什么 *(why)*

Making Equal Comparisons

The Conjunctions **yīnwèi** 因为
(because) and **suǒyǐ** 所以 *(therefore)*

Nǐ bǐ wǒ gāo hěn duō.

你比我高很多。

You are much taller than I (am).

Nàge nánhái bǐ tā de jiějie qīng hěn duō.

那个男孩比他的姐姐轻很多。

The boy is much lighter than his older sister.

Zhè piàn cǎodì bǐ nà piàn lǜ hěn duō.

这片草地比那片绿很多。

This lawn is much greener than that one.

In Chinese, you can also make comparisons between how a particular action is performed. In other words, you can compare adverbs rather than adjectives. The construction you use to do this is: A + verb + de 得 bǐ 比 + B + adverb. So, *Mary sings more beautifully than John* would literally be *Mary sings* de 得 bǐ 比 *John beautifully* in Chinese.

Wǒ zǒu de bǐ nǐ kuài.

我走得比你快。

I walk more quickly than you do.

Tā shuō de bǐ tā de mèimei màn.

她说得比她的妹妹慢。

She speaks more slowly than her younger sister.

Tā bèi shī bèi de bǐ lǎoshī liúlì.

他背诗背得比老师流利。

He recited the poem more eloquently than (his) teacher.

Remember that, in Chinese, adjectives do not change form when they are used as adverbs.

Yīnggāi 应该
(should, ought to)

The Double Conjunction
yòu ... yòu 又 ... 又

Making Comparisons

Ordinal Numbers

(II)

✎ Work Out 2

Fill in the blanks to make the appropriate comparisons based on the information and English clues provided.

1. Wáng xiǎojie yìbǎi èrshí bàng. Zhāng xiǎojie yìbǎi bàng. Wáng xiǎojie _____

   Zhāng xiǎojie zhòng. *(heavier)*

   王小姐一百二十磅。张小姐一百磅。王小姐 ___ 张小姐重。

2. Wǒ shí bā suì. Tā shí qī suì. Wǒ bǐ tā _____ . *(older)*

   我十八岁。他/她十七岁。我比他/她 ___ 。

3. Tā de mèimei piàoliang. Wǒ de mèimei bú piàoliang. Tā de mèimei bǐ wǒ de

   mèimei _____ . *(prettier)*

   他的妹妹漂亮。我的妹妹不漂亮。他的妹妹比我的妹妹 _____ 。

4. Tā de xīnshuǐ bù gāo. Wǒ de xīnshuǐ gāo. _____ bǐ

   _____ gāo. *(higher)*

   他的薪水不高。我的薪水高。我的薪水比他的 _____ 。

5. Zhège rén zuò de hěn màn. Nàge rén zuò de hěn kuài. _____

   _____ bǐ _____ kuài. *(faster)*

   这个人做得很慢。那个人做得很快。_____ 比 _____ 快。

6. Wǒ de xuésheng de chéngjì búcuò. Tā de xuésheng de chéngjì bù hǎo. Wǒ de

   xuésheng de chéngjì bǐ tā de xuésheng de chéngjì _____ . *(better)*

Functions of **huì** 会

The Interrogative
wèishénme 为什么 (*why*)

Making Equal Comparisons

The Conjunctions **yīnwèi** 因为
(*because*) and **suǒyǐ** 所以 (*therefore*)

我的学生的成绩不错。他的学生的成绩不好。我的学生的成绩比他的学生的成绩 ＿＿＿＿。

7. Tā de xuéxiào de xiàoyuán dà. Wǒ de xuéxiào de xiàoyuán xiǎo. Wǒ de xuéxiào de xiàoyuán bǐ tā de xuéxiào de xiàoyuán ＿＿＿＿＿＿. (*smaller*)

他的学校的校园大。我的学校的校园小。我的学校的校园比他的学校的校园 ＿＿＿＿。

8. Tā de kèběn hěn zāng. Wǒ de kèběn bù zāng. ＿＿＿＿＿＿＿＿＿＿＿ bǐ ＿＿＿＿＿＿＿＿＿ zāng. (*more*)

他的课本很脏。我的课本不脏。＿＿＿＿＿ 比 ＿＿＿＿ 脏。

ANSWER KEY

1. Wáng xiǎojie bǐ Zhāng xiǎojie zhòng. 王小姐比张小姐重。(*Miss Wang is heavier than Miss Zhang.*) 2. Wǒ bǐ tā dà. 我比他大。(*I'm older than he is.*) 3. Tā de mèimei bǐ wǒ de mèimei piàoliang. 他的妹妹比我的妹妹漂亮。(*His younger sister is prettier than mine.*) 4. Wǒ de xīnshuǐ bǐ tā de xīnshuǐ gāo. 我的薪水比他的薪水高。(*My salary is higher than his.*) 5. Nàge rén zuò de bǐ zhège rén kuài. 那个人做得比这个人快。(*That person works faster than this person.*) 6. Wǒ de xuésheng de chéngjì bǐ ta de xuésheng de chéngjì hǎo. 我的学生的成绩比他/她的学生的成绩好。(*My students' academic performance is better than his/her students' academic performance.*) 7. Wǒ de xuéxiào de xiàoyuán bǐ tā de xuéxiào de xiàoyuán xiǎo. 我的学校的校园比他/她的学校的校园小。(*My school's campus is smaller than his/hers.*) 8. Tā de kèběn bǐ wǒ (de) zāng. 他的课本比我的脏。(*His textbooks are dirtier than mine.*)

✎ Drive It Home

Compare two objects or persons using the verbs provided in parentheses and the word bǐ 比。 For each set of comparisons, write three sentences.

1. Zhè liàng chē/nà liàng chē (dà, xiǎo, xīn) 这辆车/那辆车 (大、小、新) ＿＿＿＿＿＿

＿＿＿＿＿＿＿＿＿＿＿＿＿＿＿＿＿＿＿＿＿＿＿＿＿＿＿＿＿＿＿＿＿＿＿

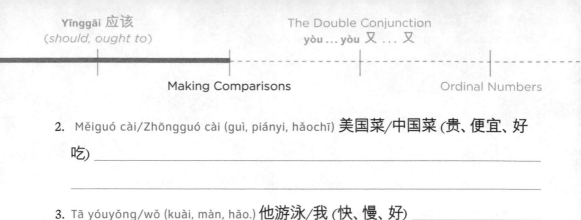

Yīnggāi 应该
(should, ought to)

The Double Conjunction
yòu … yòu 又 … 又

Making Comparisons

Ordinal Numbers

2. Měiguó cài/Zhōngguó cài (guì, piányi, hǎochī) 美国菜/中国菜 (贵、便宜、好吃) _____

_____

3. Tā yóuyǒng/wǒ (kuài, màn, hǎo.) 他游泳/我 (快、慢、好) _____

_____

ANSWER KEY

1. Zhè liàng chē bǐ nà liàng chē dà. 这辆车比那辆车大。 (*This car is bigger than that car.*) Zhè liàng chē bǐ nà liàng chē xiǎo. 这辆车比那辆车小。 (*This car is is smaller than that car.*) Zhè liàng chē bǐ nà liàng chē xīn. 这辆车比那辆车新。 (*This car is more new than that car.*) 2. Měiguó cài bǐ Zhōngguó cài guì. 美国菜比中国菜贵。 (*American cuisine is more expensive than Chinese cuisine.*) Měiguó cài bǐ Zhōngguó cài piányi. 美国菜比中国菜便宜。 (*American cuisine is cheaper than Chinese cuisine.*) Měiguó cài bǐ Zhōngguó cài hǎochī. 美国菜比中国菜好吃。 (*American cuisine is more delicious than Chinese cuisine.*) 3. Tā yóuyǒng yóu de bǐ wǒ kuài. 他游泳游得比我快。 (*He swims faster than I do.*) Tā yóuyǒng yóu de bǐ wǒ màn. 他游泳游得比我慢。 (*He swims slower than I do.*) Tā yóuyǒng yóu de bǐ wǒ hǎo. 他游泳游得比我好。 (*He swims better than I do.*)

✎ Word Recall

Match the English word in the column on the left with its appropriate translation in the column on the right.

1. *to graduate*   a. gùyuán 雇员

2. *document, file*   b. zhuānyè/zhǔxiū 专业/主修

3. *classroom*   c. huìyì 会议

4. *boss*   d. kǎoshì 考试

5. *laboratory*   e. wénjiàn 文件

6. *meeting*   f. yánjiūyuàn/yánjiūsuǒ 研究院/研究所

7. *major*   g. bìyè 毕业

8. *colleague*   h. lǎobǎn 老板

9. *university*   i. jiàoshì 教室

10. *salary*   j. shíyànshì 实验室

Functions of **huì** 会

The Interrogative
wèishénme 为什么 (*why*)

Making Equal Comparisons

The Conjunctions **yīnwèi** 因为
(*because*) and **suǒyǐ** 所以 (*therefore*)

11. *graduate school*	k. tóngshì 同事
12. *extracurricular acivity*	l. kèběn 课本
13. *employee*	m. dàxué 大学
14. *test, exam*	n. xīnshuǐ 薪水
15. *textbook*	o. kèwài huódòng 课外活动

ANSWER KEY

1. g; 2. e; 3. i; 4. h; 5. j; 6. c; 7. b; 8. k ; 9. m; 10. n; 11. f; 12. o; 13. a; 14. d; 15. l

Lesson 10: Phrases

In this lesson, you'll learn:

☐ More expressions related to work and school.

☐ How to use the double conjunction yòu … yòu 又 … 又.

☐ Ordinal numbers.

Phrase Builder 1
▶ 10A Phrase Builder 1 (CD 8, Track 18)

Here are some useful expressions for talking about your job.

jiābān	加班	*to work overtime*
qǐng bìngjià	请病假	*to take sick leave*
qǐng (shì) jià	请(事)假	*to take personal leave*
dǎ diànhuà	打电话	*to make a phone call*
fā chuánzhēn	发传真	*to send a fax*
jì xiàlái	记下来	*to jot something down*

Yīnggāi 应该
(should, ought to)

The Double Conjunction
yòu ... yòu 又 ... 又

Making Comparisons

Ordinal Numbers

✎ Work Out 1

Use the double conjunction yòu ... yòu 又 ... 又 to combine each pair of sentences into a single comparative statement:

1. Tā de lǎobǎn cōngmíng. Tā de lǎobǎn hǎo. 他的老板聪明。他的老板好。 _____
   _____

2. Wǒ de bàngōngshì dà. Wǒ de bàngōngshì piàoliang. 我的办公室大。我的办公
   室漂亮。 _____
   _____

3. Nàge guójiā xiǎo. Nàge guójiā qióng. (poor) 那个国家小。那个国家穷 _____
   _____

4. Zhège huìyì hěn cháng. Zhège huìyì hěn mèn. 这个会议很长。这个会议很
   闷。 _____
   _____

5. Xuéxiào de kèwài huódòng hěn duō. Xuéxiào de kèwài huódòng hěn hǎowán.
   (fun) 学校的课外活动很多。学校的课外活动很好玩 _____
   _____

6. Shíyànshì de shèbèi hěn xīn. Shíyànshì de shèbèi hěn hǎo. (equipment) 实验室的
   设备很新。实验室的设备很好。 _____
   _____

ANSWER KEY

1. Tā de lǎobǎn yòu cōngmíng yòu hǎo. 他的老板又聪明又好。 (His boss is intelligent and good.) 2. Wǒ de bàngōngshì yòu dà yòu piàoliang. 我的办公室又大又漂亮。 (My office is large and beautiful.) 3. Nàge guójiā yòu xiǎo yòu qióng. 那个国家又小又穷。 (That country is small and poor.) 4. Zhège huìyì yòu cháng yòu mèn. 这个会议又长又闷。 (The meeting was long and boring.) 5. Xuéxiào de kèwài huódòng yòu duō yòu hǎowán. 学校的课外活动又多又好玩。 (The

Functions of **huì** 会

The Interrogative
wèishénme 为什么 (*why*)

Making Equal Comparisons

The Conjunctions **yīnwèi** 因为
(*because*) and **suǒyǐ** 所以 (*therefore*)

extracurricular activities at school are many and fun.) 6. Shíyànshì de shèbèi yòu xīn yòu hǎo. 实验室
的设备又新又好。 (*The laboratory's equipment is new and good.*)

Phrase Builder 2

▶ 10C Phrase Builder 2 (CD 8, Track 20)

Now let's look at some useful expressions for school.

shàngkè	上课	to attend (a) class
pángtīng	旁听	to audit a class
kǎoshì	考试	exam, to take an exam
pái dì-yī míng	排第一名	to be placed first
fàngxué	放学	to finish class, after school hours
shēnqǐng	申请	to apply
fùxí	复习	to review a lesson
yùxí	预习	to prepare for a lesson
sīrén bǔxí	私人补习	private tutoring
shàngwǎng	上网	to go online
jiāo gōngkè	交功课	to submit homework
nǐ de chéngjì	你的成绩	your academic performance, your grades
shàng dàxué	上大学	to attend university
zhù zài sùshè lǐ	住在宿舍里	to live in the dorm
zài shítáng lǐ chīfàn	在食堂里吃饭	to eat in the cafeteria

⏸

Yīnggāi 应该
(should, ought to)

The Double Conjunction
yòu … yòu 又 … 又

Making Comparisons

Ordinal Numbers

✎ Phrase Practice 2

Match the English phrase in the column on the left with its appropriate translation in the column on the right.

1. *to finish class, after school hours*	a. shàngkè 上课
2. *to attend class*	b. fùxí 复习
3. *to apply*	c. fàngxué 放学
4. *to review*	d. shàng dàxué 上大学
5. *to attend university*	e. shēnqǐng 申请

ANSWER KEY
1. c; 2. a; 3. e; 4. b; 5. d

Grammar Builder 2
ORDINAL NUMBERS

▶ 10D Grammar Builder 2 (CD 8, Track 21)

You already know cardinal numbers—numbers like *one*, *sixteen*, and *forty-five*—which show quantity or are used to count. Ordinal numbers are used to describe order, so they correspond to the English *first*, *sixteenth*, and *forty-fifth*. Quite simply, cardinal numbers are transformed into ordinal numbers in Chinese by adding the prefix dì 第.

yī 一 (*one*)	dì-yī 第一 (*first*)
èr 二 (*two*)	dì-èr 第二 (*second*)
sān 三 (*three*)	dì-sān 第三 (*third*)
sì 四 (*four*)	dì-sì 第四 (*fourth*)

Here are a few examples that show how ordinal numbers are typically used in Chinese sentences. Notice the use of measure words between the ordinal numbers and the nouns they modify. Also notice the word order of the descriptive phrases and the use of de 的.

Making Equal Comparisons

The Conjunctions **yīnwèi** 因为
(*because*) and **suǒyǐ** 所以 (*therefore*)

Wǒ shì zhè gōngsī de dì-yī ge yuángōng.

我是这公司的第一个员工。

I'm the first person to work for this company. (lit., this company's first staff member)

Tā shì dì-yī ge xué Zhōngwén de Měiguórén.

他是第一个学中文的美国人。

He is the first American to study Chinese. (lit., the first-to-study-Chinese American)

⏸

✎ Work Out 2

Translate the following sentences into English.

1. Tā shì wǒ dì-yī ge lǎobǎn. _____

   _____

2. Wǒmen de dì-yī ge yuángōng shì Yīngguórén. _____

   _____

3. Zài zhège xuéxiào lǐ, wǒ shì dì-yī ge huì shuō Zhōngwén de Měiguórén. _____

   _____

4. Tā dì-èr ge nǚpéngyou (*girlfriend*) shì Zhōngguórén. _____

   _____

5. Tā pái dì-sì míng. _____

   _____

ANSWER KEY
1. *He/She is my first boss.* 2. *Our first staff member was British.* 3. *I'm the first American who knows how to speak Chinese at this school.* 4. *His second girlfriend was Chinese.* 5. *He placed fourth.*

Yīnggāi 应该
(should, ought to)

The Double Conjunction
yòu ... yòu 又 ... 又

Making Comparisons

Ordinal Numbers

Modify each sentence by incorporating ordinal numbers, using the cardinal numbers in parentheses to help you. For example, with Tāmen kàn shū 他们看书 (2), you would write: Tāmen kàn dì-èr běn shū. 他们看第二本书。 (They are reading the second book.) Write three sentences for each item. Be sure to use the appropriate measure word.

1. Zhè shì wǒ de qìchē 这是我的汽车 *(1, 2, 3)* _____

_____

2. Tā shì wǒmen de Zhōngwén lǎoshī 他是我们的中文老师 *(5, 10, 9)* _____

_____

3. Wǒ xiǎng yào nà shuāng xiézi 我想要那双鞋子 *(4, 6, 11)* _____

_____

ANSWER KEY
1. Zhè shì wǒ de dì-yī liàng qìchē. 这是我的第一辆汽车。 (*This is my first car.*) Zhè shì wǒ de dì-èr liàng qìchē. 这是我的第二辆汽车。 (*This is my second car.*) Zhè shì wǒ de dì-sān liàng qìchē. 这是我的第三辆汽车。 (*This is my third car.*) 2. Tā shì wǒmen de dì-wǔ ge Zhōngwén lǎoshī. 他是我们的第五个中文老师。 (*He is our fifth Chinese language teacher.*) Tā shì wǒmen de dì-shí ge Zhōngwén lǎoshī. 他是我们的第十个中文老师。 (*He is our tenth Chinese language teacher.*) Tā shì wǒmen de dì-jiǔ ge Zhōngwén lǎoshī. 他是我们的第九个中文老师。 (*He is our ninth Chinese language teacher.*)
3. Wǒ xiǎng yào nà dì-sì shuāng xiézi. 我想要那第四双鞋子。 (*I would like that fourth pair of shoes.*) Wǒ xiǎng yào nà dì-liù shuāng xiézi. 我想要那第六双鞋子。 (*I would like that sixth pair of shoes.*) Wǒ xiǎng yào nà dì-shíyī shuāng xiézi. 我想要那第十一双鞋子。 (*I would like that eleventh pair of shoes.*)

✎ Word Recall

Match the English phrase in the column on the left with its appropriate translation in the column on the right.

1. *exam, to take an exam*   a. yùxí 预习

2. *to take sick leave*   b. fàngjià 放假

3. *to leave a message*   c. zhù zài sùshè lǐ 住在宿舍里

4. *to make an appointment*   d. pái dì-yī míng 排第一名

Functions of huì 会

The Interrogative
wèishénme 为什么 *(why)*

Making Equal Comparisons

The Conjunctions yīnwèi 因为
(because) and suǒyǐ 所以 *(therefore)*

5. *to audit a class*   e. jiāo gōngkè 交功课

6. *your grades*   f. qǐng bìngjià 请病假

7. *to eat in the cafeteria*   g. sīrén bǔxí 私人补习

8. *to send a fax*   h. pángtīng 旁听

9. *to live in the dorm*   i. kǎoshì 考试

10. *to prepare for a lesson*   j. yùyuē 预约

11. *to submit homework*   k. liúyán 留言

12. *deadline*   l. fā chuánzhēn 发传真

13. *on vacation, time off*   m. zuìhòu qīxiàn 最后期限

14. *to be placed first*   n. nǐ de chéngjì 你的成绩

15. *private tutoring*   o. zài shítáng lǐ chīfàn 在食堂里吃饭

ANSWER KEY
1. i; 2. f; 3. k; 4. j; 5. h; 6. n; 7. o; 8. l; 9. c; 10. a; 11. c; 12. m; 13. b; 14. d; 15. g

Lesson 11: Sentences

In this lesson, you'll learn:

☐ More language for around the office and school.

☐ Some functions of huì 会.

☐ More about comparisons.

Sentence Builder 1

▶ 11A Sentence Builder 1 (CD 8, Track 22)

Tā míngtiān huì huí gōngsī.	她明天会回公司。	*She will be back in the office tomorrow.*
Nǐ míngnián huì qù Měiguó dúshū ma?	你明年会去美国读书吗？	*Will you go to America to study next year?*

Yīnggāi 应该
(*should, ought to*)

The Double Conjunction
yòu ... yòu 又 ... 又

Making Comparisons

Ordinal Numbers

Wǒmen xià ge yuè bìyè.	我们下个月毕业。	*We'll graduate next month.*
Wǒ bìyè zhīhòu bù dú yánjiūshēngyuàn.	我毕业之后不读研究生院。	*I won't be going to graduate school after graduation.*
Hěn duō xuésheng míngtiān kǎoshì.	很多学生明天考试。	*Many students will take the/an exam tomorrow.*
Xuéxiào xià ge lǐbài yī fàngjià.	学校下个礼拜一放假。	*The school will be closed next Monday.*
Xuésheng xià ge yuè kāishǐ shàngkè.	学生下个月开始上课。	*Students will begin going to school next month.*
Zhège xuéxiào jiǔyuè zhāoshēng.	这个学校九月招生。	*This school will recruit students in September.*
Tā de gōngsī xià ge lǐbài guānbì.	他的公司下个礼拜关闭。	*His company will go out of business next week.*
Nǐ huì zhǎo qítā gōngzuò ma?	你会找其他工作吗?	*Will you look for another job?*
Tā xià ge lǐbài èr huì gēn lǎobǎn chūchāi.	她下个礼拜二会跟老板出差。	*She will take a business trip with her boss next Tuesday.*

Sentence Practice 1

Fill in the blanks of the sentences. The characters are given for additional help and practice.

1. Tā de _____ xià ge lǐbài guānbì.

他的公司下个礼拜关闭。

(*His company will go out of business next week.*)

Functions of **huì** 会

The Interrogative
wèishénme 为什么 *(why)*

Making Equal Comparisons

The Conjunctions **yīnwèi** 因为
(because) and **suǒyǐ** 所以 *(therefore)*

2. Wǒmen xià ge yuè _____.

   我们下个月毕业。

   (We'll graduate next month.)

3. Xuéxiào xià ge lǐbài yī _____.

   学校下个礼拜一放假。

   (The school will be closed next Monday.)

4. Hěn duō xuésheng míngtiān _____.

   很多学生明天考试。

   (Many students will take the/an exam tomorrow.)

5. Wǒ bìyè _____ bù dú _____.

   我毕业之后不读研究生院。

   (I won't be going to graduate school after graduation.)

   ANSWER KEY

   1. gōngsī 公司; 2. bìyè 毕业; 3. fàngjià 放假; 4. kǎoshì 考试; 5. zhīhòu 之后, yánjiūshēngyuàn 研究生院

Grammar Builder 1
FUNCTIONS OF HUÌ 会

▶ 11B Grammar Builder 1 (CD 8, Track 23)

You have already been exposed to huì 会, which has different meanings in Chinese depending on how it is used. Here is a review of two of its main functions.

As you learned in *Intermediate Chinese*, one of the primary functions of huì 会 is to express the possibility that an action will take place in the future. When placed immediately before the main verb in a sentence, hùi 会 is the equivalent of *will* in

Yīnggāi 应该
(should, ought to)

The Double Conjunction
yòu ... yòu 又 ... 又

Making Comparisons

Ordinal Numbers

English. It expresses a future action that is likely or probable, but of course not guaranteed since it hasn't happened yet. If you want to stress that something is possible, use kěnéng 可能 (*maybe, perhaps*). This is the equivalent of *may*.

Wǒ míngtiān huì qù Shànghǎi.
我明天会去上海。
I'll (probably) go to Shanghai tomorrow.

Tā děng yíhuìr huì gěi nǐ.
他等一会儿会给你。
He will (most likely) give it to you in a while.

Tā kěnéng huì lái.
她可能会来。
She may come.

In the previous unit, you learned that huì 会 can also be used as a modal verb, in which case it means *can* in the sense of *know how to*.

Wǒ huì shuō Zhōngwén.
我会说中文。
I can (know how to) speak Chinese.

Wǒ bú huì shuō Zhōngwén.
我不会说中文。
I can't (don't know how to) speak Chinese.

Huì 会 can also be used as a main verb, in which case it means *to know how*.

Functions of **huì** 会

The Interrogative
wèishénme 为什么 (why)

Making Equal Comparisons

The Conjunctions **yīnwèi** 因为
(because) and **suǒyǐ** 所以 (therefore)

✎ Work Out 1

Match each Chinese sentence in the column on the left with the correct English translation on the right.

1. Nǐ míngtiān huì shàngxué ma? 你明天会上学吗?

   a. *I will (probably) go to bed in a while.*

2. Tā bú huì shuō Yīngwén. 他不会说英文。

   b. *Will he (possibly) come tonight?*

3. Wǒ děng yíhuìr (*a while*) huì qù shuìjiào. 我等一会儿会去睡觉。

   c. *He won't attend university next year.*

4. Wǒ míngtiān bú shàngxué. 我明天不上学。

   d. *Will you (most likely) go to school tomorrow?*

5. Zhāng lǎoshī huì kāichē. 张老师会开车.

   e. *He will go study in the U.S. next month.*

6. Tā jīntiān wǎnshang huì lái ma? 他今天晚上会来吗?

   f. *He doesn't know how to speak English.*

7. Tā míngnián bú shàng dàxué. 他明年不上大学。

   g. *Teacher Zhang knows how to drive.*

8. Tā xià ge yuè qù Měiguó dúshū. 他下个月去美国读书。

   h. *I won't go to school tomorrow.*

ANSWER KEY

1. d; 2. f; 3. a; 4. h; 5. g; 6. b; 7. c; 8. e

Sentence Builder 2

▶ 11C Sentence Builder 2 (CD 8, Track 24)

Tā de bàba hé wǒ de māma yíyàng dà.	他的爸爸和我的妈妈一样大。	*His father is as old as my mother.*
Zhège xuéxiào hé nàge xuéxiào yíyàng hǎo.	这个学校和那个学校一样好。	*This school is as good as that school.*

Yīnggāi 应该
(should, ought to)

The Double Conjunction
yòu … yòu 又 … 又

Making Comparisons

Ordinal Numbers

Tā de xīnshuǐ hé nǐ de yíyàng gāo.	他的薪水和你的一样高。	*His salary is as high as yours.*
Tā de gōngsī yǒu nǐ de zhème dà.	他的公司有你的这么大。	*His company is as big as yours.*
Wǒ de jiàqī méiyǒu nǐ de nàme duō.	我的假期没有你的那么多。	*My vacation is not as long as yours.*
Jīnnián de kǎoshì hé qùnián de yíyàng nán.	今年的考试和去年的一样难。	*The examination this year is as difficult as it was last year.*
Jīnnián de kǎoshì méiyǒu qùnián de róngyì.	今年的考试没有去年的容易。	*This year's examination is not as easy as last year's.*
Zài Měiguó, sīlì xiǎoxué de xuéfèi hé sīlì dàxué de xuéfèi yíyàng guì.	在美国, 私立小学的学费和私立大学的学费一样贵。	*In the U.S., the tuition fee at private elementary schools is as expensive as at universities.*
Wénkē de xuéfèi méiyǒu lǐkē de nàme guì.	文科的学费没有理科的那么贵。	*Tuition fees for the humanities majors are not as expensive as for the sciences.*
Yīngwén méiyǒu Zhōngwén nàme nán xué.	英文没有中文那么难学。	*English is not as difficult to learn as Chinese.*
Zhè běn shū hé nà běn shū yíyàng yǒu yìsi.	这本书和那本书一样有意思。	*This book is as interesting as that one.*
Tā de shēngwù lǎoshī de gōngkè hé huàxué lǎoshī de yíyàng duō.	他的生物老师的功课和化学老师的一样多。	*His biology teacher gives as much homework as his chemistry teacher.*

⏸

Functions of **huì** 会

The Interrogative
wèishénme 为什么 (why)

Making Equal Comparisons

The Conjunctions **yīnwèi** 因为
(because) and **suǒyǐ** 所以 (therefore)

✎ Sentence Practice 2

Translate the following sentences into English.

1. Wǒ de jiàqī méiyǒu nǐ de nàme duō. 我的假期没有你的那么多。 _____

_____

2. Jīnnián de kǎoshì hé qùnián de yíyàng nán. 今年的考试和去年的一样难。 ___

_____

3. Tā de xīnshuǐ hé nǐ de yíyàng gāo. 他的薪水和你的一样高。 _____

_____

4. Jīnnián de kǎoshì méiyǒu qùnián de róngyì. 今年的考试没有去年的容易。 ___

_____

5. Zhège xuéxiào hé nàge xuéxiào yíyàng hǎo. 这个学校和那个学校一样好。 ___

_____

ANSWER KEY
1. *I don't have as many days of vacation as you have.* 2. *The examination this year is as difficult as it was last year.* 3. *His salary is as high as yours.* 4. *This year's examination is not as easy as last year's.* 5. *This school is as good as that school.*

Grammar Builder 2
MAKING EQUAL COMPARISONS

▶ 11D Grammar Builder 2 (CD 8, Track 25)

There are two ways in Chinese to express equal comparisons, corresponding to the English construction as … as. The first is to use yǒu … zhème/nàme 有 . . . 这么/那么 to show that separate entities share the same characteristics and are comparatively very similar.

Yīnggāi 应该
(*should, ought to*)

The Double Conjunction
yòu ... yòu 又 ... 又

Making Comparisons

Ordinal Numbers

Wǒ yǒu nǐ nàme gāo.
我有你那么高。
I am as tall as you.

Nǐ yǒu wǒ zhème gāo.
你有我这么高。
You are as tall as I am.

Zhège hézi yǒu nàge nàme dà.
这个盒子有那个那么大。
This box is as big as that one.

Whether you use zhème 这么 or nàme 那么 depends on the relative location of the speaker. As you can see from the examples above, zhème 这么 is used to refer to someone or something close to the speaker, while nàme 那么 is used to refer to someone or something that is farther away from the speaker. In other words, zhème 这么 is used in the sentence Nǐ yǒu wǒ zhème gāo 你有我这么高 (*You are as tall as I am*) because it modifies the word *I*, which refers to the speaker himself. On the other hand, nàme 那么 is used in the sentence Wǒ yǒu nǐ nàme gāo 我有你那么高 (*I am as tall as you*) because it modifies the word *you*, which is separate and apart from the speaker.

The second way of expressing equal comparisons in Chinese is by using the word yíyàng 一样(*same*) to form the grammatical construct: A + hé 和 + B + yíyàng 一样 + adjective.

This indicates a more precise level of exact comparison and literally means that two things are the same:

Wǒ hé nǐ yíyàng gāo.
我和你一样高。
I am as tall as you. (We are the same height.)

Functions of **huì** 会

The Interrogative
wèishénme 为什么 (*why*)

Making Equal Comparisons

The Conjunctions **yīnwèi** 因为
(*because*) and **suǒyǐ** 所以 (*therefore*)

Wǒ de wèikǒu hé nǐ de yíyàng dà.

我的胃口和你的一样大。

My appetite is as big as yours. (Our appetites are equally big.)

Zhè kē shù hé zhège fángzi yíyàng lǎo.

这棵树和这个房子一样老。

The tree is as old as the house. (The tree and the house are the same age.)

Likewise, there are two different ways in Chinese to show similarity when comparing two different actions or activities. You can use either of the following constructions:

A + verb + de 得 + yǒu 有 + B + zhème/nàme 这么/那么 + adverb
or
A + hé 和 + B + verb + de 得 + yíyàng 一样 + adverb

Wǒ chī de yǒu nǐ nàme kuài.

我吃得有你那么快。

I eat as quickly as you do.

Wǒ hé nǐ chī de yíyàng kuài.

我和你吃得一样快。

I eat as quickly as you do.

Both of these forms are equally correct and are used interchangeably in colloquial Chinese. Here are some more examples:

Tā pǎo de hé tāmen yíyàng kuài.

她跑得和他们一样快。

She runs as fast as they do.

Yīnggāi 应该
(should, ought to)

The Double Conjunction
yòu … yòu 又 … 又

Making Comparisons

Ordinal Numbers

Wǒ de māma zuòfàn zuò de hé chúshī yíyàng hǎo.

我的妈妈做饭做得和厨师一样好。

My mother cooks as well as a professional chef.

There are different rules in Chinese for negating equal comparisons. In constructions that use the verb yǒu 有, simply replace yǒu 有 with méiyǒu 没有 in order to form the negative. But in constructions that don't use yǒu 有, place the negative particle bù in front of yíyàng 一样 + adjective/adverb.

Wǒ méiyǒu nǐ nàme gāo.

我没有你那么高。

I'm not as tall as you.

Wǒ hé nǐ bù yíyàng gāo.

我和你不一样高。

I'm not as tall as you. (You and I are not of the same height.)

Wǒ chī de méiyǒu nǐ nàme kuài.

我吃得没有你那么快。

I don't eat as quickly as you do.

Wǒ hé nǐ chī de bù yíyàng kuài.

我和你吃得不一样快。

I don't eat as quickly as you do. (You and I do not eat at the same speed.)

Ⓟ

Functions of **huì** 会

The Interrogative
wèishénme 为什么 (*why*)

Making Equal Comparisons

The Conjunctions **yīnwèi** 因为
(*because*) and **suǒyǐ** 所以 (*therefore*)

✎ Work Out 2

Using the word or phrase in parentheses, rewrite and combine each pair of
sentences into a single comparative statement. Then translate your answers.

1. Wǒ shuō Zhōngwén hěn kuài. Tā shuō Zhōngwén hěn kuài. (yíyàng) 我说中文很
快。他说中文很快。(一样) _____

   _____

2. Wǒ de bàba hěn gāo. Nǐ de bàba hěn gāo. (yǒu ... zhème/nàme) 我的爸爸很高。
你的爸爸很高。(有 ... 这么/那么) _____

   _____

3. Nàge rén de fángzi hěn piàoliang. Wǒ de péngyou de fángzi hěn piàoliang. (yǒu ...
zhème/nàme) 那个人的房子很漂亮。我的朋友的房子很_____
么/那么) _____

   _____

4. Huáng xiānsheng zǒu de hěn kuài. Wáng xiǎojie zǒu de hěn kuài. (yíyàng) 黄先生
走得很快。王小姐走得很快。(一样) _____

   _____

5. Nà liàng chē hěn guì. Zhè liàng chē hěn guì. (yíyàng) 那辆车很贵。这辆车很
贵。(一样) _____

   _____

6. Zhāng lǎoshī hěn hǎo. Lǐ lǎoshī hěn hǎo. (yíyàng) 张老师很好。李老师很好。
(一样) _____

   _____

Yīnggāi 应该
(should, ought to)

The Double Conjunction
yòu ... yòu 又 ... 又

Making Comparisons

Ordinal Numbers

7. Jiānádà *(Canada)* hěn dà. Zhōngguó búshì hěn dà. (méiyǒu ... zhème) 加拿大 *(Canada)* 很大。中国不是很大。(没有 ... 这么) _____

_____

8. Tā de chéngjì hěn hǎo. Wǒ de chéngjī hěn hǎo. (yíyàng) 他的成绩很好。我的成绩很好。(一样) _____

_____

ANSWER KEY

1. Wǒ shuō Zhōngwén hé tā yíyàng kuài. 我说中文和他/她一样快。 *(I speak Chinese as quickly as he/she does.)* 2. Wǒ de bàba yǒu nǐ de bàba nàme gāo. 我的爸爸有你的爸爸那么高。 *(My father is as tall as your father.)* 3. Nàge rén de fángzi yǒu wǒ de péngyou de fángzi nàme piàoliang. 那个人的房子有我的朋友的房子那么漂亮。 *(That person's house is as pretty/beautiful as my friend's house.)* 4. Huáng xiānsheng zǒu de hé Wáng xiǎojie yíyàng kuài. 黄先生走得和王小姐一样快。 *(Mr. Huang walks as fast as Miss Wang.)* 5. Nà liàng chē hé zhè liàng chē yíyàng guì. 那辆车和这辆车一样贵。 *(That car is as expensive as this car.)* 6. Zhāng lǎoshī hé Lǐ lǎoshī yíyàng hǎo. 张老师和李老师一样好。 *(Teacher Zhang is as good as Teacher Li.)* 7. Zhōngguó méiyǒu Jiānádà nàme dà. 中国没有加拿大那么大。 *(China is not as big as Canada.)* 8. Tā de chéngjì hé wǒ de chéngjì yíyàng hǎo. 他的成绩和我的成绩一样好。 *(His grades are as good as my grades.)*

✎ Drive It Home

Practice writing sentences expressing equal or unequal comparisons. For each sentence, you are given two things or actions to compare, along with an adjective. Write an appropriate comparison of the two things or actions for each of the constructions provided in parentheses.

1. Tā de chéngjì, nǐ de chéngjì, hǎo (yǒu ... zhème, hé ... yíyàng, méiyǒu) 他的成绩、你的成绩、好(有 ... 这么、和 ... 一样、没有) _____

_____

2. Wǒ de fángzi, tāmen de fángzi, dà (yǒu ... nàme, hé ... yíyàng, méiyǒu) 我的房子、他们的房子、大 (有 ... 那么、和 ... 一样、没有) _____

_____

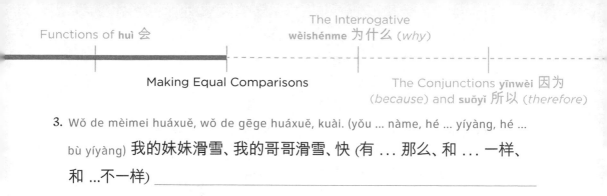

Functions of **huì** 会

The Interrogative
wèishénme 为什么 (*why*)

Making Equal Comparisons

The Conjunctions **yīnwèi** 因为
(*because*) and **suǒyǐ** 所以 (*therefore*)

3. Wǒ de mèimei huáxuě, wǒ de gēge huáxuě, kuài. (yǒu ... nàme, hé ... yíyàng, hé ...

bù yíyàng) 我的妹妹滑雪、我的哥哥滑雪、快 (有 ... 那么、和 ... 一样、
和 ...不一样) _____

ANSWER KEY

1. Tā de chéngjì yǒu nǐ de chéngjì zhème hǎo. 他的成绩有你的成绩这么好。(*His grades are as good as yours.*) Tā de chéngjì hé nǐ de chéngjì yíyàng hǎo. 他的成绩和你的成绩一样好。(*His grades are as good as yours.*) Tā de chéngjì méiyǒu nǐ de chéngjì hǎo. 他的成绩没有你的成绩好。(*His grades are not as good as yours.*) 2. Wǒ de fángzi yǒu tāmen de fángzi dà. 我的房子有他们的房子大。(*My house is as big as their house.*) Wǒ de fángzi hé tāmen de fángzi yíyàng dà. 我的房子和他们的房子一样大。(*My house is as big as their house.*) Wǒ de fángzi méiyǒu tāmen de fángzi dà. 我的房子没有他们的房子大。(*My house is not as big as their house.*) 3. Wǒ de mèimei huáxuě huá de yǒu wǒ de gēge nàme kuài. 我的妹妹滑雪滑得有我的哥哥那么快。(*My younger sister skis as fast as my older brother.*) Wǒ de mèimei huáxuě huá de hé wǒ de gēge yíyàng kuài. 我的妹妹滑雪滑得和我的哥哥一样快。(*My younger sister skis as fast as my older brother.*) Wǒ de mèimei huáxuě huá de hé wǒ de gēge bù yíyàng kuài. 我的妹妹滑雪滑得和我的哥哥不一样快。(*My younger sister doesn't ski as fast as my older brother.*)

✎ Sentence Recall

Match the English sentence in the column on the left with its appropriate translation in the column on the right.

1. *This book is as interesting as that one.*

a. Tā míngtiān huì huí gōngsī. 他明天会回公司。

2. *Many students will take the/an exam tomorrow.*

b. Tā xià ge lǐbài èr huì gēn lǎobǎn chūchāi. 他下个礼拜二会跟老板出差。

3. *His salary is as high as yours.*

c. Jīnnián de kǎoshì méiyǒu qùnián de róngyì. 今年的考试没有去年的容易。

4. *His company is as big as yours.*

d. Zài Měiguó, sīlì xiǎoxué de xuéfèi hé sīlì dàxué de xuéfèi yíyàng guì. 在美国, 私立小学的学费和私立大学的学费一样贵。

Yīnggāi 应该
(should, ought to)

The Double Conjunction
yòu ... yòu 又 ... 又

Making Comparisons

Ordinal Numbers

5. *Students will begin going to school next month.*

e. Hěn duō xuésheng míngtiān kǎoshì. 很多学生明天考试。

6. *English is not as difficult to learn as Chinese.*

f. Zhè běn shū hé nà běn shū yíyàng yǒu yìsi. 这本书和那本书一样有意思。

7. *He will be back in the office tomorrow.*

g. Tā de xīnshuǐ hé nǐ de yíyàng gāo. 他的薪水和你的一样高。

8. *Will you go to America to study next year?*

h. Xuésheng xià ge yuè kāishǐ shàngkè. 学生下个月开始上课。

9. *In the U.S., the tuition at private elementary schools is as expensive as at universities.*

i. Wǒ de jiàqī méiyǒu nǐ de nàme duō. 我的假期没有你的那么多。

10. *He will take a business trip with his boss next Tuesday.*

j. Wǒmen xià ge yuè bìyè. 我们下个月毕业。

11. *This year's examination is not as easy as last year's.*

k. Tā de bàba hé wǒ de māma yíyàng dà. 他的爸爸和我的妈妈一样大。

12. *My vacation is not as long as yours.*

l. Nǐ huì zhǎo qítā gōngzuò ma? 你会找其他工作吗?

13. *His father is as old as my mother.*

m. Nǐ míngnián huì qù Měiguó dúshū ma? 你明年会去美国读书吗?

14. *We'll graduate next month.*

n. Yīngwén méiyǒu Zhōngwén nàme nán xué. 英文没有中文那么难学.

15. *Will you look for another job?*

o. Tā de gōngsī yǒu nǐ de zhème dà. 他的公司有你的这么大。

ANSWER KEY

1. f; 2. e; 3. g; 4. o; 5. h; 6. n; 7. a; 8. m; 9. d; 10. b; 11. c; 12. i; 13. k; 14. j; 15. l

Functions of huì 会

The Interrogative
wèishénme 为什么 (why)

Making Equal Comparisons

The Conjunctions yīnwèi 因为
(because) and suǒyǐ 所以 (therefore)

Lesson 12: Conversations

In this lesson, you'll learn:

☐ How to talk about future plans.

☐ How to use the interrogative wèishénme 为什么 (why).

☐ How to use the conjunctions yīnwèi 因为 (because) and suǒyǐ 所以 (therefore).

🎧 Conversation 1

▶ 12A Conversation 1 (CD 9, Track 1-Chinese, Track 2-Chinese and English)

Wang Hai and Jess are talking about their plans after graduation.

Hai:	Jiéxī, nǐ bìyè zhīhòu dǎsuan zěnyàng?
海:	洁希, 你毕业之后打算怎样?
Jiéxī:	Wǒ dǎsuan liú zài Zhōngguó gōngzuò yì nián, zhīhòu qù lǚxíng, ránhòu cái huí guó. Nǐ ne?
洁希:	我打算留在中国工作一年, 之后去旅行, 然后才回国。你呢?
Hai:	Wǒ xiǎng zài Zhōngguó jiāo liǎng sān nián Yīngwén, cún yìdiǎnr qián, zài shēnqǐng chūguó dúshū. Tīngshuō zài Měiguó dúshū, shēnghuófèi hěn gāo.
海:	我想在中国教两三年英文, 存一点儿钱, 再申请出国读书。听说在美国读书, 生活费很高。
Jiéxī:	Nà yào kàn nǐ zài nǎ yí ge chéngshì, dà chéngshì de shēnghuófèi bǐ xiǎo zhèn de gāo, hěn duō dàxuéshēng dōu yào zuò jiānzhí bāngbǔ yí xià.
洁希:	那要看你在哪一个城市, 大城市的生活费比小镇的高, 很多大学生都要做兼职帮补一下。

Yīnggāi 应该
(should, ought to)

The Double Conjunction
yòu ... yòu 又 ... 又

Making Comparisons

Ordinal Numbers

Hai: Nà wǒ xiànzài kāishǐ yào shěng yìdiǎnr qián le. Nǐ xiǎng zuò shénme gōngzuò?

海: 那我现在开始要省一点儿钱了。你想做什么工作？

Jiéxī: Wǒ yě xiǎng zài zhèlǐ jiāo Yīngwén, hěn duō Zhōngguó xuésheng dōu xǐhuan xué hǎo Yīngwén.

洁希: 我也想在这里教英文，很多中国学生都喜欢学好英文。

Hai: Nǐ de Zhōngwén shuō de hěn hǎo, miànshì de shíhou yídìng huì yǒu bāngzhù.

海: 你的中文说得很好，面试的时候一定会有帮助。

Jiéxī: Xièxie!

洁希: 谢谢！

Hai: *Jess, what do you plan to do after graduation?*

Jess: *I'm planning to stay in China for a year. Then I'll travel, and after that I'll go back to my own country. How about you?*

Hai: *I want to teach English in China for two to three years. Meanwhile, I'll save some money and apply to study abroad. I hear that the cost of living is very high in the U.S.*

Jess: *Well, it depends on which city you live in. The cost of living in a big city is higher than in a small town, and a lot of undergraduates have part-time jobs to help cover the expenses.*

Hai: *Then I have to start saving money now. What's your plan for staying in China?*

Jess: *I'd also like to teach English here. A lot of Chinese students want to improve their English.*

Hai: *You speak Chinese very well. It will definitely help you when you interview for a job.*

Jess: *Thanks!*

Ⅱ

Functions of **huì** 会

The Interrogative
wèishénme 为什么 (*why*)

Making Equal Comparisons

The Conjunctions **yīnwèi** 因为
(*because*) and **suǒyǐ** 所以 (*therefore*)

Take It Further

The verb dǎsuan 打算 (*to plan*) can be used with another verb to mean *to plan to do something*.

The verb liú 留 (*to stay*) is usually combined with the preposition zài 在 to indicate where one is staying or intends to stay.

The word ránhòu 然后 can be translated as *then*, or *afterwards*.

The verb chǔ 储 (or cún 存) means *to save* or *to store up*, as in money, food, and so on.

The verb chūguó 出国 may be translated as *to leave one's own country* or *to go abroad*.

The word nà 那 is used as a conversational flavoring word in the same way as *Well* … It can also be used to mean *in this case* or *in that case*.

✎ Conversation Practice 1

Fill in the blanks with the missing words in pīnyīn. Refer to Hai and Jess' conversation.

1. Jiéxī bìyè zhīhòu _____ liú zài Zhōngguó gōngzuò yì nián, zhīhòu qù

   _____.

   洁希毕业之后打算留在中国工作一年, 之后去旅行。

   (*Jess plans to stay in China to work for a year after graduation, then to go travel.*)

2. Hǎi _____ zhīhòu xiǎng zài Zhōngguó jiāo jǐ nián Yīngwén, ránhòu

   _____ chūguó dúshū.

   海毕业之后想在中国教几年英文, 然后申请出国读书。

   (*Hai wants to teach English in China for a few years after graduation, then apply to study abroad.*)

3. Měiguó de dà chéngshì de _____ bǐ xiǎo zhèn de gāo.

美国的大城市的生活费比小镇的高。

(The cost of living in a big city in America is higher than in a small town.)

4. Jiéxī xiǎng zài Zhōngguó _____ Yīngwén.

洁希想在中国教英文。

(Jess wants to teach English in China.)

5. Jiéxī de Zhōngwén shuō de hěn hǎo, _____ de shíhou huì yǒu

_____.

洁希的中文说得很好, 面试的时候会有帮助。

(Jess speaks Chinese very well, which will help when she interviews for a job.)

ANSWER KEY

1. dǎsuan 打算, lǚxíng 旅行; 2. bìyè 毕业, shēnqǐng 申请; 3. shēnghuófèi 生活费; 4. jiāo 教; 5. miànshì 面试, bāngzhù 帮助

Grammar Builder 1
THE INTERROGATIVE WÈISHÉNME 为什么 (WHY)

▶ 12B Grammar Builder 1 (CD 9, Track 3)

In previous lessons, you learned how a number of interrogatives are used in Chinese to ask basic questions like *how, what, where, who,* and *which.* Another important interrogative is wèishénme 为什么, which means *why.* In questions, wèishénme 为什么 can take one of several different positions. It can be placed at the head of a sentence immediately in front of the subject, or else it can come right after the subject:

Wèishénme nǐ bù xǐhuan kàn diànyǐng?

为什么你不喜欢看电影?

Why don't you like going to the movies?

Functions of huì 会

The Interrogative
wèishénme 为什么 (*why*)

Making Equal Comparisons

The Conjunctions **yīnwèi** 因为
(*because*) and **suǒyǐ** 所以 (*therefore*)

Nǐ wèishénme bù xǐhuan kàn diànyǐng?

你为什么不喜欢看电影?

Why don't you like going to the movies?

In cases where a time period is specified, there are a few different word order possibilities with respect to wèishénme 为什么, the subject, and the time expression:

- wèishénme 为什么 + subject + time expression + verb

- subject + time expression + wèishénme 为什么 + verb

- time expression + subject + wèishénme 为什么 + verb

Wèishénme nǐ jīntiān chídào?

为什么你今天迟到?

Why were you late today?

Nǐ jīntiān wèishénme chídào?

你今天为什么迟到?

Why were you late today?

Jīntiān nǐ wèishénme chídào?

今天你为什么迟到?

Why were you late today?

The choice depends on what you want to stress. Put the word that is receiving the most emphasis first. If wèishénme 为什么 starts the sentence, you are emphasizing that you want to know *why* something happened. If the subject comes first, then you're emphasizing that you want to know why *a particular person* is responsible for doing something. And if the time expression begins the sentence, you are emphasizing that you want to know why someone did something *at a particular time*. Take another look at our examples. The underlined word is the element of the question that is being emphasized.

Yīnggāi 应该
(should, ought to)

The Double Conjunction
yòu ... yòu 又 ... 又

Making Comparisons

Ordinal Numbers

Wèishénme nǐ jīntiān chídào?

为什么你今天迟到?

Why were you late today?

Nǐ jīntiān wèishénme chídào?

你今天为什么迟到?

Why were you late today?

Jīntiān nǐ wèishénme chídào?

今天你为什么迟到?

Why were you late today?

✎ Work Out 1

Use wèishénme 为什么 to turn the following statements into questions.

1. Wǒmen bú qù Měiguó dúshū le. 我们不去美国读书了。 _____

   _____

2. Tā míngtiān bú shàngbān. 他明天不上班。 _____

   _____

3. Jīntiān xiàwǔ fàngxué zhīhòu wǒmen bú yìqǐ fùxí. 今天下午放学之后我们不一

   起复习。 _____

   _____

4. Wǒ de lǎobǎn xǐhuan yuángōng jiābān. 我的老板喜欢员工加班。 _____

   _____

5. Wǒ de xīnshuǐ méiyǒu nǐ de gāo. 我的薪水没有你的高。 _____

_____

6. Zhāng xiǎojie bìyè zhīhòu bù gōngzuò. 张小姐毕业之后不工作。 _____

_____

7. Nǐmen yīnggāi zhǔnshí shàngxué. 你们应该准时上学。 _____

_____

8. Wǒ yào yìbǎi kuài qián. 我要一百块钱。 _____

_____

ANSWER KEY

1. Wèishénme nǐmen bú qù Měiguó dúshū le? 为什么你们不去美国读书了? (*Why aren't you (pl.) going to America to study?*) 2. Tā wèishénme míngtiān bú shàngbān? 他为什么明天不上班? (*Why won't he go to work tomorrow?*) 3. Wèishénme jīntiān xiàwǔ fàngxué zhīhòu wǒmen bú yìqǐ fùxí? 为什么今天下午放学之后我们不一起复习? (*Why aren't we reviewing the lessons together after school this afternoon?*) 4. Nǐ de lǎobǎn wèishénme xǐhuan yuángōng jiābān? 你的老板为什么喜欢员工加班? (*Why does your boss like the staff to work overtime?*) 5. Nǐ de xīnshuǐ wèishénme méiyǒu wǒ de gāo? 你的薪水为什么没有我的高? (*Why isn't your salary as high as mine?*) 6. Wèishénme Zhāng xiǎojie bìyè zhīhòu bù gōngzuò? 为什么张小姐毕业之后不工作? (*Why won't Miss Zhang work after graduation?*) 7. Wǒmen wèishénme yīnggāi zhǔnshí shàngxué? 我们为什么应该准时上学? (*Why should we go to school on time?*) 8. Nǐ wèishénme yào yìbǎi kuài qián? 你为什么要一百块钱? (*Why do you need a hundred yuan?*)

🎧 Conversation 2

▶ 12C Conversation 2 (CD 9, Track 4-Chinese, Track 5-Chinese and English)

Jess and Wang Hai are talking about university life.

Jiéxī: Zǎoshang hǎo! Zuótiān zài xuéxiào méiyǒu kànjiàn nǐ, nǐ dào nǎli qùle?
洁希: 早上好! 昨天在学校没有看见你, 你到哪里去了?

Hai: Zuótiān wǒ xiàkè hòu qù bāng wǒ de biǎodì bǔxí.
海: 昨天我下课后去帮我的表弟补习。

Jiéxī: Zhēn de? Wèishénme?
洁希: 真的? 为什么?

Yīnggāi 应该
(should, ought to)

The Double Conjunction
yòu … yòu 又 … 又

Making Comparisons

Ordinal Numbers

Hai: Yīnwèi tā de chéngjì bú tài hǎo, míngnián tā yào kǎo dàxué, suǒyǐ tā māma yào wǒ guòqù bāngmáng.

海: 因为他的成绩不太好，明年他要考大学，所以他妈妈要我过去帮忙。

Jiéxī: Guàibude zuìjìn nǐ zǒu de zhème cōngmáng. Tā xiǎng dú shénme zhuānyè?

洁希: 怪不得最近你走得这么匆忙。他想读什么专业？

Hai: Tā xǐhuan zhéxué. Kěshì, tā māma yào tā dú gōngchéng.

海: 他喜欢哲学。可是，他妈妈要他读工程。

Jiéxī: Wèishénme Zhōngguó jiāzhǎng dōu xiǎng zǐnǚ dú gōngchéng, yīkē, fǎlǜ?

洁希: 为什么中国家长都想子女读工程、医科、法律？

Hai: Búshì měi yí ge jiāzhǎng dōu zhèyàng de. Xiàng wǒ fùmǔ, tāmen jiù méiyǒu yào wǒ dú lǐkē. Wǒ yīnwéi xǐhuan yǔwén, suǒyǐ xiànzài dú wàiyǔ xì.

海: 不是每一个家长都这样的。像我父母，他们就没有要我读理科。我因为喜欢语文，所以现在读外语。

Jiéxī: Rúguǒ měi yí ge fùmǔ dōu hé nǐ de bàba māma yíyàng kāimíng jiù hǎo le.

洁希: 如果每一个父母都和你的爸爸妈妈一样开明就好了。

Jess: *Good morning! I didn't see you after school yesterday. Where did you go?*

Hai: *I went to tutor my cousin.*

Jess: *Really? Why?*

Hai: *Since his academic performance is not very good and he has to take the college entrance exam next year, his mother wants me to help him.*

Jess: *No wonder you've been leaving school so quickly lately. What major does he intend to choose?*

Hai: *He likes philosophy. But his mother wants him to study engineering.*

Functions of **huì** 会

The Interrogative
wèishénme 为什么 (why)

Making Equal Comparisons

The Conjunctions **yīnwèi** 因为
(because) and **suǒyǐ** 所以 (therefore)

Jess:	*Why do so many Chinese parents want their children to study engineering, medicine or law?*
Hai:	*Not every parent thinks that way. Take my parents; they didn't ask me to study science. I like language studies, so I now study in the foreign language department.*
Jess:	*It would be wonderful if every parent were as open-minded as your parents!*

✎ Conversation Practice 2

Fill in the blanks with the missing words in pīnyīn. Use the Chinese characters for additional help and practice. Refer to the second conversation.

1. Hǎi zuótiān _____ hòu qù bāng tā de biǎodì _____.

   海昨天下课后去帮他的表弟补习。

   (Hai went to tutor his cousin yesterday.)

2. Hǎi de biǎodì _____ bú tài hǎo, míngnián yào _____ dàxué.

   海的表弟成绩不太好, 明年要考大学。

   (Hai's cousin's grades are not very good and he has to take the college entrance exam next year.)

3. Biǎodì xǐhuan _____, kěshì tā māma yào tā dú

   _____.

   表弟喜欢哲学, 可是他妈妈要他读工程。

   (The cousin likes philosophy. But his mother wants him to study engineering.)

4. Búshì měi yí ge Zhōngguó _____ dōu xiǎng _____ dú gōngchéng, yīkē, fǎlǜ.

Yīnggāi 应该
(*should, ought to*)

The Double Conjunction
yòu ... yòu 又 ... 又

Making Comparisons

Ordinal Numbers

不是每一个中国家长都想子女读工程、医科、法律。

(*Not every Chinese parent wants their children to study engineering, medicine, and law.*)

5. Yīnwéi Hǎi xǐhuan _____, suǒyǐ xiànzài dú _____ xì.

因为海喜欢语文，所以现在读外语系。

(*Because Hai likes language studies, (so) he now studies in the foreign languages department.*)

ANSWER KEY
1. xiàkè 下课, bǔxí 补习; 2. chéngjī 成绩, kǎo 考; 3. zhéxué 哲学, gōngchéng 工程; 4. jiāzhǎng 家长, zǐnǚ 子女; 5. yǔwén 语文, wàiyǔ 外语

Grammar Builder 2
THE CONJUNCTIONS YĪNWÈI 因为 (*BECAUSE*) AND SUǑYǏ 所以 (*THEREFORE*)

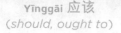 12D Grammar Builder 2 (CD 9, Track 6)

Questions that use the word wèishénme 为什么 (*why*) are often answered with yīnwèi 因为 ... (*because* ...). For example:

Wèishénme nǐ bú qù kàn diànyǐng?
为什么你不去看电影？
Why don't you go to the movie?

Yīnwèi wǒ hěn máng.
因为我很忙。
Because I am very busy.

Yīnwèi 因为 is also often used with the word suǒyǐ 所以 (*therefore, consequently*) to convey a sense of cause and effect. This results in a two-part sentence in

Functions of **huì** 会

The Interrogative
wèishénme 为什么 (why)

Making Equal Comparisons

The Conjunctions **yīnwèi** 因为
(because) and **suǒyǐ** 所以 (therefore)

which yīnwèi 因为 first establishes a reason, and then suǒyǐ 所以 identifies the consequence. This can be translated into English as *since ... , because ... , ... so, ... therefore*, and so on.

Yīnwèi méiyǒu rén bāng wǒ, suǒyǐ wǒ zìjǐ zuò.
因为没有人帮我，所以我自己做。
Since no one's going to help me, I'll do it myself.

Yīnwèi tā méiyǒu dúshū, suǒyǐ tā bù jígé.
因为他没有读书，所以他不及格。
He didn't study, so he failed the exam.

(II)

✎ Work Out 2

Match the Chinese sentences in the column on the left with their English translations on the right.

1. Tā yīnwèi méiyǒu qián, suǒyǐ bù kěyǐ shàng dàxué. 他因为没有钱，所以不可以上大学。

2. Yīnwèi méiyǒu dìtiě, suǒyǐ wǒ yào zǒulù shàngbān. 因为没有地铁，所以我要走路上班。

3. Tā yīnwèi chídào, suǒyǐ bù kěyǐ kǎoshì. 他因为迟到，所以不可以考试。

4. Yīnwèi xuéxiào lí wǒ jiā yuǎn, suǒyǐ wǒ zhù zài sùshè. 因为学校离我家远，所以我住在宿舍。

a. *Since he's late, he can't take the exam.*

b. *Since she doesn't have money, she can't attend university.*

c. *We don't like him, so we won't go tonight.*

d. *Since they are good friends, they ride to school together.*

Yīnggāi 应该
(*should, ought to*)

The Double Conjunction
yòu ... yòu 又 ... 又

Making Comparisons

Ordinal Numbers

5. Yīnwèi tiānqì bù hǎo, suǒyǐ wǒ bù xiǎng qù yóuyǒng le. 因为天气不好, 所以我不想去游泳了。

e. *There was no subway, so I had to go to work on foot.*

6. Wǒmen yīnwèi bù xǐhuan tā, suǒyǐ jīntiān wǎnshang wǒmen bú qù le. 我们因为不喜欢他, 所以今天晚上我们不去了。

f. *Since the weather isn't good, I don't want to go swimming.*

7. Yīnwèi tāmen shì hǎo péngyou, tāmen yìqǐ zuò chē shàngxué. 因为他们是好朋友, 他们一起坐车上学。

g. *The school is far from my home, so I live in the dorm.*

ANSWER KEY
1. b; 2. e; 3. a; 4. g; 5. f; 6. c; 7. d

⊕ Culture Note

Chinese parents usually steer their children in the direction of practical, well-respected professions, and therefore recommend that they study law, medicine or one of the sciences. Parents feel that this guarantees their children a good job after graduating from college.

Because so much depends on how well one does at school, the pressure to succeed is great, and students learn at an early age to take their studies quite seriously. Generally speaking, admission to schools is very competitive in China and, once you are enrolled, you have to study really hard. From elementary school onward, curricula are performance-based and high grades and long hours of study are prerequisites for success. Chinese students are given a lot of homework, even at the elementary school level, and must constantly prepare for tests, quizzes and dictations that are administered quite frequently throughout the school year.

Functions of **huì** 会

The Interrogative
wèishénme 为什么 (*why*)

Making Equal Comparisons

The Conjunctions **yīnwèi** 因为
(*because*) and **suǒyǐ** 所以 (*therefore*)

The school year in China is also longer than the typical school year in the United States. It is divided into two consecutive semesters that begin in September and end in mid-July.

High school students have a particularly rigorous schedule since they must take a yearly public examination called gāokǎo 高考 (*lit., high exam*) in order to be admitted to a university. In order to do well on this examination, many students take special cramming classes after the regular school day ends.

Such an intense regimen of study leaves little time for extracurricular activities. Extracurricular activities do exist in China, but in smaller quantity and with far less variety than at American schools. Extracurricular activities are mainly limited to sports, singing and the playing of musical instruments, and are designed for talented students, which means that not everyone has the opportunity to enjoy them.

✎ Drive It Home

Practice writing *because ... so* sentences. Link each set of two separate sentences with yīnwei 因为 ... suǒyǐ 所以。 Then translate each sentence into English.

1. Wǒ zǒu lù màn. Wǒ shàngkè chídào. 我走路慢。我上课迟到。 _____

   _____

2. Tāmen bù xǐhuan chī shuǐguǒ. Tāmen chī tiándiǎn. 他们不喜欢吃水果。他们吃
   甜点。 _____

   _____

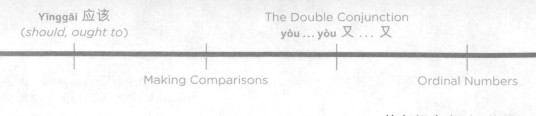

Yīnggāi 应该
(should, ought to)

The Double Conjunction
yòu ... yòu 又 ... 又

Making Comparisons

Ordinal Numbers

3. Tā yǒu hěnduō kǎoshì. Tā měitiān wǎnshang fùxí hěn wǎn. 他有很多考试。他每天晚上复习很晚。 _____

_____

4. Nǐ de gōngzuò hěn máng. Nǐ méiyǒu shíjiān qù lǚxíng. 你的工作很忙。你没有时间去旅行。 _____

_____

5. Wǒ bù shūfu. Wǒ qù kàn yīsheng. 我不舒服。我去看医生。 _____

_____

ANSWER KEY

1. Yīnwèi wǒ zǒu lù màn, suǒyǐ wǒ shàngkè chídào. 因为我走路慢, 所以我上课迟到。 (*Because I walk slowly, (so) I'm late to class.*) 2. Yīnwèi tāmen bù xǐhuan chī shuǐguǒ, suǒyǐ tāmen chī tiándiǎn. 因为他们不喜欢吃水果, 所以他们吃甜点。 (*Because they don't like to eat fruit, (so) they are eating dessert.*) 3. Yīnwèi tā yǒu hěnduō kǎoshì, suǒyǐ tā měitiān wǎnshang fùxí hěn wǎn. 因为他有很多考试, 所以他每天晚上复习很晚。 (*Because he has a lot of exams, (so) he studies very late every night.*) 4. Yīnwèi nǐ de gōngzuò hěn máng, suǒyǐ nǐ méiyǒu shíjiān qù lǚxíng. 因为你的工作很忙, 所以你没有时间去旅行。 (*Because your work is very busy, (so) you don't have time to go travel.*) 5. Yīnwèi wǒ bù shūfu, suǒyǐ wǒ qù kàn yīsheng. 因为我不舒服, 所以我去看医生。 (*Because I don't feel well, (so) I'm going to see the doctor.*)

✎ Word Recall

Match the English word in the column on the left with its appropriate translation in the column on the right.

1. *open-minded, enlightened*   a. miànshì 面试

2. *to stay, to keep*   b. zěnyàng 怎样

3. *city*   c. xiǎo zhèn 小镇

4. *interview*   d. dǎsuan 打算

5. *how*   e. cōngmáng 匆忙

6. *to economize*   f. liú 留

7. *in a hurry, in a rush*   g. shěng 省

Functions of **huì** 会

The Interrogative
wèishénme 为什么 (*why*)

Making Equal Comparisons

The Conjunctions **yīnwèi** 因为
(*because*) and **suǒyǐ** 所以 (*therefore*)

8. *cost of living*

9. *to go abroad*

10. *small town*

11. *to plan to*

12. *then, afterwards*

13. *to supplement (money)*

14. *to save (money)*

15. *parent*

h. ránhòu 然后

i. bāngbǔ 帮补

j. cún 存

k. chūguó 出国

l. jiāzhǎng 家长

m. shēnghuófèi 生活费

n. chéngshì 城市

o. kāimíng 开明

ANSWER KEY

1. o; 2. f; 3. n; 4. a; 5. b; 6. g; 7. e; 8. m; 9. k; 10. c; 11. d; 12. h; 13. i; 14. j; 15. l

Don't forget to practice and reinforce what you've learned by visiting **www.livinglanguage.com/languagelab** for flashcards, games, and quizzes.

Unit 3 Essentials

Vocabulary Essentials

Test your knowledge of the key material in this unit by filling in the blanks in the following charts. Once you've completed these pages, you'll have tested your retention, and you'll have your own reference for the most essential vocabulary. This is also a great time to practice a few Chinese characters. Fill in the middle column with the characters that you remember. Or, if you only remember the pīnyīn, go back through the unit to find the character.

WORK AND OFFICE

PĪNYĪN	CHARACTER	
		telephone
		computer
		office
		document, file
		company
		meeting
		salary
		boss
		holiday, vacation
		part-time job
		to work overtime
		to take sick leave
		to make a phone call
		on the phone
		to leave a message
		to make an appointment

SCHOOL

PĪNYĪN	CHARACTER	
		classroom
		university
		graduate school
		to graduate
		major
		philosophy
		foreign language
		biology
		physics
		chemistry
		history
		textbook
		campus
		bookstore
		academic performance, grades
		examination, to take an exam
		to attend (a) class
		to finish class
		to review a lesson
		to prepare for a lesson

If you're having a hard time remembering this vocabulary, don't forget to check out the flashcards, games and quizzes for this unit online. Go to **www.livinglanguage.com/languagelab** for a great way to help you practice what you've learned.

Grammar Essentials

Here is a reference for the key grammar that was covered in Unit 3. Make sure you understand the summary and can use all of the grammar it covers.

COMPARISONS WITH ADJECTIVES

- A + bǐ 比 + B + adjective

- A + bǐ 比 + B + adjective + amount of difference

- A + bǐ 比 + B + adjective + hěn duō

Ta bǐ wǒ dà.	他/她比我大。	He/She is older/bigger than I (am).
Tāmen de cǎodì bǐ nǐmen de lǜ.	他们的草地比你们的绿。	Their lawn is greener than yours.
Wǒ bǐ nǐ dà sān suì.	我比你大三岁。	I am three years older than you.
Nàge nánhái bǐ tā de jiějie qīng shí bàng.	那个男孩比他的姐姐轻十磅。	The boy is ten pounds lighter than his older sister.
Nǐ bǐ wǒ gāo hěn duō.	你比我高很多。	You are much taller than I (am).
Nàge nánhái bǐ tā de jiějie qīng hěn duō.	那个男孩比他的姐姐轻很多。	The boy is much lighter than his older sister.

COMPARISONS WITH ADVERBS

- A + verb + de 得 bǐ 比 + B + adverb

Wǒ zǒu de bǐ nǐ kuài.	我走得比你快。	I walk more quickly than you do.

Tā shuō de bǐ tā de mèimei màn.	她说得比她的妹妹慢。	*She speaks more slowly than her younger sister.*
Tā bèi shī bèi de bǐ lǎoshī liúlì.	他背诗背得比老师流利。	*He recited the poem more eloquently than (his) teacher.*

MAKING EQUAL COMPARISONS

- yǒu ... zhème/nàme 有 ... 这么/那么

- A + hé 和 + B + yíyàng 一样 + adjective (more exact)

- A + verb + de 得 + yǒu 有 + B + zhème/nàme 这么/那么 + adverb

- A + hé 和 + B + verb + de 得 + yíyàng 一样 + adverb

Wǒ yǒu nǐ nàme gāo.	我有你那么高。	*I am as tall as you.*
Wǒ hé nǐ yíyàng gāo.	我和你一样高。	*I am as tall as you. (We are the same height.)*
Wǒ chī de yǒu nǐ nàme kuài.	我吃得有你那么快。	*I eat as quickly as you do.*
Wǒ hé nǐ chī de yíyàng kuài.	我和你吃得一样快。	*I eat as quickly as you do.*

NEGATING EQUAL COMPARISONS

Wǒ méiyǒu nǐ nàme gāo.	我没有你那么高。	*I'm not as tall as you.*
Wǒ hé nǐ bù yíyàng gāo.	我和你不一样高。	*I'm not as tall as you. (You and I are not of the same height.)*
Wǒ chī de méiyǒu nǐ nàme kuài.	我吃得没有你那么快。	*I don't eat as quickly as you do.*

Wǒ hé nǐ chī de bù yíyàng kuài.	我和你吃得不一样快。	*I don't eat as quickly as you do. (You and I do not eat at the same speed.)*

DOUBLE CONJUNCTION WITH YOU ... YOU 又 ... 又

- yòu + adjective + yòu + adjective

- verb + de + yòu + adjective + yòu + adjective

Tā yòu dà yòu gāo.	他/她又大又高。	*He/She is big and tall.*
Nàge rén zuò de yòu kuài yòu hǎo.	那个人做得又快又好。	*That man works quickly and well.*

ASKING WHY

- wèishénme 为什么 + subject + verb

- subject + wèishénme 为什么 + verb

Wèishénme nǐ bù xǐhuan kàn diànyǐng?	为什么你不喜欢看电影?	*Why don't you like going to the movies?*
Nǐ wèishénme bù xǐhuan kàn diànyǐng?	你为什么不喜欢看电影?	*Why don't you like going to the movies?*

ASKING WHY WITH TIME EXPRESSIONS

- wèishénme 为什么 + subject + time expression + verb

- subject + time expression + wèishénme 为什么 + verb

- time expression + subject + wèishénme 为什么 + verb

Wèishénme nǐ jīntiān chídào?	为什么你今天迟到?	*Why were you late today?*

Advanced Chinese

Nǐ jīntiān wèishénme chídào?	你今天为什么迟到?	*Why were you late today?*
Jīntiān nǐ wèishénme chídào?	今天你为什么迟到?	*Why were you late today?*

Unit 3 Quiz

A. Rewrite the following sentences using yīnggāi 应该 (*should*) or bù yīnggāi 不应该 (*shouldn't*) as indicated.

1. Tā shàngke. 她上课。(*should*) _____

   _____

2. Tā de péngyou zài dàxué xué lìshǐ. 他的朋友在大学学历史。(*should*) _____

   _____

3. Tā jīntiān qù yóuyǒng. 他今天去游泳。(*shouldn't*) _____

   _____

4. Tā yǒu sān tiān de jiàqī. 他有三天的假期。(*shouldn't*) _____

   _____

5. Gōngsī de gùyuán shàngbān chídào. 公司的雇员上班迟到。(*shouldn't*) _____

   _____

B. Use the double conjunction yòu ... yòu 又 ... 又 to combine each pair of sentences into a single comparative statement.

1. Tā de xuéxiào xīn. Tā de xuéxiào dà. 他的学校新。他的学校大。_____

   _____

2. Wǒ de qúnzi cháng. Wǒ de qúnzi lán. 我的裙子长。我的裙子蓝。_____

   _____

3. Nàge chéngshì xiǎo. Nàge chéngshì yuǎn. 那个城市小。那个城市远。 _____

   _____

4. Zhè tái diànnǎo hěn jiù. Zhè tái diànnǎo hěn zhòng. 这台电脑很旧。这台电脑很重。 _____

   很重。 _____

   _____

5. Xuéxiào de kèwài huódòng hěn duō. Xuéxiào de kèwài huódòng hěn hǎowán (*fun*).
   学校的课外活动很多。学校的课外活动很好玩。 _____

   _____

C. Translate the following sentence featuring the word huì 会 into English.

1. Nǐ huì qí zìxíngchē ma? 你会骑自行车吗? _____

   _____

2. Wǒmen míngtiān huì kǎoshì. 我们明天会考试。 _____

   _____

3. Nàge rén huì qù jiàn tā de péngyou. 那个人会去见他的朋友。 _____

   _____

4. Wǒ huì shāo Fǎguó cài. 我会烧法国菜。 _____

   _____

5. Xià ge xīngqī wǒ huì shāo Fǎguó cài. 下个星期我会烧法国菜。 _____

   _____

D. Use wèishénme 为什么 to turn the following statements into questions.

1. Wǒ de lǎobǎn xǐhuan yuángōng jiābān. 我的老板喜欢员工加班。 _____

   _____

2. Wǒ de wòfáng méiyǒu nǐ de gānjing. 我的卧房没有你的干净。 _____

_____

3. Zhāng xiǎojie bìyè zhīhòu huì chūguó. 张小姐毕业之后会出国。 _____

_____

4. Nǐmen yīnggāi měitiān kàn kèběn. 你们应该每天看课本。 _____

_____

5. Wǒ bú yào chī ròu. 我不要吃肉。 _____

_____

ANSWER KEY

A. 1. Tā yīnggāi shàngke. 她应该上课。 (*She should go to class.*) 2. Tā de péngyou yīnggāi zài dàxué xué lìshǐ. 他的朋友应该在大学学历史。 (*His friend should study history in university.*) 3.Tā jīntiān bù yīnggāi qù yóuyǒng. 他今天不应该去游泳。 (*He shouldn't go swimming today.*) 4. Tā bù yīnggāi yǒu sān tiān de jiàqī. 他不应该有三天的假期。 (*He shouldn't have three days' vacation.*) 5. Gōngsī de gùyuán bù yīnggāi shàngbān chídào. 公司的雇员不应该上班迟到。 (*A company's employees shouldn't be late to work.*)

B. 1. Tā de xuéxiào yòu xīn yòu dà. 他的学校又新又大。 (*His school is new and big.*) 2.Wǒ de qúnzi yòu cháng yòu lán. 我的裙子又长又蓝。 (*My skirt is long and blue.*) 3. Nàge chéngshì yòu xiǎo yòu yuǎn. 那个城市又小又远。 (*That city is small and faraway.*) 4. Zhè tái diànnǎo yòu jiù yòu zhòng. 这台电脑又旧又重。 (*This computer is old and heavy.*) 5. Xuéxiào de kèwài huódòng yòu duō yòu hǎowán. 学校的课外活动又多又好玩。 (*The school's extracurricular activities are many and fun.*)

C. 1. *Do you know how to ride a bicycle?* 2. *We will take an exam tomorrow.* 3. *That person will go see his friend.* 4. *I know how to cook French dishes.* 5. *Next week, I will cook French dishes.*

D. 1. Nǐ de lǎobǎn wèishénme xǐhuan yuángōng jiābān? 你的老板为什么喜欢员工加班？ (*Why does your boss like the staff to work overtime?*) 2. Wèishénme nǐ de wòfáng méiyǒu wǒ de gānjing? 为什么你的卧房没有我的干净？ (*Why is your bedroom not as clean as mine?*) 3. Wèishénme Zhāng xiǎojie bìyè zhīhòu huì chūguó? 为什么张小姐毕业之后会出国？ (*Why will Miss Zhang go abroad after graduation?*) 4. Wǒmen wèishénme yīnggāi měitiān kàn kèběn? 我们为什么应该每天看课本？ (*Why should we read the textbook everyday?*) 5. Nǐ wèishénme bú yào chī ròu? 你为什么不要吃肉？ (*Why don't you want to eat meat?*)

How Did You Do?

Give yourself a point for every correct answer, then use the following key to tell whether you're ready to move on:

0-7 points: It's probably a good idea to go back through the lesson again. You may be moving too quickly, or there may be too much "down time" between your contact with Chinese. Remember that it's better to spend 30 minutes with Chinese three or four times a week than it is to spend two or three hours just once a week. Find a pace that's comfortable for you, and spread your contact hours out as much as you can.

8-12 points: You would benefit from a review before moving on. Go back and spend a little more time on the specific points that gave you trouble. Re-read the Grammar Builder sections that were difficult, and do the Work Outs one more time. Don't forget about the online supplemental practice material, either. Go to **www.livinglanguage.com/languagelab** for games and quizzes that will reinforce the material from this unit.

13-17 points: Good job! There are just a few points that you might consider reviewing before moving on. If you haven't worked with the games and quizzes on **www.livinglanguage.com/languagelab**, please give them a try.

18-20 points: Great! You're ready to move on to the next unit.

 points

The Verb dǎ qiú 打球
(to play ball)

Expressing Frequency
with cì 次 or biàn 遍

Uses of bǎ 把

Expressing duration

Unit 4: Sports and Leisure Activities

Tǐyù he kèwài huódòng
体育和课外活动

Are you ready for your last unit of Chinese? Since you've put so much hard work into this course, we'll end on an enjoyable and relaxing topic: sports, recreational activities, hobbies, and things people do for fun. That means that you'll learn a lot of new vocabulary that will come in handy when you talk about your interests, plan social events, or just plain relax.

For grammar, you'll learn useful constructions for talking about sports and games, and you'll also learn indefinites like *anyone, anything, someone, something*, and so on. This last unit will also highlight *if* conditional constructions and other expressions that will help make your Chinese sound more natural.

Lesson 13: Words

In this lesson you'll learn:

☐ Sports and hobbies vocabulary.

☐ The verb dǎ qiú 打球 (to play ball).

☐ Uses of bǎ 把.

Indefinite Pronouns

Making Comparisons with
gèng 更 *(even)*

Expressing Conditions with
rúguǒ 如果 *(if)*

Intensifying Comparisons

Word Builder 1

13A Word Builder 1 (CD 9, Track 7)

Here is some vocabulary that will come in handy when you want to talk about sports.

tǐyù	体育	*sports*
lánqiú	篮球	*basketball*
bàngqiú	棒球	*baseball*
qūgùnqiú	曲棍球	*hockey*
zúqiú	足球	*soccer (football)*
gǎnlǎnqiú	橄榄球（美式足球）	*(American) football*
yǔmáoqiú	羽毛球	*badminton*
páiqiú	排球	*volleyball*
wǎngqiú	网球	*tennis*
mànpǎo/huǎnbùpǎo	慢跑/缓步跑	*jogging*
qí zìxíngchē	骑自行车	*cycling*
yújiā	瑜伽	*yoga*
yuǎnzú	远足	*hiking*
yóuyǒng	游泳	*swimming*
yěyíng/lùyíng	野营/露营	*camping*
Májiàng	麻将	*Mahjong*
tàijíquán	太极拳	*Taiji/tai chi*

Word Practice 1

Match the English word in the column on the left with its appropriate translation in the column on the right.

| 1. camping | *a.* lánqiú 篮球 |
| 2. basketball | *b.* Májiàng 麻将 |

The Verb **dǎ qiú** 打球
(to play ball)

Expressing Frequency
with **cì** 次 or **biàn** 遍

Uses of **bǎ** 把

Expressing duration

3. yoga	c. yěyíng/lùyíng 野营/露营
4. Mahjong	d. páiqiú 排球
5. volleyball	e. yújiā 瑜伽

ANSWER KEY
1. c; 2. a; 3. e; 4. b; 5. d

Grammar Builder 1
THE VERB DĂ QIÚ 打球 (TO PLAY BALL)

▶ 13B Grammar Builder 1 (CD 9, Track 8)

The expression dǎ qiú 打球 can be translated as *to play ball*, and it refers to games that require using one's hands to manipulate a ball. The expression literally translates as *to hit (a) ball*.

Wǒ zuótiān dǎ qiú.
我昨天打球。
I played ball yesterday.

Tāmen xǐhuan dǎ qiú.
他们喜欢打球。
They like to play ball.

You can specify a particular type of game by replacing qiú 球 with the name of the game. Here are some examples of the games you can use with the basic verb dǎ 打:

dǎ bàngqiú 打棒球	*to play baseball*
dǎ wǎngqiú 打网球	*to play tennis*
dǎ lánqiú 打篮球	*to play basketball*
dǎ yǔmáoqiú 打羽毛球	*to play badminton*

Indefinite Pronouns

Making Comparisons with
gèng 更 *(even)*

Expressing Conditions with
rúguŏ 如果 *(if)*

Intensifying Comparisons

dǎ pīngpāngqiú 打乒乓球	*to play ping pong*
dǎ májiàng 打麻将	*to play Mahjong*
dǎ tàijíquán 打太极拳	*to do tai chi*

Note that the game of soccer (football) is not included in the list above. Since soccer is played with the feet, the verb tī 踢 *(to kick)* is substituted for dǎ 打 *(to hit)*. As a result, tī zúqiú 踢足球 means *to play soccer*. Here are a few more example sentences with both dǎ 打 and tī 踢:

Wŏmen zŏngshì zài gōngyuán tī zúqiú.
我们总是在公园踢足球。
We always play soccer in the park.

Háizimen fàngxué zhīhòu dǎ lánqiú.
孩子们放学之后打篮球。
The children play basketball after school.

Nĭ huì dǎ wăngqiú ma?
你会打网球吗?
Do you play tennis? (lit., Do you know how to play tennis?)

Wŏ hěn xǐhuan dǎ pīngpāngqiú, dànshì wŏ dǎ de bùhǎo.
我很喜欢打乒乓球, 但是我打得不好。
I love to play ping pong, but I'm not very good at it. (lit., I like to play ping pong very much, but I don't play well.)

Ⓟ

The Verb **dǎ qiú** 打球
(to play ball)

Expressing Frequency
with **cì** 次 or **biàn** 遍

Uses of **bǎ** 把

Expressing duration

✎ Work Out 1

Match each Chinese word or expression with its equivalent in English:

1. dǎ wǎngqiú 打网球
2. dǎ yǔmáoqiú 打羽毛球
3. yuǎnzú 远足
4. dǎ lánqiú 打篮球
5. tī zúqiú 踢足球
6. dǎ gǎnlǎnqiú 打橄榄球
7. qí zìxíngchē 骑自行车
8. yújiā 瑜伽

a. *cycling*
b. *yoga*
c. *to play basketball*
d. *to play (American) football*
e. *hiking*
f. *to play badminton*
g. *to play tennis*
h. *to play soccer*

ANSWER KEY
1. g; 2. f; 3. e; 4. c; 5. h; 6. d; 7. a; 8. b

Word Builder 2

▶ 13C Word Builder 2 (CD 9, Track 9)

Here are some helpful words you can use when talking about hobbies.

àihào	爱好	*hobbies*
kàn shū	看书	*reading*
shī	诗	*poetry*
xiǎoshuō	小说	*novel*
yīnyuè	音乐	*music*
gǔdiǎn yīnyuè	古典音乐	*classical music*
liúxíng yīnyuè	流行音乐	*pop music*
diànyǐng	电影	*film, movie*
xiězuò	写作	*writing*
diàoyú	钓鱼	*fishing*
biānzhī	编织	*knitting*

Indefinite Pronouns

Making Comparisons with
gèng 更 (*even*)

Expressing Conditions with
rúguǒ 如果 (*if*)

Intensifying Comparisons

pēngrèn	烹饪	*cooking*
lǚxíng	旅行	*travel*
huà huà	画画	*painting*
chànggē	唱歌	*singing*

✏ Word Practice 2

Fill in the blanks of the following conversation.

A: Nǐ yǒu shénme _____?

你有什么爱好?

(*What kind of hobbies do you have?*)

B: Wǒ xǐhuan _____ shū, _____ yīnyuè.

我喜欢看书、听音乐。

(*I like to read, listen to music.*)

A: Nǐ xǐhuan kàn shénme _____ ?

你喜欢看什么书?

(*What do you like to read?*)

B: Wǒ xǐhuan kàn _____.

我喜欢看小说。

(*I like to read novels.*)

A: Nǐ tīng _____ yīnyuè ma?

你听流行音乐吗?

(*Do you listen to pop music?*)

The Verb **dǎ qiú** 打球
(*to play ball*)

Expressing Frequency
with **cì** 次 or **biàn** 遍

Uses of **bǎ** 把

Expressing duration

B: Yì diǎnr. Wǒ zuì xǐhuan _____ yīnyuè.

一点儿。我最喜欢古典音乐。

(*A little. I like classical music the best.*)

ANSWER KEY
A. àihào 爱好; B. kàn 看, tīng 听; A. shū 书; B. xiǎoshuō 小说; A. liúxíng 流行; B. gǔdiǎn 古典

Grammar Builder 2
USES OF BǍ 把

▶ 13D Grammar Builder 2 (CD 9, Track 10)

As you know, basic word order in Chinese is the same as it is in English: subject + verb + object. But it's possible to move the object of a sentence in front of the verb by adding the word bǎ 把. This gives you the word order: subject + bǎ 把 + object + verb (+ le 了). The verb must always follow the object in sentences with bǎ 把.

Wǒ chīle píngguǒ.
我吃了苹果。
I ate an apple.

Wǒ chīle nàge píngguǒ.
我吃了那个苹果。
I ate the apple. (lit., I ate that apple.)

Wǒ bǎ píngguǒ chīle.
我把苹果吃了。
I ate the apple.

Wǒ bǎ nàge píngguǒ chīle.
我把那个苹果吃了。
I ate the apple. (lit., I ate that apple.)

Indefinite Pronouns

Making Comparisons with
gèng 更 (*even*)

Expressing Conditions with
rúguǒ 如果 (*if*)

Intensifying Comparisons

Remember that, in Chinese, there is no real equivalent for the English word *the*. However, bǎ 把 can be used to make your reference more specific, as in Wǒ bǎ píngguǒ chīle 我把苹果吃了 (*I ate the apple*). However, the words *this* (zhège 这个) and *that* (nàge 那个) are usually used in place of *the* in Chinese. If you want to tell someone *I ate the apple*, you can say Wǒ chīle nàge píngguǒ 我吃了那个苹果 (*lit., I ate that apple*). Of course, these sentences can also take on their literal meanings.

Bǎ 把 is also used in more complex constructions. Compare these two examples:

Tā ná zhe nà běn shū.
他拿着那本书。
He is holding that book.

Tā bǎ nà běn shū cóng shūjià shàng ná zǒu.
他把那本书从书架上拿走。
He took that book away from the shelf. (lit., He [bǎ 把] that book from the bookshelf take off.)

The first example is simple, and the English is a literal translation of the Chinese. If, however, you want to explain specifically how his action of taking resulted in the book being off of the shelf, you need to use the word bǎ 把, followed by the complex phrase nà běn shū cóng shūjià shàng ná zǒu 那本书从书架上拿走, which can literally be translated as *that book from the shelf take off*.

Generally speaking, the word bǎ 把 (which literally means *to grasp*) is introduced to show the intention or consequence of a deliberate action, or it can clarify the location, time frame or manner in which something is purposely done. These constructions are often built very differently in Chinese than they are in English, but comparing a few examples both with and without bǎ 把 will help make them clearer.

Uses of **bǎ** 把

Wǒ nále zhè xiē xiézi.
我拿了这些鞋子。
I took these shoes.

Wǒ bǎ zhè xiē xiézi ná huí jiā lǐ lái.
我把这些鞋子拿回家里来。
I took these shoes home.

Wǒ chīle wǎncān.
我吃了晚餐。
I ate dinner.

Wǒ huāle yí ge zhōngtóu bǎ wǎncān chī wán.
我花了一个钟头把晚餐吃完。
I spent an hour eating dinner.

Nàge xuésheng gǎile dáàn.
那个学生改了答案。
The student changed his answer.

Nàge xuésheng bǎ dáàn gǎile sān cì.
那个学生把答案改了三次。
The student changed his answer three times.

Wǒ xǐle pánzi.
我洗了盘子。
I washed the plate.

Wǒ bǎ pánzi xǐ de hěn gānjìng.
我把盘子洗得很干净。
I washed the plate clean.

Indefinite Pronouns

Making Comparisons with
gèng 更 (even)

Expressing Conditions with
rúguǒ 如果 (if)

Intensifying Comparisons

One issue to keep in mind is that bǎ 把 is only used in contexts with some kind of action verb where there's a tangible result, such as ná 拿 (to take), chī 吃 (to eat), or xǐ 洗 (to wash). In our last example above, *wash* expresses a tangible activity, and the result of the washing is that the plates are clean. So you wouldn't use bǎ 把 with a verb that expresses a state or a psychological condition, such as xǐhuan 喜欢 (to like) or ài 爱 (to love). Nor would you use it with sensory verbs such as gǎndào 感到 (to feel), zhīdao 知道 (to know), kànjian 看见 (saw), or tīngdào 听到 (heard); with stative verbs such as shì 是 (to be) or yǒu 有 (to have); or with verbs that describe movement to and from a location such as lái 来 (to come) or qù 去 (to go).

⑪

✎ Work Out 2

Each of the following sentences has been broken down into its grammatical components to help you identify the subject, object, verb and time phrase. Restate these sentences using bǎ 把, and don't forget to change the word order. Then see if you can give an English translation. As an example, the answer to the first one is: Wǒmen zuótiān bǎ jiā lǐ de shuǐ hē guāng le. 我们昨天把家里的水喝光了。 (*Yesterday we drank all the water at home.*) Guāng 光 literally means *all used up, all gone.*

Subject	Time Phrase/ Modal	Action	Object
1. Wǒmen 我们	zuótiān 昨天	hē guāng le 喝光了	jiā lǐ de shuǐ 家里的水
2. Nǐ 你	yīnggāi 应该	ná zǒu 拿走	nà bǎ yǐzi 那把椅子
3. Tā 他	-	huā guāng le 花光了	qián 钱

| 4. Nàge rén
那个人 | - | zuò hǎo le
做好了 (made) | zhège dàngāo
这个蛋糕 |
| 5. Wǒ
我 | jīntiān
今天 | kàn wán (finish) le
看完了 | nǐ de shū
你的书 |

ANSWER KEY

2. Nǐ yīnggāi bǎ nà bǎ yǐzi ná zǒu. 你应该把那把椅子拿走。 (*You ought to take away that chair.*) 3. Tā bǎ qián huā guāng le. 他把钱花光了。 (*He spent all his money.*) 4. Nàge rén bǎ zhège dàngāo zuò hǎo le. 那个人把这个蛋糕做好了。 (*That person made this cake.*) 5. Wǒ jīntiān bǎ nǐ de shū kàn wán le. 我今天把你的书看完了。 (*I finished reading your book today.*)

✎ Drive It Home

Practice the bǎ 把 construction by using it in each sentence.

1. Wǒ shāole niúròu. 我烧了牛肉。(*I cooked beef.*) _____

_____

2. Tā kàn wán le diànyǐng. 他看完了电影。(*He finished watching the movie.*) _____

_____

3. Tāmen mǎile nàge fángzi. 他们买了那个房子。(*They bought that house.*) _____

_____

4. Wǒmen ná qùle nǐ de kèběn. 我们拿去了你的课本。(*We took away your*

textbook.) _____

_____

5. Nà xiē rén chīle júzi. 那些人吃了橘子。(*Those people ate oranges.*) _____

_____

6. Wǒ de jiějie xǐle chē. 我的姐姐洗了车。(*My older sister washed the car.*) _____

_____

Indefinite Pronouns

Making Comparisons with
gèng 更 (*even*)

Expressing Conditions with
rúguǒ 如果 (*if*)

Intensifying Comparisons

7. Nǐ shénme shíhou fùxí le gōngkè? 你什么时候复习了功课? (*When did you review the homework?*) _____

_____

ANSWER KEY

1. Wǒ bǎ niúròu shāo le. 我把牛肉烧了。 (*I cooked the beef.*) 2. Tā bǎ diànyǐng kàn wán le. 他把电影看完了。 (*He finished watching the movie.*) 3. Tāmen bǎ nàge fángzi mǎi le. 他们把那个房子买了。 (*They bought that house.*) 4. Wǒmen bǎ nǐ de kèběn ná qù le. 我们把你的课本拿去了。 (*We took away your textbook.*) 5. Nà xiē rén bǎ júzi chī le. 那些人把橘子吃了。 (*Those people ate the oranges.*) 6. Wǒ de jiějie bǎ chē xǐ le. 我的姐姐把车洗了。 (*My older sister washed the car.*) 7. Nǐ shénme shíhou bǎ gōngkè fùxí le? 你什么时候把功课复习了? (*When did you review the homework?*)

✎ Word Recall

Match the English word in the column on the left with its appropriate translation in the column on the right.

1. *classical music*	a. tàijíquán 太极拳
2. *sports*	b. àihào 爱好
3. *novel*	c. yuǎnzú 远足
4. *hiking*	d. gǔdiǎn yīnyuè 古典音乐
5. *writing*	e. yùndòng 运动
6. *badminton*	f. xiǎoshuō 小说
7. *fishing*	g. wǎngqiú 网球
8. *soccer (football)*	h. huà huà 画画
9. *poetry*	i. shī 诗
10. *travel*	j. bàngqiú 棒球
11. *tennis*	k. xiězuò 写作
12. *taiji/tai chi*	l. yǔmáoqiú 羽毛球
13. *baseball*	m. lǚxíng 旅行
14. *painting*	n. zúqiú 足球
15. *hobbies*	o. diàoyú 钓鱼

ANSWER KEY
1. d; 2. e; 3. f; 4. c; 5. k; 6. l; 7. o; 8. n; 9. i; 10. m; 11. g; 12. a; 13. j; 14. h; 15. b

Lesson 14: Phrases

In this lesson, you'll learn:

☐ More vocabulary related to sports and hobbies.

☐ Frequency words cì 次 or biàn 遍.

☐ How to express duration and frequency.

Phrase Builder 1

▶ 14A Phrase Builder 1 (CD 9, Track 11)

Here are some phrases related to leisure activities and entertainment.

kàn diànyǐng	看电影	*to go to a movie/the movies*
qù hǎitān	去海滩	*to go to the beach*
kàn xìjù	看戏剧	*to see a play*
kàn diànshì	看电视	*to watch TV*
wán de kāixīn	玩得开心	*to have fun*
qù tǐyùguǎn	去体育馆	*to go to a stadium*
zuò yùndòng	做运动	*to play a sport*
wán yóuxì	玩游戏	*to play a game*
dǎ chéng píngshǒu	打成平手	*to tie the score*
tán gāngqín	弹钢琴	*to play piano*
lā xiǎotíqín	拉小提琴	*to play violin*
dǎ gǔ	打鼓	*to play drums*

Indefinite Pronouns

Making Comparisons with
gèng 更 (*even*)

Expressing Conditions with
rúguǒ 如果 (*if*)

Intensifying Comparisons

chuī dízi	吹笛子	*to play the flute*

⏸

✏️ Phrase Practice 1

Translate the following sentences into pīnyīn.

1. *When are we going to the beach?* _____

_____

2. *He is going to the stadium today.* _____

_____

3. *Do you know how to play the piano?* _____

_____

4. *Let's play a game.* _____

_____

5. *We often play sports.* _____

_____

ANSWER KEY
1. Wǒmen/zánmen shénme shíhou qù hǎitān? 我们/咱们什么时候去海滩？ 2. Tā jīntiān qù
tǐyùguǎn. 他今天去体育馆。 3. Nǐ huì tán gāngqín ma? 你会弹钢琴吗？ 4. Wǒmen/zánmen wán
yóuxì ba. 我们/咱们玩游戏吧。 5. Wǒmen jīngcháng zuò yùndòng. 我们经常做运动。

The Verb **dǎ qiú** 打球
(to play ball)

Expressing Frequency
with **cì** 次 or **biàn** 遍

Uses of **bǎ** 把

Expressing duration

Grammar Builder 1
EXPRESSING FREQUENCY WITH cì 次 OR biàn 遍

▶ 14B Grammar Builder 1 (CD 9, Track 12)

You can use the word cì 次 or biàn 遍 (*times*) along with a number to express how many times something happened. The word order is number + cì/biàn 次/遍, and this phrase is positioned after the verb.

Wǒ qùle sān cì.
我去了三次。
I went three times.

Lǎoshī shuōle liǎng biàn.
老师说了两遍。
The teacher said it twice. (lit., The teacher spoke twice.)

Note that biàn 遍 is usually used to describe how many times a completed action has been done (for example, the teacher's action of saying something was completed twice), while cì 次 can generally be used with any event.

If an object that comes after the verb is not a personal pronoun or a place name, the phrase 'number + cì/biàn 次/遍' comes between the verb and the object.

Wǒ jīntiān huànle sì cì yīfu.
我今天换了四次衣服。
I've changed clothing four times today.

Tā zhège lǐbài fāle liǎng cì shāo.
他这个礼拜发了两次烧。
He had a fever twice this week.

In cases where the object is a personal pronoun or place name, the phrase 'number + cì/biàn 次/遍' comes after the pronoun or place name.

Indefinite Pronouns

Making Comparisons with
gèng 更 (*even*)

Expressing Conditions with
rúguǒ 如果 (*if*)

Intensifying Comparisons

Wǒ jiànguò tā yí cì.

我见过他一次。

I saw him once.

Tāmen qùle Shànghǎi liǎng cì.

他们去了上海两次。

They went to Shanghai twice.

✎ Work Out 1

Match the Chinese sentences in the right column with the English translations on the left.

1. *I have seen his teacher twice.*

   a. Wǒ yí ge lǐbài yóu liǎng cì yǒng.
     我一个礼拜游两次泳。

2. *They have been to China once.*

   b. Tā měitiān dǎ liǎng cì diànhuà gěi māma.
     他每天打两次电话给妈妈。

3. *I swim twice a week.*

   c. Wǒ jiàn guò tā de lǎoshī liǎng cì.
     我见过他的老师两次。

4. *He has been late ten times this year.*

   d. Wǒ jīntiān zǎoshang chīle sān cì.
     我今天早上吃了三次。

5. *He gives his mother a call twice every day.*

   e. Qǐng nǐ zài shuō yí cì.
     请你再说一次.

6. *Please say it (once) again.*

   f. Tāmen qù guò Zhōngguó yí cì.
     他们去过中国一次。

7. *I ate three times this morning.*

   g. Tā jīnnián chídào le shí cì.
     他今年迟到了十次。

ANSWER KEY

1. c; 2. f; 3. a; 4. g; 5. b; 6. e; 7. d

The Verb **dǎ qiú** 打球
(*to play ball*)

Uses of **bǎ** 把

Expressing Frequency
with **cì** 次 or **biàn** 遍

Expressing duration

Phrase Builder 2

14C Phrase Builder 2 (CD 9, Track 13)

Here are some phrases that express duration and frequency.

hěn jiǔ	很久	*a long time*
hěn duō cì	很多次	*many times*
jǐ cì	几次	*several times*
cónglái méiyǒu …	从来没有…	*never*
yì nián	一年	*one year*
liǎng ge lǐbài	两个礼拜	*two weeks*
sān ge yuè	三个月	*three months*
jǐ tiān	几天	*several days*
wǔ nián	五年	*five years*
yì fēnzhōng	一分钟	*one minute*
bàn ge xiǎoshí	半个小时	*half an hour*
liǎng ge zhōngtóu	两个钟头	*two hours*

Phrase Practice 2

Match the English phrase in the column on the left with its appropriate
translation in the column on the right.

1. *a long time*
2. *several times*
3. *several days*
4. *many times*
5. *never*

a. hěn duō cì 很多次
b. jǐ tiān 几天
c. hěn jiǔ 很久
d. cónglái méiyǒu … 从来没有 …
e. jǐ cì 几次

ANSWER KEY
1. c; 2. e; 3. b; 4. a; 5. d

Indefinite Pronouns

Making Comparisons with
gèng 更 (*even*)

Expressing Conditions with
rúguǒ 如果 (*if*)

Intensifying Comparisons

Grammar Builder 2
EXPRESSING DURATION

▶ 14D Grammar Builder 2 (CD 9, Track 14)

Phrases that express how long an activity lasted are generally placed after the verb in Chinese, at the end of the sentence:

Wǒmen děngle yí ge zhōngtóu.
我们等了一个钟头。
We waited for an hour.

Tā lǚxíng le liǎng nián.
他旅行了两年。
He traveled for two years.

As with the phrase 'number + cì/biàn 次/遍,' in cases where an object follows the verb and the object is neither a personal pronoun nor a place name, the expression of duration is put between the verb and the object, and the object goes last.

Wǒ xuéle sān nián Zhōngwén.
我学了三年中文。
I have studied Chinese for three years.

Tā kànle wǔ ge zhōngtóu diànshì.
她看了五个钟头电视。
She watched TV for five hours.

If the object is a personal pronoun or place name, the expression of duration comes after the object.

The Verb **dǎ qiú** 打球
(*to play ball*)

Expressing Frequency
with **cì** 次 or **biàn** 遍

Uses of **bǎ** 把

Expressing duration

Tā děngle wǒ bàn ge xiǎoshí.

他等了我半个小时。

He waited for me for half an hour.

Wǒ de péngyou láile Niǔ Yuē yí ge lǐbài.

我的朋友来了纽约一个礼拜。

My friend has come to New York for a week.

Take It Further

In English, the verb *to play* is used with all musical instruments: *play the flute*, *play the piano*, *play the violin*, and so on. In Chinese, however, different verbs are used for each instrument depending on how that instrument is actually played. Since a drum is hit or struck, the verb dǎ 打 (*to hit*) is used in the expression dǎ gǔ 打鼓 (*to play the drums*). Similarly, the verb used with a piano is tán 弹 (*to pluck*), lā 拉 (*to pull*) is used with a violin, and chuī 吹 (*to blow*) is used with a flute.

✎ Work Out 2

Match the Chinese sentences in the column on the left with the English translations on the right.

1. Tāmen xuéle liǎng nián Zhōngwén. 他们学了两年中文。

    a. *My mother and father have danced for an hour.*

2. Wǒ de péngyou qùle Zhōngguó sān ge yuè. 我的朋友去了中国三个月。

    b. *I have been living in the U.S. for a year.*

Indefinite Pronouns

Making Comparisons with
gèng 更 (*even*)

Expressing Conditions with
rúguǒ 如果 (*if*)

Intensifying Comparisons

3. Māma hé bàba tiàole yí ge zhōngtóu wǔ. 妈妈和爸爸跳了一个钟头舞。

c. *They played ball for an hour today.*

4. Wǒ zài Měiguó zhùle yì nián. 我在美国住了一年。

d. *They have studied Chinese for two years.*

5. Wǒ de dìdi wánle bàn ge xiǎoshí diànnǎo yóuxì. 我的弟弟玩了半个小时电脑游戏。

e. *My friend went to China for three months.*

6. Wǒ jīntiān wǎnshang dúle liǎng ge zhōngtóu shū. 我今天晚上读了两个钟头书。

f. *I read for two hours tonight.*

7. Tā chàngle sān ge zhōngtóu gē. 他唱了三个钟头歌。

g. *My younger brother has played computer games for half an hour.*

8. Tāmen jīntiān dǎle yí ge zhōngtóu qiú. 他们今天打了一个钟头球。

h. *He has been singing for three hours.*

ANSWER KEY
1.d; 2. e; 3. a; 4. b; 5. g; 6. f; 7. h; 8. c

✎ Drive It Home

Practice writing sentences featuring the duration of an activity. For each verb phrase given, write three sentences using the duration phrase provided in parentheses. Be aware of where the duration phrase goes if there is an object involved.

1. Nǐ chàngle 你唱了 (shí fēnzhōng 十分钟, hěn jiǔ 很久, hěn duō cì 很多次) _____

_____

2. Tā lāle xiǎotíqín 他拉了小提琴 (qī nián 七年, èrshí nián 二十年, sān tiān 三天)

_____

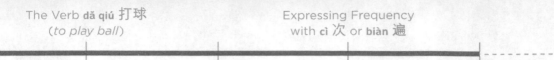

The Verb **dǎ qiú** 打球
(*to play ball*)

Expressing Frequency
with **cì** 次 or **biàn** 遍

Uses of **bǎ** 把

Expressing duration

3. Wǒ zài Yīngguó zhùle 我在英国住了 (bàn nián 半年, bā ge yuè 八个月, jǐ cì 几
   次) _____

ANSWER KEY

1. Nǐ chàngle shí fēnzhōng. 你唱了十分钟。 (*You sang for ten minutes.*) Nǐ chàngle hěn jiǔ. 你唱了
很久。 (*You sang for a long time.*) Nǐ chàngle hěn duō cì. 你唱了很多次。 (*You sang many times.*)
2. Tā lāle qī nián xiǎotíqín. 他拉了七年小提琴。 (*He played the violing for seven years.*) Tā lāle
èrshí nián xiǎotíqín. 他拉了二十年小提琴。 (*He played the violin for twenty years.*) Tā lāle sān tiān
xiǎotíqín. 他拉了三天小提琴。 (*He played the violin for three days.*)
3. Wǒ zài Yīngguó zhùle bàn nián. 我在英国住了半年。 (*I lived in the England for half a year.*) Wǒ
zài Yīngguó zhùle bā ge yuè. 我在英国住了八个月。 (*I lived in England for eight months.*) Wǒ zài
Yīngguó zhùle jǐ cì. 我在英国住了几次。 (*I lived in England several times.*)

✎ Phrase Recall

Match the English word in the column on the left with its appropriate translation
in the column on the right.

1. *a long time*

2. *to go to a movie/the movies*

3. *to tie the score*

4. *several days*

5. *to watch TV*

6. *to play the violin*

7. *to go to the beach*

8. *to play the flute*

9. *to have fun*

10. *many times*

11. *to see a play*

12. *to play drums*

13. *several times*

14. *to play a sport*

a. dǎ chéng píngshǒu 打成平手

b. hěn jiǔ 很久

c. wán de kāixīn 玩得开心

d. lā xiǎotíqín 拉小提琴

e. dǎ gǔ 打鼓

f. kàn diànyǐng 看电影

g. jǐ cì 几次

h. hěn duō cì 很多次

i. kàn xìjù 看戏剧

j. zuò yùndòng 做运动

k. cónglái méiyǒu ... 从来没有...

l. qù hǎitān 去海滩

m. chuī dízi 吹笛子

n. kàn diànshì 看电视

Indefinite Pronouns

Making Comparisons with
gèng 更 (even)

Expressing Conditions with
rúguǒ 如果 (if)

Intensifying Comparisons

15. *never*

o. jǐ tiān 几天

ANSWER KEY
1. b; 2. f; 3. a; 4. o; 5. n; 6. d; 7. l; 8. m; 9. c; 10. h; 11. i; 12. e; 13. g; 14. j; 15. k.

Lesson 15: Sentences

In this lesson, you'll learn:

☐ Indefinite pronouns.

☐ How to express conditions with rúguǒ 如果 (*if*).

Sentence Builder 1

▶ 15A Sentence Builder 1 (CD 9, Track 15)

Wǒ shénme shū yě bú kàn.	我什么书也不看。	*I don't read (any) books.*
Wǒ shéi yě bù xiǎng jiàn.	我谁也不想见。	*I don't want to see anyone.*
Wǒ nǎli yě bù xiǎng qù.	我哪里也不想去。	*I don't want to go anywhere.*
Wǒ hěn lèi, shénme yě bù xiǎng zuò.	我很累, 什么也不想做。	*I'm tired and don't want to do anything.*
Wǒ yǒu diǎn dōngxi gěi nǐ.	我有点东西给你。	*I have something to give you.*
Wǒ xiànzài yǒukòng, shénme shíhou yě kěyǐ péi nǐ qù.	我现在有空, 什么时候也可以陪你去。	*I'm free now and can go with you anytime.*

The Verb **dǎ qiú** 打球
(*to play ball*)

Expressing Frequency
with **cì** 次 or **biàn** 遍

Uses of **bǎ** 把

Expressing duration

Shéi yě kěyǐ jìn zhè ge dàxué dúshū.	谁也可以进这个大学读书。	*Anyone can (go) study at this university.*
Wǒ yǒu qián, zhù zài nǎr yě kěyǐ.	我有钱, 住在哪儿也可以。	*I have money and can live anywhere.*
Xiànzài shénme xuéxiào yě yǒu diànnǎo kè le.	现在什么学校也有电脑课了。	*Now there is a computer course in every school.*
Tā de chéngjì hěn hǎo, shénme dàxué yě kěyǐ shēnqǐng.	他的成绩很好, 什么大学也可以申请。	*His grades are very good, so he/she can apply to any university.*

Ⓘ

✎ Sentence Practice 1

Fill in the blanks of the following sentences. The characters are provided for additional help and practice.

1. Wǒ _____ yě bù xiǎng _____ .

   我谁也不想见。

   (*I don't want to see anyone.*)

2. Shéi _____ kěyǐ _____ zhè ge dàxué dúshū.

   谁也可以进这个大学读书。

   (*Anyone can [go] study at this university.*)

3. Wǒ yǒu qián , zhù zài _____ yě _____ .

   我有钱, 住在哪儿也可以。

   (*I have money and can live anywhere.*)

Indefinite Pronouns

Making Comparisons with
gèng 更 (*even*)

Expressing Conditions with
rúguǒ 如果 (*if*)

Intensifying Comparisons

4. Wǒ _____ shū _____ bú kàn.

我什么书也不看。

(*I don't read [any] books.*)

5. Wǒ hěn lèi, _____ yě bù _____ zuò.

我很累, 什么也不想做。

(*I'm tired and don't want to do anything.*)

ANSWER KEY

1. shéi 谁, jiàn 见; 2. yě 也, jìn 进; 3. nǎr 哪儿, kěyǐ 可以; 4. shénme 什么, yě也; 5. shénme 什么, xiǎng 想

Grammar Builder 1
INDEFINITE PRONOUNS

▶ 15B Grammar Builder 1 (CD 9, Track 16)

Indefinite pronouns refer to people, places and things that are not specifically identified. The indefinite pronouns *anyone, anything, anywhere,* and *anytime* are made in Chinese using question words + yě 也:

shéi 谁 (*who*)	shéi yě 谁也 (*anyone*)
shénme dōngxi 什么东西 (*what thing*)	shénme dōngxi yě 什么东西也 (*anything*)
shénme shíhou 什么时候 (*when*)	shénme shíhou yě 什么时候也 (*anytime*)
nǎr/nǎli 哪儿/哪里 (*where*)	nǎr/nǎli yě 哪儿/哪里也 (*anywhere*)

Let's see some example sentences:

Shéi yě kěyǐ lái zhè ge wǔhuì.

谁也可以来这个舞会。

Anyone can come to the party.

The Verb **dǎ qiú** 打球
(*to play ball*)

Expressing Frequency
with **cì** 次 or **biàn** 遍

Uses of **bǎ** 把

Expressing duration

Nǐ shénme shíhou guòlái yě kěyǐ.
你什么时候过来也可以。
You can come over anytime.

Wǒ shénme dōngxi yě huì chī.
我什么东西也会吃。
I'll eat anything.

Rúguǒ nǐ huì shuō Yīngwén, nǐ nǎli yě kěyǐ qù.
如果你会说英文, 你哪里也可以去。
If you know how to speak English, you can go anywhere.

The indefinites *someone/somebody* and *something* are not formed this way.
Someone is expressed by yǒu rén 有人, and *something* by (yì) diǎn dōngxi (一) 点
东西 or (yì) xiē dōngxi (一) 些 东西.

Yǒu rén qùle xuéxiào zhǎo Zhāng lǎoshī.
有人去了学校找张老师。
Someone went to the school to look for Teacher Zhang.

Wǒ de shūbāo lǐ yǒu diǎn dōngxi.
我的书包里有点东西。
There is something in my schoolbag.

The indefinites *nothing* or *nowhere* are expressed in Chinese by using shénme
dōngxi yě 什么东西也 (*anything*) or nǎr/nǎli yě 哪儿/哪里也 (*anywhere*) in a
negative sentence. In this way they're very similar to the English *not … anything*
and *not … anywhere*.

Jīntiān wǒ shénme dōngxi yě méiyǒu chī.
今天我什么东西也没有吃。
Today I ate nothing. (lit., Today I anything didn't eat.)

Indefinite Pronouns

Making Comparisons with
gèng 更 (even)

Expressing Conditions with
rúguǒ 如果 (if)

Intensifying Comparisons

Tāmen nǎr yě bú qù.
他们哪儿也不去。
They go nowhere./They don't go anywhere.

Nobody is expressed in a similar way, using the indefinite pronoun shénme rén yě
什么人也(*anyone*) and negation with bù 不 or méiyǒu 没有。

Wǒ zài jiàoshì lǐ shénme rén yě méiyǒu kànjiàn.
我在教室里什么人也没有看见。
I saw nobody in the classroom./I didn't see anyone in the classroom.

Tā shénme rén yě bú shì.
她什么人也不是。
She is nobody./She isn't anybody.

The indefinites shéi yě 谁也 (*anyone*) and shénme dōngxi yě 什么东西也
(*anything*) can also be translated into English as *everyone* and *everything*:

Shéi yě xǐhuan wǒ.
谁也喜欢我。
Everyone loves me.

Shénme dōngxi zuìhòu yě huì sǐ.
什么东西最后也会死。
Everything eventually dies.

(II)

The Verb **dǎ qiú** 打球
(*to play ball*)

Expressing Frequency
with **cì** 次 or **biàn** 遍

Uses of **bǎ** 把

Expressing duration

✎ Sentence Practice 2

Translate the following sentences into pīnyīn.

1. *If I were you, I wouldn't go.* _____

_____

2. *If you want to learn Chinese, I can teach you.* _____

_____

3. *If you're late again, you can't take the exam this year.* _____

_____

4. *If you're free, could you come to my home?* _____

_____

5. *If you had money, what would you buy?* _____

_____

ANSWER KEY

1. Rúguǒ wǒ shì nǐ, wǒ bú huì qù. 如果我是你, 我不会去。 2. Rúguǒ nǐ xiǎng xué Zhōngwén, wǒ kěyǐ jiāo nǐ. 如果你想学中文, 我可以教你。 3. Rúguǒ nǐ zài chídào, jīnnián jiù bù kěyǐ kǎoshì. 如果你再迟到, 今年就不可以考试。 4. Rúguǒ nǐ yǒu kòng, kěyǐ lái wǒ jiā ma? 如果你有空, 可以来我家吗? 5. Rúguǒ nǐ yǒu qián, nǐ huì mǎi shénme dōngxi? 如果你有钱, 你会买什么东西?

Grammar Builder 2
EXPRESSING CONDITIONS WITH RÚGUǑ 如果 (*IF*)

▶ 15D Grammar Builder 2 (CD 9, Track 18)

The conjunction rúguǒ 如果 is the equivalent of the English word *if* and is used in Chinese to indicate a conditional relationship between an action or event and its consequence. In other words, rúguǒ 如果 is used to form conditional

Indefinite Pronouns

Making Comparisons with
gèng 更 (even)

Expressing Conditions with
rúguǒ 如果 (if)

Intensifying Comparisons

sentences that show what requirements must be met in order for something to happen, or how one action occurs as the consequence of another.

As in English, conditional sentences in Chinese are comprised of two clauses. One is the *if* or conditional clause (beginning with rúguǒ 如果); the other is the main or consequence clause. Rúguǒ 如果 is typically placed at the head of a sentence, so this construction is similar to *if … then* in English although *then* is not always overtly expressed. Jiù 就 is the equivalent of *then* in English and when present is placed either directly after the subject or, if there is no subject, at the front of the main clause.

Rúguǒ nǐ qù, wǒ jiù bú qù.
如果你去，我就不去。
If you go, (then) I won't go.

Rúguǒ nǐ yònggōng dúshū, jiù huì chénggōng.
如果你用功读书，就会成功。
If you study hard, (then) you'll succeed.

If you want to express a possible future consequence of a condition, use the particle huì 会 in the consequence clause.

Rúguǒ wǒ yǒukòng, wǒ huì dǎ pīngpāngqiú.
如果我有空，我会打乒乓球。
If I'm free, I'll play ping pong.

Rúguǒ tā kāi zhe diànshì, tā huì zhěngtiān zuò zài jiā lǐ kàn diànshì.
如果她开着电视，她会整天坐在家里看电视。
If she turns on the TV, she'll sit at home and watch it all day long.

Note that, unlike English, there is no conditional verb tense (*would, could,* etc.) in Chinese, so a conditional meaning in a sentence is therefore determined mainly

The Verb **dǎ qiú** 打球
(to play ball)

Expressing Frequency
with **cì** 次 or **biàn** 遍

Uses of **bǎ** 把

Expressing duration

by context. Occasionally, the word le 了, which is sometimes used to end a sentence, helps to emphasize a change in condition.

Rúguǒ wǒ qù nián méiyǒu kāishǐ zuò yùndòng, xiànzài wǒ de shēntǐ kěnéng huì hěn chā.

如果我去年没有开始做运动, 现在我的身体可能会很差。

If I hadn't started to exercise last year, my body would've been very weak now.

Rúguǒ nǐ méiyǒu pǎo de nàme kuài, jiù bú huì shòushāng le.

如果你没有跑得那么快, 就不会受伤了。

If you hadn't run so fast, you wouldn't have gotten hurt.

Rúguǒ tā yǒu qián, wǒ huì jiào tā mǎi yí ge fángzi.

如果他有钱, 我会叫他买一个房子。

If he had money, I would ask him to buy a house.

Rúguǒ wǒ huì dǎ qiú, wǒ huì gēn tāmen qù.

如果我会打球, 我会跟他们去。

If I knew how to play ball, I'd go with them.

Rúguǒ tāmen rènzhēn dúshū, jiù bú huì bù jígéle.

如果他们认真读书, 就不会不及格了。

If they had taken their studies seriously, they wouldn't have failed.

Rúguǒ nǐ xiǎoxīn, jiù bú huì nòng cuò le.

如果你小心, 就不会弄错了。

If you were careful, you wouldn't make mistakes.

Rúguǒ nǐ zuò qítā gōngzuò, nǐ jiù huì kāixīn yì diǎnr.

如果你做其他工作, 你就会开心一点儿。

If you had a different job, you would be (a little) happier.

Rúguǒ tiānqì hǎo yì diǎnr jiù hǎo le.

如果天气好一点儿就好了。

It would be great if the weather were a little better.

Rúguǒ wǒ yǒu duō yì xiē qián jiù hǎo le.

如果我有多一些钱就好了。

It would be wonderful if I had more money.

✎ Work Out 2

Match the Chinese sentences in the column on the left with the English translations on the right.

1. Rúguǒ nǐ xiǎng shěng (*save*) qián, nà nǐ jiù bù yīnggài mǎi nà liàng chē. 如果你想省钱, 那你就不应该买那辆车。

   a. *If you had money, what would you like to do?*

2. Rúguǒ wǒmen yǒu liù ge rén, jiù kěyǐ dǎ lánqiú le. 如果我们有六个人, 就可以打篮球了。

   b. *If we had six people, we could play basketball.*

3. Rúguǒ nǐ chídào, wǒmen huì bù děng nǐ. 如果你迟到, 我们会不等你。

   c. *If the weather is bad today, I won't go swimming.*

4. Rúguǒ nǐ yǒu qián, nǐ xiǎng zuò shénme? 如果你有钱, 你想做什么?

   d. *If you're late, we won't wait for you.*

5. Rúguǒ jīntiān de tiānqì bù hǎo, wǒ bú huì qù yóuyǒng. 如果今天的天气不好, 我不会去游泳。

   e. *If you wanted to save money, you shouldn't have bought the car.*

ANSWER KEY

1. e; 2. b; 3. d; 4. a; 5. c

The Verb **dǎ qiú** 打球
(*to play ball*)

Expressing Frequency
with **cì** 次 or **biàn** 遍

Uses of **bǎ** 把

Expressing duration

✎ Drive It Home

Practice forming sentences with rǔguǒ 如果. For each set of phrases below, form a sentence using the rǔguǒ 如果 ... jiù 就 construction.

1. Wǒ fāshāo, wǒ míngtiān bú shàngbān.我发烧, 我明天不上班。 _____

   _____

2. Nǐ kāichē, wǒ kàn dìtú. 你开车, 我看地图。 _____

   _____

3. Tāmen bú lái, wǒmen zǎo chīfàn. 他们不来, 我们早吃饭。 _____

   _____

4. Nǐmen qù dǎ qiú, wǒ qù kàn.你们去打球, 我去看。 _____

   _____

5. Wǒ chī tàiduō, wǒ huì bù shūfu. 我吃太多, 我会不舒服。 _____

   _____

6. Tā bú dài bǐ, tā bùnéng xiězì.她不带笔, 她不能写字。 _____

   _____

7. Wǒmen mǎi zhè shuāng xiézi, wǒmen yīnggāi mǎi wàzi.我们买这双鞋子, 我们
   应该买袜子。 _____

   _____

ANSWER KEY

1.Rǔguǒ wǒ fāshāo, wǒ míngtiān jiù bú shàngbān. 如果我发烧, 我明天就不上班。 (*If I have a fever, I will not go to work tomorrow.*) 2. Rǔguǒ nǐ kāichē, wǒ jiù kàn dìtú. 如果你开车, 我就看地图。 (*If you drive, I will read the map.*) 3. Rǔguǒ tāmen bú lái, wǒmen jiù zǎo chīfàn. 如果他们不来, 我们就早吃饭。 (*If they don't come, we will eat early.*) 4. Rǔguǒ nǐmen qù dǎ qiú, wǒ jiù qù kàn.如果你们去打球, 我就去看。 (*If you go to play ball, I will go watch.*) 5. Rǔguǒ wǒ chī tàiduō, wǒ jiù huì bù shūfu.如果我吃太多, 我就会不舒服。 (*If I eat too much, I will not feel well.*) 6. Rǔguǒ tā bú dài

Indefinite Pronouns

Making Comparisons with
gèng 更 (even)

Expressing Conditions with
rúguǒ 如果 (if)

Intensifying Comparisons

bǐ, tā jiù bùnéng xiězì. 如果她不带笔，她就不能写字。 (*If she doesn't bring a pen, she would not be able to write.*) 7. Rúguǒ wǒmen mǎi zhè shuāng xiézi, wǒmen jiù yīnggāi mǎi wàzi. 如果我们买这双鞋子，我们就应该买袜子。 (*If we buy this pair of shoes, we should buy socks.*)

✎ Word Recall

Let's review some of the words and phrases having to do with direction and place that you've learned so far. Match the English word in the column on the left with its appropriate translation in the column on the right.

1. *in, inside*

2. *under*

3. *here*

4. *next to*

5. *street*

6. *in front of*

7. *on*

8. *there*

9. *outside*

10. *intersection*

11. *on the left side of*

12. *where*

13. *on the right side of*

14. *corner*

15. *behind*

a. shàngbiān/shàng 上边/上

b. shízì lùkǒu 十字路口

c. pángbiān 旁边

d. lǐ/lǐbiaān 里/里边

e. wàibian 外边

f. zhèlǐ 这里

g. lùkǒu 路口

h. qiánbian 前边

i. nǎli 哪里

j. xiàbian/xià 下边/下

k. nàli 那里

l. zuǒbian 左边

m. jiē 街

n. hòubian 后边

o. yòubian 右边

ANSWER KEY

1. d; 2. j; 3. f; 4. c; 5. m; 6. h; 7. a; 8. k; 9. e; 10. b; 11. l; 12. i; 13. o; 14. g; 15. n.

The Verb **dǎ qiú** 打球
(*to play ball*)

Expressing Frequency
with **cì** 次 or **biàn** 遍

Uses of **bǎ** 把

Expressing duration

Lesson 16: Conversations

In this lesson, you'll learn:

☐ More about talking about hobbies and studying.

☐ How to make comparisons with gèng 更 (*even*).

☐ How to use intensifying comparisons.

Conversation 1

16A Conversation 1 (CD 9, Track 19-Chinese, Track 20-Chinese and English)

Jess and Hai are talking about their hobbies.

Jiéxī:
Nǐ yǒukòng de shíhou xǐhuan zuò shénme?

洁希: 你有空的时候喜欢做什么?

Hai:
Wǒ xǐhuan gēn péngyou qù dǎ qiú.

海: 我喜欢跟朋友去打球。

Jiéxī:
Nǐ xǐhuan dǎ shénme qiú? Lánqiú háishì bàngqiú?

洁希: 你喜欢打什么球? 篮球还是棒球?

Hai:
Bàngqiú zài Zhōngguó bú tài liúxíng. Wǒ hé péngyou háishì bǐjiào xǐhuan dǎ lánqiú. Wǒmen tōngcháng yí ge lǐbài dǎ yí cì. Wǒ hái qù yóuyǒng. Xiàtiān de shíhou, chàbuduō měitiān dōu qù. Nǐ ne?

海: 棒球在中国不太流行。我和朋友还是比较喜欢打篮球。我们通常一个礼拜打一次。我还去游泳。夏天的时候, 差不多每天都去。你呢?

Jiéxī:
Wǒ shénme yùndòng yě bù xǐhuan. Wǒ zhǐ xǐhuan kàn diànyǐng hé kànshū. Zài Měiguó, yīnwèi diànyǐng piào hěn guì, suǒyǐ, wǒ yí ge yuè zhǐ néng kàn yì liǎng cì. Zài zhèr, diànyǐng piào bǐjiào piányi, wǒ kěyǐ yí ge lǐbài qù kàn yí cì diànyǐng.

洁希:　我什么运动也不喜欢。我只喜欢看电影和看书。在
美国，因为电影票很贵，所以，我一个月只能看一、两
次。在这儿，电影票比较便宜，我可以一个礼拜去看一
次电影。

Hai:　Nǐ zhīdao ma? Chéng lǐ yǒu yì jiā diànyǐngyuàn de piào bǐ zhèlǐ gèng

p
iányi, tāmen fàng de diànyǐng yě hěn hǎo kàn.

海:　你知道吗？　城里有一家电影院的票比这里更便宜，他
们放的电影也很好看。

Jiéxī:　Zhēn de ma? Nà nǐ xià cì dài wǒ qù ba.

洁希:　真的吗？　那你下次带我去吧。

Hai:　Hǎo, méi wèntí.

海:　好，没问题。

Jess:　What do you like to do when you have free time?

Hai:　I like to play ball with my friends.

Jess:　Which game do you play? Basketball or baseball?

Hai:　Baseball is not popular in China. My friends and I like to play
basketball instead. We usually play once a week. I also like
swimming. During the summer, I swim almost everyday. How about
you?

Jess:　I don't like any sports. I only like going to the movies and reading.
In the U.S., movie tickets are very expensive, so I was only able to go
one or two times a month. Since tickets are comparatively cheaper
here, now I can go to the movies once a week.

Hai:　You know what? There's a movie theater in the city whose tickets
are even cheaper than they are here, and the movies they show are
very interesting.

Jess:　Really? Can you take me there next time?

Hai:　Sure! No problem.

Ⓘ

The Verb **dǎ qiú** 打球
(*to play ball*)

Expressing Frequency
with **cì** 次 or **biàn** 遍

Uses of **bǎ** 把

Expressing duration

✎ Conversation Practice 1

Fill in the blanks with the missing words in pīnyīn. The Chinese characters are provided for additional help and practice. Refer to the conversation between Jess and Hai.

1. Hǎi _____ de shíhou xǐhuan gēn _____ qù dǎ qiú.

   海有空的时候喜欢跟朋友去打球。

   (*When Hai has free time, he likes to play ball with friends.*)

2. _____ zài Zhōngguó bú tài _____.

   棒球在中国不太流行。

   (*Baseball is not popular in China.*)

3. Hǎi hé tā de péngyou _____ yí ge lǐbài dǎ yí cì

   _____.

   海和他的朋友通常一个礼拜打一次篮球。

   (*Hai and his friends usually play basketball once a week.*)

4. Jiéxī _____ yùndòng _____ bù xǐhuan.

   洁希什么运动也不喜欢。

   (*Jess doesn't like any sports.*)

5. Zài Zhōngguó, diànyǐng piào _____ piányi, Jiéxī _____ yí ge

   lǐbài qù kàn yí cì diànyǐng.

   在中国, 电影票比较便宜, 洁希可以一个礼拜去看一次电影。

   (*In China, movie tickets are comparatively cheaper, and Jess can go to the movies*

   once a week.)

Indefinite Pronouns

Making Comparisons with
gèng 更 (even)

Expressing Conditions with
rúguǒ 如果 (if)

Intensifying Comparisons

Grammar Builder 1
MAKING COMPARISONS WITH GÈNG 更 (EVEN)

▶ 16B Grammar Builder 1 (CD 9, Track 21)

In English, you can clarify the degree of a comparison by using *even*, as in *even colder* or *even more expensive*. In Chinese, this is done with gèng 更 using the construction A + bǐ 比 + B + gèng 更 + adjective. Here are some examples of how gèng 更 combines with various comparative adjectives.

Wǒ bǐ tā gèng gāo.
我比他更高。
I'm even taller than he is.

Zhè běn shū bǐ nà běn shu gèng hǎokàn.
这本书比那本书更好看。
This book is even more interesting than that one.

Dàxué lǐ lǎoshī bǐ yǐqián gèng shǎo.
大学里老师比以前更少。
There are even fewer teachers at the university than before.

Zhèlǐ de miàn diàn bǐ Shànghǎi de gèng dà.
这里的面店比上海的更大。
The noodle shops here are even larger than those in Shanghai.

Wǒ xiǎng yào gèng xiǎo yìdiǎn de dàngāo.
我想要更小一点的蛋糕。
I'd like an even smaller piece of cake.

The Verb **dǎ qiú** 打球
(*to play ball*)

Expressing Frequency
with **cì** 次 or **biàn** 遍

Uses of **bǎ** 把

Expressing duration

Jiānglái zhèlǐ de rén huì gèng duō.

将来这里的人会更多。

There will be even more people here in the future.

Yǐqián hé lǐ de yú gèng duō.

以前河里的鱼更多。

In the past, there were even more fish in the river.

Work Out 1

Translate the following sentences into English.

1. Jīnnián gèng duō Zhōngguó rén kàn Měiguó diànyǐng. 今年更多中国人看美国
电影。 _____

2. Tā mǎile chē hòu gèng qióng. 他买了车后更穷。 _____

3. Wǒ yòngle (*used*) gèng duō qián mǎi zhè běn shū. 我用了更多钱买这本。 ____

4. Tāmen jīntiān zǎoshang lái de gèng zǎo (*early*). 他们今天早上来得更早。 ____

5. Nàge dàxué xiànzài yǒu gèng duō Měiguó xuésheng. 那个大学现在有更多美国
学生。 _____

6. Nǐ bǐ píngshí (*usual*) gèng xiǎoxīn. 你比平时更小心。 _____

_____

7. Yīnwèi tā qùnián kǎoshì bù jígé, suǒyǐ tā jīnnián gèng yònggōng. 因为他去年考试不及格，所以他今年更用功。 _____

_____

ANSWER KEY

1.*This year even more Chinese people are watching American movies. 2. After he bought the car, he became even poorer. 3. I used even more money to buy this book. 4. They came even earlier this morning. 5. The university has even more American students now. 6. You've been even more careful than usual. 7. Since he failed the exam last year, he is studying even harder this year.*

◖◗ Conversation 2

▶ 16C Conversation 2 (CD 9, Track 22-Chinese, CD 10-Track 23)

Jess and Hai are talking about their studies.

Hai:	Kuài kǎoshì le. Wǒ dǎsuan xiàwǔ qù túshūguǎn wēnxí, nǐ yào yìqǐ lái ma?
海:	快考试了。我打算下午去图书馆温习，你要一起来吗?
Jiéxī:	Wǒ bú qùle. Wǒ xǐhuan zìjǐ yí ge rén zài sùshè lǐ wēnxí. Túshūguǎn lǐ de rén tài duō, wǒ bù néng jízhōng jīngshén. Érqiě zuìjìn yuè lái yuè duō xuéshēng qù túshūguǎn, wǒ hěn nán zhǎo dào zuòwèi.
洁希:	我不去了。我喜欢自己一个人在宿舍里温习。图书馆里的人太多，我不能集中精神。而且最近越来越多学生去图书馆，我很难找到座位。
Hai:	Nǐ shuō de duì. Túshūguǎn zǒngshì zài kǎoshì qián hěn yōngjǐ. Hěn duō xuéshēng yào zhǔnbèi kǎoshì de shíhou cái qù nàli. Dànshì, yīnwèi wǒ jiā lǐ tài chǎo, suǒyǐ wǒ xǐhuan qù túshūguǎn dúshū.
海:	你说得对。图书馆总是在考试前很拥挤。很多学生要准备考试的时候才去那里。但是，因为我家里太吵，所以我喜欢去图书馆读书。
Jiéxī:	Nǐ píngshí zài nàr dāi duōjiǔ?

The Verb dǎ qiú 打球
(to play ball)

Expressing Frequency
with cì 次 or biàn 遍

Uses of bǎ 把

Expressing duration

洁希: 你平时在那儿呆多久？

Hai: Zhège hěn nán shuō. Rúguǒ wǒ yǒu kè, wǒ měi cì dàgài zuò sān ge xiǎoshí, bú yòng shàngkè de shíhou, wǒ kěyǐ zài nàr zuò yì zhěng tiān.

海: 这个很难说。如果我有课，我每次大概坐三个小时，不用上课的时候，我可以在那儿坐一整天。

Jiéxī: Kuài wǔ diǎn le. Wǒ yuēle péngyou qù kàn diànyǐng. Wǒ yào zǒule. Míngtiān jiàn.

洁希: 快五点了。我约了朋友去看电影。我要走了。明天见。

Hai: Míngtiān jiàn.

海: 明天见。

Hai: It's almost time for exams. I'm planning to go to the library this afternoon to start reviewing my course notes. Do you want to go with me?

Jess: No. I'd rather stay in the dorm and study by myself. There are too many people at the library, and I can't concentrate. Furthermore, more and more students have been going to the library recently and I can't find a seat.

Hai: You're right. The library always gets really crowded before exam time. A lot of students don't go there until they have to prepare for their examinations. But I like to study at the library because it's too noisy at home.

Jess: How long do you usually stay there?

Hai: It's hard to say. On days when I have classes, I probably stay at the library for three hours. When there's no class, I can stay there the whole day.

Jess: It's almost five o'clock! I made an appointment with friends to go to a movie, so I have to run. See you tomorrow.

Hai: See you tomorrow.

Indefinite Pronouns

Making Comparisons with
gèng 更 (*even*)

Expressing Conditions with
rúguǒ 如果 (*if*)

Intensifying Comparisons

Take It Further

Kuài … le 快 … 了 is a phrase which literally means *quickly … as of now*. When a verb is added between kuài 快 and le 了, kuài … le 快 … 了 takes on the meaning of *it's almost time to do something*. The following examples show how this works:

Kuài xiàbān le.
快下班了。
It's almost time to leave work.

Kuài kāishǐ le.
快开始了。
It's almost time to start.

Kuài chīfàn le.
快吃饭了。
It's almost time to eat.

✎ Conversation Practice 2

Fill in the blanks with the missing words in pīnyīn. The Chinese characters are provided for additional help and practice. Refer to the conversation.

1. Hǎi _____ xiàwǔ qù túshūguǎn _____.

   海打算下午去图书馆温习。

2. Jiéxī xǐhuan _____ yí ge rén zài _____ lǐ wēnxí.

   洁希喜欢自己一个人在宿舍里温习。

The Verb **dǎ qiú** 打球
(*to play ball*)

Expressing Frequency
with **cì** 次 or **biàn** 遍

Uses of **bǎ** 把

Expressing duration

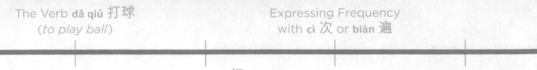

3. Túshūguǎn lǐ de rén tài duō, Jiéxī bù néng _____ jīngshén.

图书馆里的人太多, 洁希不能集中精神。

4. Túshūguǎn zǒngshì zài kǎoshì _____ hěn _____.

图书馆总是在考试前很拥挤。

5. Bú yòng _____ de shíhou, Hǎi kěyǐ zài túshūguǎn zuò yì

_____ tiān.

不用上课的时候, 海可以在图书馆坐一整天。

ANSWER KEY
1. dǎsuan 打算, wēnxí 温习; 2. zìjǐ 自己, sùshè 宿舍; 3. jízhōng 集中; 4. qián 前, yōngjǐ 拥挤; 5. shàngkè 上课, zhěng 整

Grammar Builder 2
INTENSIFYING COMPARISONS

▶ 16D Grammar Builder 2 (CD 9, Track 24)

In English, you can show a gradual increase or decrease in intensity with the phrases *more and more* or *less and less*. In Chinese, this is done by combining yuè lái yuè 越来越 with a descriptive adjective in a sentence whose main verb expresses a state of being. Take a look at these examples.

Tiānqì yuè lái yuè huài.
天气越来越坏。
The weather is getting worse and worse.

Zài Niǔ Yuē, yào zhǎo yí ge piányi de gōngyù yuè lái yuè nán.
在纽约, 要找一个便宜的公寓越来越难。
It's harder and harder to find a cheap apartment in New York.

Indefinite Pronouns

Making Comparisons with
gèng 更 (even)

Expressing Conditions with
rúguǒ 如果 (if)

Intensifying Comparisons

Tāmen yuè lái yuè lèi.
他们越来越累。
They (gradually) became more and more tired.

Hú lǐ de qīngwā yuè lái yuè shǎo.
湖里的青蛙越来越少。
There are fewer and fewer frogs in this lake.

The phrase yuè lái yuè 越来越 can also be combined with an adverb to express the change in intensity that an action undergoes over a given or implied period of time. In this case, the sentence must include an action rather than a state of being.

Tā pǎo de yuè lái yuè kuài.
他跑得越来越快。
He ran more and more quickly.

Nà xiē é fēi de yuè lái yuè gāo.
那些鹅飞得越来越高。
The geese flew higher and higher.

(II)

✎ Work Out 2

Translate the following phrases into English.

1. Fángzi yuè lái yuè guì. 房子越来越贵。 _____

   _____

2. Tā zǒu de yuè lái yuè màn. 他走得越来越慢。 _____

   _____

The Verb **dǎ qiú** 打球
(to play ball)

Expressing Frequency
with **cì** 次 or **biàn** 遍

Uses of **bǎ** 把

Expressing duration

3. Tā zuò (*works*) de yuè lái yuè kuài. 他做得越来越快。 _____

_____

4. Yuè lái yuè shǎo rén xiǎng zuò lǎoshī. 越来越少人想做老师。 _____

_____

5. Yuè lái yuè duō Měiguórén xué Zhōngwén. 越来越多美国人学中文。 _____

_____

6. Yuè lái yuè duō Zhōngguó yímín (*immigrants*) lái Měiguó. 越来越多中国移民来
美国。 _____

_____

7. Xiàtiān yuè lái yuè rè. 夏天越来越热。 _____

_____

ANSWER KEY

1. Houses are becoming more and more expensive. 2. He walked more and more slowly. 3. He works faster and faster. 4. Fewer and fewer people want to be a teacher. 5. More and more Americans are learning to speak Chinese. 6. More and more Chinese immigrants are coming to America. 7. The summer is getting hotter and hotter.

⊕ Culture Note

In China, the most popular sports are ping pong and badminton, although basketball has gained popularity over the years. Ping pong is so widely played that it is considered by many to be China's national sport, and competitions are held throughout the year in every part of the country. Given such a high level of interest in ping pong, it's not surprising that some of the best players in the world come from China.

Indefinite Pronouns

Making Comparisons with
gèng 更 (*even*)

Expressing Conditions with
rúguǒ 如果 (*if*)

Intensifying Comparisons

✎ Drive It Home

Modify each phrase to express gradual change by using the yuè lai yuè 越来越 construction.

1. Tā de chéngjì gāo 他的成绩高 _____

   _____

2. Lǐbian de rén duō 里边的人多 _____

   _____

3. Diànnǎo piányi 电脑便宜 _____

   _____

4. Fángzi jiù 房子旧 _____

   _____

5. Nǐ zǒu de kuài 你走得快 _____

   _____

6. Píngguǒ xiǎo 苹果小 _____

   _____

7. Wǒ kuàilè 我快乐 _____

   _____

8. Tāmen lèi 他们累 _____

   _____

ANSWER KEY

1.Tā de chéngjì yuè lai yuè gāo. 他的成绩越来越高。(*His academic performance is getting better.*)
2. Lǐbian de rén yuè lai yuè duō. 里边的人越来越多。(*More and more people are inside.*) 3. Diànnǎo yuè lai yuè piányi. 电脑越来越便宜。(*Computers are getting less expensive.*) 4. Fángzi yuè lai yuè jiù. 房子越来越旧。(*The house is becoming older and older.*) 5. Nǐ zǒu de yuè lai yuè kuài. 你走得越来

The Verb dǎ qiú 打球
(to play ball)

Expressing Frequency
with cì 次 or biàn 遍

Uses of bǎ 把

Expressing duration

越快。 *(You're walking faster and faster.)* 6. Píngguǒ yuè lai yuè xiǎo. 苹果越来越小。 *(Apples are getting smaller.)* 7. Wǒ yuè lai yuè kuàilè. 我越来越快乐。 *(I am becoming more and more happy.)* 8. Tāmen yuè lai yuè lèi. 他们越来越累。 *(They are getting more and more tired.)*

✎ Word Recall

Match the English word in the column on the left with its appropriate translation in the column on the right.

1. *together*	a. túshūguǎn 图书馆
2. *noisy*	b. yōngjǐ 拥挤
3. *even more*	c. liúxíng 流行
4. *crowded*	d. yuē 约
5. *to stay*	e. nán 难
6. *library*	f. bǐjiào 比较
7. *popular, trendy*	g. dāi 待
8. *to review*	h. gèng 更
9. *to prepare*	i. jízhōng jīngshén 集中精神
10. *relatively, comparatively*	j. chǎo 吵
11. *self*	k. tōngcháng 通常
12. *to concentrate*	l. zhǔnbèi 准备
13. *to make an appointment, to make a date*	m. yìqí 一齐
14. *usually*	n. wēnxí 温习
15. *difficult*	o. zìjǐ 自己

ANSWER KEY
1. m; 2. j; 3. h; 4. b; 5. g; 6. a; 7. c; 8. n; 9. l; 10. f; 11. o; 12. i; 13. d; 14. k; 15. e

Don't forget to practice and reinforce what you've learned by visiting **www.livinglanguage.com/languagelab** for flashcards, games, and quizzes.

Unit 4 Essentials

Vocabulary Essentials

Test your knowledge of the key material in this unit by filling in the blanks in the following charts. Once you've completed these pages, you'll have tested your retention, and you'll have your own reference for the most essential vocabulary. This is also a great time to practice a few Chinese characters. Fill in the middle column with the characters that you remember. Or, if you only remember the pīnyīn, go back through the unit to find the character.

SPORTS

PĪNYĪN	CHARACTER	
		sports
		basketball
		baseball
		hockey
		soccer (football)
		(American) football
		badminton
		volleyball
		tennis
		swimming
		Mahjong
		taiji/tai chi
		to go to a stadium
		to play a sport
		to play a game

HOBBIES

PĪNYĪN	CHARACTER	
		hobbies
		reading
		poetry
		novel
		music
		film, movie
		writing
		cooking
		travel
		singing
		to go to a movie/the movies
		to watch TV
		to have fun
		to play piano
		to play violin
		to play drums
		to play the flute

TIME AND FREQUENCY EXPRESSIONS

PĪNYĪN	CHARACTER	
		a long time
		many times
		several times
		never
		one year
		two weeks

PĪNYĪN	CHARACTER	
		three months
		several days
		five years
		one minute
		half an hour
		two hours

If you're having a hard time remembering this vocabulary, don't forget to check out the flashcards, games and quizzes for this unit online. Go to **www.livinglanguage.com/languagelab** for a great way to help you practice what you've learned.

Grammar Essentials

Here is a reference for the key grammar that was covered in Unit 4. Make sure you understand the summary and can use all of the grammar it covers.

USES OF BǍ 把

- Bǎ changes the verb-object order: subject + bǎ 把 + object + verb (+ le 了).

- It can be used to make your reference more specific.

- It shows the intention or consequence of a deliberate action, or clarifies the location, time frame or manner in which something is purposely done.

Wǒ bǎ píngguǒ chīle.	我把苹果吃了。	*I ate the apple.*
Wǒ bǎ nàge píngguǒ chīle.	我把那个苹果吃了。	*I ate the apple. (lit., I ate that apple.)*

Tā bǎ nà běn shū cóng shūjià shàng ná zǒu.	他把那本书从书架上拿走。	He took that book away from the shelf. (lit., He [bǎ 把] that book from the bookshelf take off.)
Wǒ xǐle pánzi.	我洗了盘子。	I washed the plate.
Wǒ bǎ pánzi xǐ de hěn gānjìng.	我把盘子洗得很干净。	I washed the plate clean.

EXPRESSING FREQUENCY

Wǒ qùle sān cì.	我去了三次。	I went three times.
Lǎoshī shuōle liǎng biàn.	老师说了两遍。	The teacher said it twice. (lit., The teacher spoke twice.)
Wǒ jīntiān huànle sì cì yīfu.	我今天换了四次衣服。	I've changed clothing four times today.
Wǒ jiànguò tā yí cì.	我见过他一次。	I saw him once.
Tāmen qùle Shànghǎi liǎng cì.	他们去了上海两次。	They went to Shanghai twice.

INDEFINITE PRONOUNS

shéi 谁 (who)	shéi yě 谁也 (anyone)
shénme dōngxi 什么东西 (what thing)	shénme dōngxi yě 什么东西也 (anything)
shénme shíhou 什么时候 (when)	shénme shíhou yě 什么时候也 (anytime)
nǎr/nǎli 哪儿/哪里 (where)	nǎr/nǎli yě 哪儿/哪里也 (anywhere)
yǒu rén 有人 (someone/somebody)	yì diǎn dōngxi 一点东西 or yì xiē dōngxi 一些东西 (something)

shénme dōngxi yě 什么东西也 *in a negative sentence (nothing)*	nǎr/nǎli yě 哪儿/哪里也 *in a negative sentence (nowhere)*
shénme rén yě 什么人也 *in a negative sentence (nobody)*	

EXPRESSING CONDITIONS

- To express the conditional: Rúguǒ 如果 + clause denoting some action or event, (jiù 就) clause denoting the consequence of the first clause

- Possible future consequences of a condition are expressed with the particle huì 会 in the consequence clause.

- There is no conditional tense; le 了 sometimes used to emphasize a change in condition.

Rúguǒ nǐ qù, wǒ jiùbú qù.	如果你去，我就不去。	*If you go, I won't go.*
Rúguǒ nǐ yònggōng dúshū, nǐ huì chénggōng.	如果你用功读书，你会成功。	*If you study hard, you'll succeed.*
Rúguǒ nǐ xiǎoxīn, jiù bú huì nòng cuò le.	如果你小心，就不会弄错了。	*If you were careful, then (you) wouldn't make mistakes.*
Rúguǒ wǒ yǒu duō yì xiē qián jiù hǎo le.	如果我有多一些钱就好了。	*It would be wonderful if I had more money.*

Unit 4 Quiz

A. Restate the following sentences using bǎ 把. Then give an English translation.

1. Tāmen shàng ge lǐbai xǐle pánzi. 他们上个礼拜洗了盘子。 _____

_____

2. Nǐ shénme shíhou ná zǒule nà zhāng zhuōzi? 你什么时候拿走那张桌子？ ____

_____

3. Tā chī guāng le tiándiǎn. 他吃光了甜点。 _____

_____

4. Nàge rén qùnián mǎile chē. 那个人去年买了车。 _____

_____

5. Wǒ jīntiān zǎoshang chīle nǐ zuò de dàngāo. 我今天早上吃了你做的蛋糕。 ____

_____

B. Modify each sentence with the frequency phrase in parentheses. Be aware of the word order depending on whether the object after the verb is a personal pronoun or place name.

1. Tāmen láile (liǎng cì) 他们来了 (两次) _____

_____

2. Wǒmen chàngle gē (sān biàn) 我们唱了歌 (三遍) _____

_____

3. Zhège diànyǐng wǒ kànle (liù biàn) 这个电影我看了 (六遍) _____

_____

4. Tāmen qù guò Zhōngguó (yí cì) 他们去过中国 (一次) _____

_____

5. Tā měitiān dǎ diànhuà gěi māma (liǎng cì) 他每天打电话给妈妈 (两次) _____

_____

C. Modify each sentence with the indefinite pronoun in parentheses and yě 也.

1. Wǒ míngtiān kěyǐ lái (shénme shíhou) 我明天可以来 (什么时候) _____

_____

2. Tā yào mǎi (shénme dōngxi) 他要买 (什么东西) _____

_____

3. Wǒmen qù shàngbān (nǎli) 我们去上班 (哪里) _____

_____

4. ... xǐhuan gēn wǒ dǎ qiú (shéi) ...喜欢跟我打球 (谁) _____

_____

5. Nǐ bú yào chī (shénme dōngxi) 你不要吃 (什么东西) _____

_____

D. Translate the following sentences into English.

1. Jīnnián gèng duō Měiguórén xué Zhōngwén. 今年更多美国人学中文。 _____

_____

2. Tā kǎoshì le zhīhòu gèng lèi. 他考试之后更累。 _____

_____

3. Nǎinai de qúnzi gèng piàoliang. 奶奶的裙子更漂亮。 _____

_____

4. Zuótiān wǎnshang wǒmen shuì de gèng zǎo. 昨天晚上我们睡得更早。 _____

_____

5. Nàge dàxué xiànzài yǒu gèng duō Měiguó xuésheng. 那个大学现在有更多美国
学生。 _____

_____

How Did You Do?

Give yourself a point for every correct answer, then use the following key to tell whether you're ready to move on:

0-7 points: It's probably a good idea to go back through the lesson again. You may be moving too quickly, or there may be too much "down time" between your contact with Chinese. Remember that it's better to spend 30 minutes with Chinese three or four times a week than it is to spend two or three hours just once a week. Find a pace that's comfortable for you, and spread your contact hours out as much as you can.

8-12 points: You would benefit from a review before moving on. Go back and spend a little more time on the specific points that gave you trouble. Re-read the Grammar Builder sections that were difficult, and do the work out one more time. Don't forget about the online supplemental practice material, either. Go to **www. livinglanguage.com/languagelab** for games and quizzes that will reinforce the material from this unit.

13-17 points: Good job! There are just a few points that you might consider reviewing before moving on. If you haven't worked with the games and quizzes on **www.livinglanguage.com/languagelab**, please give them a try.

18-20 points: Great! You're ready to move on to the next unit.

points

Pronunciation and Pīnyīn Guide

The Chinese language does not have an alphabet. Each word is represented by a character, which may be composed of just one stroke (line) or as many as several dozen. To represent Chinese sounds for those who do not read characters, various systems of romanization have been devised, including pīnyīn, the standard system used in China and the one most commonly used in the United States.

Each syllable in Chinese has an initial consonant sound and a final vowel sound. There are twenty-three initial sounds (consonants) and thirty-six final sounds (vowels or combinations of vowels and consonants). Here is how each sound is written in pīnyīn, with its approximate English equivalent.

INITIAL SOUNDS

PĪNYĪN	ENGLISH
b	*b* in *bear*
p	*p* in *poor*
m	*m* in *more*
f	*f* in *fake*
d	*d* in *dare*
t	*t* in *take*
n	*n* in *now*
l	*l* in *learn*
z	*ds* in *yards*
c	*ts* in *its*
s	*s* in *sing*
zh	*j* in *judge*
ch	*ch* in *church*
sh	hard *sh* in *shhhh!*
r	*r* in *rubber*
j	*dy* in *and yet*

PĪNYĪN	ENGLISH
q	*ty* in *won't you*
x	*sh* in *shoe*
g	*g* in *get*
k	*k* in *keep*
h	*h* in *help*
y	*y* in *yes*
w	*w* in *want*

FINAL SOUNDS

a	*a* in *ma*
ai	*y* in *my*
ao	*ou* in *pout*
an	*an* in *élan*
ang	*ong* in *throng*
o	*o* in *or*
ou	*oa* in *flout*
ong	*ong* in *long*
e	*e* in *nerve*
ei	*ay* in *day*
en	*un* in *under*
eng	*ung* in *mung*
i (after z, c, s, zh, ch, sh)	*r* in *thunder*
i	*ee* in *see*
ia	*yah*
iao	*eow* in *meow*
ian	*yan*
iang	*yang*
ie	*ye* in *yes*

iu	*yo-yo*
iong	*young*
in	*in* in *sin*
ing	*ing* in *sing*
u	*u* in *flu*
ua	*ua* in *suave*
uai	*wi* in *wide*
uan	*wan*
uang	*wong*
uo	*wo* in *won't*
ui	*weigh*
un	*won*
ü	*like ee in see, but with lips rounded into a pout (German hübsch, French tu.)*
üan	*like ü above with an*
üe	*like ü above with e in net*
ün	*like ü above with n in an*
er	*are*

Tone Marks

Each syllable in Mandarin Chinese must be pronounced with a tone—there are four, plus a neutral tone. Here are the tone marks as they are written in pīnyīn. They're written here over the vowel *a*, which is pronounced similarly to the vowel in *John*. Imagine saying the name *John* in the following contexts:

First Tone	ā	*High and neutral, no accent. Sing "John."*
Second Tone	á	*From middle to high, as in asking a question. "John? Is that you?"*
Third Tone	ǎ	*From middle to low, and then to high, as if stretching out a question: "Jo-o-o-hn, what do you think?"*
Fourth Tone	à	*From high to low, as if answering a question. "Who's there?" "John."*

Syllables pronounced with the neutral tone are unmarked. The tones are placed over the final vowel sound of a syllable. In the case of compound vowels, such as ai, uo, ao, etc., the tone is placed over the primary vowel.

Grammar Summary

1. NUMBERS

a. Cardinal numbers 1 to 10

yī 一	*one*	liù 六	*six*
èr 二	*two*	qī 七	*seven*
sān 三	*three*	bā 八	*eight*
sì 四	*four*	jiǔ 九	*nine*
wǔ 五	*five*	shí 十	*ten*

b. Cardinal numbers 11 to 100

shíyī (10 + 1) 十一	*eleven*	shíliù (10 + 6) 十六	*sixteen*
shí'èr (10+ 2) 十二	*twelve*	shíqī (10 + 7) 十七	*seventeen*
shísān (10+ 3) 十三	*thirteen*	shíbā (10 + 8) 十八	*eighteen*
shísì (10 + 4) 十四	*fourteen*	shíjiǔ (10 + 9) 十九	*nineteen*
shíwǔ (10 + 5) 十五	*fifteen*	èrshí (2 x 10) 二十	*twenty*
sānshí (3 x 10) 三十	*thirty*	qīshí (7 x 10) 七十	*seventy*
sìshí (4 x 10) 四十	*forty*	bāshí (8 x 10) 八十	*eighty*
wǔshí (5x 10) 五十	*fifty*	jiǔshí (9 x 10) 九十	*ninety*
liùshí (6x 10) 六十	*sixty*	yībǎi (1 x 100) 一百	*one hundred*

Note: The word yī 一 is added before shí 十 in numbers ending in the numerals 10 through 19.

èrshísān (20 + 3) 二十三	twenty-three	wǔshíliù (50+ 6) 五十六	fifty-six
sìshíjiǔ (40 + 9) 四十九	forty-nine	jiǔshíjiǔ (90 + 9) 九十九	ninety-nine

Note: The word yī 一 is added before shí 十 in numbers ending in the numerals 10 through 19.

c. Cardinal numbers from 200 to 100,000,000

yībǎi líng sì 一百零四	one hundred four	yīwàn 一万	ten thousand
èrbǎi/liǎngbǎi 二百	two hundred	yībǎiwàn 一百万	one million
yīqiān 一千	one thousand	yīqiānwàn 一千万	ten million
yīqiān líng sì 一千零四	one thousand four	yīyì 一亿	one hundred million
yīqiān líng sānshí'èr 一千零 三十二	one thousand thirty-two	shíyì 十亿	one billion
yībǎi yīshíyī 一百一十一	one hundred eleven	sānbǎi yīshí'èr 三百一十二	three hundred twelve
èrbǎi yīshí 二百一十	two hundred ten	wǔbǎi yīshíjiǔ 五百一十九	five hundred nineteen

Note: Líng 零 is used to express the zero in numbers. Also, the number two is expressed in two different ways in Chinese. Èr 二 is used for counting and numeric expressions, such as twelve (shí'èr 十二) or two hundred (èrbǎi 二百). Liǎng 两 is used in combination with nouns.

d. Ordinal numbers (dì 第 + cardinal number)

yī 一	one	dì-yī 第一	the first
jiǔ 九	nine	dì-jiǔ 第九	the ninth

2. NOUNS

There is no distinction in form between singular and plural nouns in Chinese. To designate a plural noun use a number or a measure word in front of the noun or the ending -men for nouns referring to human beings.

yī ge píngguǒ 一个苹果	one apple
liǎng ge píngguǒ 两个苹果	two apples
Háizimen ài chī tángguǒ. 孩子们爱吃糖果。	The children like eating candy.

3. PERSONAL PRONOUNS

1st person (sg.)	wǒ 我	I/me
2nd person (sg.)	nín (fml.) 您 nǐ (infml.) 你	you
3rd person (sg.)	tā 他 / 她	he, she, it/him, her, it
1st person (pl.)	wǒmen 我们	we/us
2nd person (pl.)	nǐmen 你们	you
3rd person (pl.)	tāmen 他们	they/them

Note: There is no special polite form for 2nd person plural pronoun nǐmen 你们. Instead, phrases nín liǎng wèi 您两位 (you two/both of you) or nín jǐ wèi 您几位 (several of you) can be used.

4. POSSESSIVE PRONOUNS (PERSONAL PRONOUN + DE)

1st person (sg.)	wǒ de 我的	my/mine
2nd person (sg.)	nín de (fml.) 您的 nǐ de (infml.) 你的	your/yours
3rd person (sg.)	tā de 他的 / 她的	his, her, its/his, hers, its
1st person (pl.)	wǒmen de 我们的	our/ours
2nd person (pl.)	nǐmen de 你们的	your/yours
3rd person (pl.)	tāmen de 他们的	their/theirs

5. DEMONSTRATIVE PRONOUNS (ZHÈ 这 / NÀ 那 + MEASURE WORD + NOUN)

zhè běn shū 这本书	*this book*
nà běn shū 那本书	*that book*
zhèxiē shū 这些书	*these books*
nàxiē shū 那些书	*those books*

Note: Xiē 些 both makes the noun plural and serves as a measure word. Also, in colloquial language, zhè 这 and nà 那 are pronounced as zhèi 这 and nèi 那 when combined with a measure word.

6. INDEFINITE PRONOUNS

Indefinite pronouns such as anyone, anybody, anything, or anytime consist of question words + yě 也.

Rènhé 任何 (any) + yě 也 can also be used when the indefinite is a subject.

The indefinite pronouns someone and somebody are expressed with yǒu rén 有人, while the indefinite pronoun something is expressed with diǎn dōngxi 点东西.

shéi + yě (*anyone*) 谁 + 也	Wǒ shéi yě bù jiàn. 我谁也不见。	*I don't see anyone.*
shénme dōngxi + yě (*anything*) 什么东西 + 也	Tā shénme dōngxi yě chī. 他什么东西也吃。	*He eats anything.*
nǎr + yě (*anywhere*) 哪儿 + 也	Nǐ nǎr yě bù zhù. 你哪儿也不住。	*You don't live anywhere.*
shénme shíhou + yě (*anytime*) 什么时候 + 也	Nǐ xǐhuan shénme shíhou lái yě kěyǐ. 你喜欢什么时候来也可以。	*Come over anytime you like.*

shénme rén + yě (*anybody*) 什么人 + 也	Shénme rén yě kěyǐ qù. 什么人也可以去。	*Anybody can go.*
rènhé rén + yě (*anyone*) 任何人 + 也	Rènhé rén yě kěyǐ qù. 任何人也可以去。	*Anyone can go.*
rènhé dōngxi + yě (*anything*) 任何东西 + 也	Rènhé dōngxi yě huì biàn. 任何东西也会变。	*Anything can change.*
rènhé shíhou + yě (*anytime*) 任何时候 + 也	Rènhé shíhou yě kěyǐ. 任何时候也可以。	*Anytime is fine.*
rènhé dìfang + yě (*anywhere*) 任何地方 + 也	Rènhé dìfang yě kěyǐ. 任何地方也可以。	*Anywhere is fine. (lit., Anywhere can be.)*
yǒu rén (*someone/somebody*) 有人	Yǒu rén zài zhèr. 有人在这儿。	*Someone is here. (lit., There is person here.)*
méiyǒu rén (*nobody*) 没有人	Gōngchēzhàn méiyǒu rén. 公车站没有人。	*Nobody is at the bus stop./There are no people at the bus stop.*
diǎn dōngxi (*something*) 点东西	Wǒ yǒu diǎn dōngxi gěi nǐ. 我有点东西给你。	*I have something to give you.*

The indefinites shéi yě 谁也 (*anyone*) and shénme dōngxi yě 什么东西也 (*anything*) can also be translated as *everyone* and *everything*.

Shéi yě xǐhuan wǒ. 谁也喜欢我。	*Everyone loves me.*
Shénme dōngxi zùihòu yě huì sǐ. 什么东西最后也会死。	*Everything eventually dies.*

7. MEASURE WORDS

Nouns modified by a number word or a demonstrative pronoun require a measure word (number word or demonstrative pronoun + measure word + noun). Here are some categories of measure words:

a. Nature of the object

MEASURE WORD	CATEGORY	EXAMPLES
zhī 只	*animals*	yī zhī jī 一只鸡 *(one/a chicken)* yī zhī māo 一只猫 *(one/a cat)* yī zhī niǎo 一只鸟 *(one/a bird)*
zhī 只	*utensils*	yī zhī bēi 一只杯 *(one/a cup/glass)* yī zhī wǎn 一只碗 *(one/a bowl)* yī zhī guō 一只锅 *(one/a pot)*
tái 台	*machinery*	yī tái jīqì 一台机器 *(one/a machine)* yī tái diànnáo 一台电脑 *(one/a computer)* yī tái diànshì 一台电视 *(one/a television)*
jiàn 件	*clothing (top)*	yī jiàn chènshān 一件衬衫 *(one/a shirt)* yī jiàn fēngyī 一件风衣 *(one/a wind break)*
tiáo 条	*clothing (bottom)*	yī tiáo qúnzi 一条裙子 *(one/a skirt)*

MEASURE WORD	CATEGORY	EXAMPLES
bǎ 把	*something with handle*	yī bǎ cháhú 一把茶壶 *(one/a teapot)* yī bǎ yǔsǎn 一把雨伞 *(one/an umbrella)* yī bǎ shànzi 一把扇子 *(one/a Chinese fan)* yī bǎ yǐzi 一把椅子 *(one/a chair)*
zuò 座	*large and imposing objects*	yī zuò sān 一座山 *(one/a mountain)* yī zuò dàlóu 一座大楼 *(one/a building)*
liàng 辆	*vehicles*	yī liàng qìchē 一辆汽车 *(one/a car)*
jiā 家	*families or enterprises*	yī jiā fànguǎn 一家饭馆 *(one/a restaurant)* liǎng jiā rénjia 两家人家 *(two families)*
ge 个	*people*	yī ge rén 一个人 *(one/a person)* liǎng ge lǎoshī 两个老师 *(two teachers)*

b. Shape of the object

MEASURE WORD	CATEGORY	EXAMPLES
zhāng 张	*flat surface*	yī zhāng zhǐ 一张纸 (*one/a piece of paper*) yī zhāng bàozhǐ 一张报纸 (*one/a newspaper*) yī zhāng zhàopiàn 一张照片 (*one/a photo*) yī zhāng chuáng 一张床 (*one/a bed*)
zhī 支	*pointed and thin or like a branch*	yī zhī bǐ 一支笔 (*one/a pen*) yī zhī qiāng 一支枪 (*one/a gun*) yī zhī jūnduì 一支军队 (*one/a troop*)
lì 粒	*granular*	yī lì mǐ 一粒米 (*one/a grain of rice*) yī lì zhǒngzi 一粒种子 (*one/a seed*)
kē 颗	*small and round*	yī kē yǎnlèi 一颗眼泪 (*one/a tear drop*) yī kē hóngdòu 一颗红豆 (*one/a red bean*)
tiáo 条	*long and thin*	yī tiáo lù 一条路 (*one/a road*) yī tiáo sījīn 一条丝巾 (*one/a silk scarf*) yī tiáo xiàn 一条线 (*one/a string*)

MEASURE WORD	CATEGORY	EXAMPLES
pán 盘	*something round and flat or shaped like a plate*	yī pán wéiqí 一盘围棋 (*one/a game of Chinese checkers*) yī pán cídài 一盘磁带 (*one/a tape*)

c. Containers that function as measure words

MEASURE WORD	CATEGORY	EXAMPLES
bēi 杯	*cup*	yī bēi shuǐ 一杯水 (*one/a cup of water*)
dài 袋	*bag*	yī dài píngguǒ 一袋苹果 (*one/a bag of apples*)
pán 盘	*plate*	yī pán cài 一盘菜 (*one/a dish*)
xiāng 箱	*box*	yī xiāng lājī 一箱垃圾 (*one/a box of rubbish*)

d. Measure words denoting quantity

MEASURE WORD	CATEGORY	EXAMPLES
duì 对	*pair*	yī duì ěrhuán 一对耳环 (*a pair of earrings*)
shuāng 双	*pair*	yī shuāng wàzi 一双袜子 (*one/a pair of socks*) yī shuāng yǎnjing 一双眼睛 (*one/a pair of eyes*)
fù 副	*pair*	yī fù yǎnjìng 一副眼镜 (*one/a pair of glasses*)

MEASURE WORD	CATEGORY	EXAMPLES
qún 群	group	yī qún yāzi 一群鸭子 (one/a group of ducks) yī qún rén 一群人 (one/a group of people)
dá 打	dozen	yī dá jīdàn 一打鸡蛋 (one/a dozen eggs)
chuàn 串	cluster	yī chuàn pútáo 一串葡萄 (one/a cluster of grapes)

f. Amounts or portions of things

MEASURE WORD	CATEGORY	EXAMPLES
kuài 块	piece	yī kuài dàngāo 一块蛋糕 (one/a piece of cake)
dī 滴	drop	yī dī shuǐ 一滴水 (one/a drop of water)
cè 册	volume	yī cè shū 一册书 (one/a volume of a set of books)

j. Units of measurement

cùn 寸	inch	chǐ 尺	foot
yīnglǐ 英里	mile	gōngchǐ/mǐ 公尺 / 米	meter
gōnglǐ 公里	kilometer	gōngjīn 公斤	kilogram
jīn 斤	catty	bàng 磅	pound

The table below shows the different units of measure used in mainland China, Taiwan and Hong Kong.

UNITS OF MEASURE	MAINLAND CHINA	TAIWAN	HONG KONG
Length	mǐ 米 *(meter)/* gōnglǐ 公里 *(kilometer)*	mǐ 米 *(meter)/* gōnglǐ 公里 *(kilometer)*	chǐ 尺 *(foot)/* gōnglǐ 公里 *(kilometer)*
Weight	gōngjīn 公斤 *(kilogram)*	gōngjīn 公斤 *(kilogram)*	bàng 磅 *(pound)/* gōngjīn 公斤 *(kilogram)/* jīn 斤 *(catty)*

k. The measure word gè 个

Used especially with those nouns that don't have particular measure words assigned or abstract things

yī ge píngguǒ 一个苹果	*one/an apple*
yī ge zhàoxiàngjī 一个照相机	*one/a camera*
yī ge xīngqī 一个星期	*one/a week*
yī ge mèng 一个梦	*one/a dream*
yī ge zhǔyi 一个主意	*one/an idea*

l. More than one measure word may be possible.

yī tái diànnǎo 一台电脑 *or* yī bù diànnǎo 一部电脑	*one/a computer*
yī ge diànyǐng 一个电影 *or* yī bù diànyǐng 一部电影	*one/a film*

8. VERB-OBJECT VERBS VS. TWO-SYLLABLE VERBS

"Verb-object" verbs, such as chīfàn 吃饭 (*lit., to eat cooked rice*), consist of a verb plus an implicit (often not translated) object in that order. They differ from ordinary two syllable verbs such as míngbái 明白 (*to understand*) and rènshi 认识 (*to know someone*) in that:

Only "verb-object" verbs can be split by a particle, such as le 了.

In adverbial constructions that follow the pattern verb + object + duplicated verb + de 得, only the verb of "verb-object" verbs is repeated.

Wǒ chīfàn. 我吃饭。	*I eat.*
Wǒ chīle fàn. 我吃了饭。	*I ate.*
Wǒ jiǎnchá le. 我检查了。	*I examined (someone or something).*
Wǒ (de) māma zuòfàn zuò de hěn hǎo. 我(的)妈妈做饭做得很好。	*My mother cooks very well.*

9. EXPRESSING *TO BE*

Use hěn 很 (*very*) not shì 是 to connect nouns and adjectives.

Tā hěn gāo. 他很高。	*He is tall. (lit., he very tall)*

Use shì 是 between a subject noun and a predicate noun in an equational sentence.

Měiguó de shǒudū shì Huáshèngdùn. 美国的首都是华盛顿。	*America's capital is Washington.*
Jīngyú shì yī zhǒng dòngwù. 鲸鱼是一种动物。	*The whale is one kind of animal.*

Shì 是 is used to indicate existence or a state of being (see 19 below).

10. VERB PARTICLES

In Chinese, time expressions often fulfill the role that tense endings and
auxiliaries do in English.

Míngtiān wǒ chūchāi.	明天我出差。	*Tomorrow I'm going on a business trip.*

Verbal particles are used to encode information related to verbs such as
completion, duration, and future intent.

a. Completed actions: Le 了

Le 了 indicates something is different from the way it was in the past and can be
used to refer to things that have not yet happened.

Tā qùle Shànghǎi. 他去上海。	*He went to Shanghai.*
Qiūtiān láile. 秋天来了。	*Now it's autumn.*
Fēijī kuài qǐfēi le. 飞机快起飞了。	*The plane is about to take off.*

b. Actions that took place from a time in the past to now: Guò 过

Wǒ qù guò Zhōngguó. 我去过中国。	*I have been to China.*
Nǐ qù guò Zhōngguó méiyǒu? 你去过中国没有？	*Have you ever been to China?*
Wǒ qù guò. 我去过。	*Yes, I have been.*
Wǒ hái méi qùguò. 我还没去过。	*No, I haven't been yet.*
Wǒ méi(yǒu) qùguò. 我没（有）去过。	*No, I have never been before.*

c. Continuous actions and states: Zài 在 and Zhe 着

Zài 在 refers to a continuous activity.

Wǒ zài kànshū. 我在看书。	*I am reading.*
Tāmen zài gōngzuò. 他们在工作。	*They are working.*
Tā zài chuān yīfu. 她在穿衣服。	*She is putting on clothes.*

Zhe 着 refers to a state of events that continues in time.

Tā zhànzhe. 他站着。	*He is standing.*
Nǐ názhe yī běn shū. 你拿着一本 书。	*You are holding a book.*
Tā chuānzhe yī jiàn hóngsè de yīfu. 她穿着一件红色的衣服。	*She is wearing a red piece of clothing.*

d. Future actions: Huì 会

One use of huì is to express that an action will (possibly) take place in the future.

Wǒ míngtiān huì qù Shànghǎi.	我明天会去上海。	*I'll (probably) go to Shanghai tomorrow.*

11. NEGATION

Bù 不 is used with the present, future or continuous tense and zài.

Méiyǒu 没有 is used with completed actions (translated into present perfect in English).

Wǒ bù xǐhuan yú. 我不喜欢鱼。	*I don't like fish.*
Wǒ de māma hái méiyǒu chīfàn. 我的妈妈还没有吃饭。	*My mother hasn't eaten yet.*

12. COMMANDS

Commands are formed by simply using a verb without any subject. You can soften the tone of a command by using the particle ba 吧 after the verb. To make a negative command add bié 别 (or bùyào 不要) in front of the verb.

Shuì! 睡*!*	*Sleep!*
Shuì ba. 睡吧。	*Go to sleep.*
Bié shuì. 别睡。	*Don't sleep.*

13. ADVERBIAL USE OF DE 得

verb + de 得 + adjective

Tā chī de hěn kuài. 他吃得很快。	*He eats very fast.*
Nǐ shuō de hěn hǎo. 你说得很好。	*You speak very well.*

verb + object + verb + de 得 + adjective

Wǒ shuō Zhōngwén shuō de hěn bù hǎo. 我说中文说得很不好。	*I don't speak Chinese very well. (lit., I speak Chinese not very well.)*

Note that, in Chinese characters, de 得 differs from the possessive de 的, although both have the same pronunciation.

14. QUANTIFIERS (*MANY, SOME, ALL, EVERY*)

hěn duō 很多 (*many*)	Zhōngguó yǒu hěn duō ré. 中国有很多人。	*There are a lot of people in China.*
bù shǎo 不少 (*many*)	Wǒ yǒu bù shǎo gǒu. 我有不少狗。	*I have quite a few dogs.*
yīxiē 一些 (*some*)	Tā yǒu yīxiē wèntí. 他有一些问题。	*He has some questions.*
quánbù 全部 (*all*)	Quánbù rén dōu zǒu le. 全部人都走了。	*All the people are gone.*
měi 每 (*every*) + measure word	Měi ge rén dōu zǒu le. 每个人都走了。	*Everyone is gone.*

All and *every* can formed by duplicating a measure word and using dōu 都 before the main verb. Used with subjects that denote two things or people, dōu 都 means both.

Měi ge rén dōu xǐhuan tā. 每个人都喜欢他。	*Everyone likes him. (lit., All the people like him.)*

Běnběn shū dōu hěn guì. 本本书都很贵。	*Every book is expensive./All books are expensive.*
Huáng xiānsheng hé Huáng tàitai dōu bù zài. 黄先生和黄太太都不在。	*Both Mr. Huang and Mrs. Huang are not here.*
Bob, Bill hé Susie dōu shì xuésheng. 鲍勃，比尔和苏西是学生。	*Bob, Bill, and Susie are all students.*
Wǒmen dōu shì Měiguórén. 我们都是美国人。	*We are all American.*

15. COMPARISON

a. Comparative adjectives: A bǐ 比 B + adjective + (exact degree of difference)

Wǒ bǐ nǐ dà. 我比你大。	*I am older than you. (lit., I am bigger than you.)*
Zhè běn shū bǐ nà běn shū guì. 这本书比那本书贵。	*This book is more expensive than that one.*
Wǒ bǐ nǐ dà sān suì. 我比你大三岁。	*I am three years older than you.*

b. Comparative adverbs: A + verb + de bǐ 的比 + B + adverb

Wǒ zǒu de bǐ nǐ kuài. 我走得比你快。	*I walk faster than you do.*

c. Expressing similarity: yǒu ... nàme 有... 那么 (*as ... as*) or A + hé 和 + B + yīyàng 一样 + adjective

Wǒ yǒu nǐ nàme gāo. 我有你那么高。	*I am as tall as you.*
Wǒ hé nǐ yīyàng gāo. 我和你一样高。	*I am as tall as you. (lit., I and you are the same height.)*

d. Superlative: zuì 最 + adjective

Zhè jiā lǚdiàn zuì hǎo. 这家旅店最好。	*This hotel is the best.*
Tā de chē zuì kuài. 他的车最快。	*His car is the fastest.*

16. YES/NO QUESTIONS

a. The question particle ma 吗 (declarative sentence + ma 吗)

Nǐ qù ma? 你去吗?	*Do you go?*
Wǒ qù. 我去。	*Yes, I do.*
Zhāng xiānsheng zhù zài zhèr ma? 张先生住在这儿吗?	*Does Mr. Zhang live here?*
Tā zhù zài zhèr. 他住在这儿。	*Yes, he does.*
Tā pǎo de kuài ma? 他跑得快吗?	*Does he run fast?*
Tā pǎo de kuài. 他跑得快。	*Yes, he does.*

b. verb/adverb + bù 不 + verb/adverb

Nǐ qù bù qù? 你去不去?	*Do you go or not?*
Wǒ qù. 我去。	*Yes, I do.*
Tā pǎo de kuài bù kuài? 他跑得快不快?	*Does he run fast?*
Tā pǎo de kuài. 他跑得快。	*Yes, he does.*

c. ne 呢 (*how about … ?*)

Nǐ xǐhuan hē chá ma? 你喜欢喝茶吗?	*Do you like drinking tea?*
Wǒ xǐhuan. Nǐ ne? 我喜欢，你呢?	*Yes, I do. How about you?*

d. Answering yes/no questions

Repeat the (auxliary) verb in positive or negative form.

Nǐ shì Zhāng xiǎojie ma? 你是张小姐吗?	*Are you Miss Zhang?*
Wǒ shì. 我是。	*Yes, I am.*
Wǒ bù shì. 我不是。	*No, I am not.*
Nǐ huì shuō Yīngwén ma? 你会说英文吗?	*Do you know how to speak English?*
Wǒ huì. 我会。	*Yes, I do.*
Wǒ bù huì. 我不会。	*No, I don't.*

e. Answering negative questions

Opposite of English pattern

Nǐ méiyǒu qián ma? 你没有钱吗?	*Don't you have money?*
Bù shì. Wǒ yǒu. 不是。我有。	*Yes. I have (money). (lit., No. I have money.)*
Shì. Wǒ méiyǒu. 是。我没有。	*No. I don't (have money). (lit., Yes. I don't have money.)*

17. QUESTION WORDS

shénme 什么	*what*
shénme shíhou 什么时候	*when*
nǎli/nǎr 哪里／那儿	*where*
nǎ/něi + *measure word* 哪	*which (sg.)*
nǎ/něi + xiē 哪＋些	*which (pl.)*
shéi 谁	*who/whom*
duōshǎo qián 多少钱	*how much (money)*
duōshǎo/jǐ + *measure word* 多少／几	*how many*
duōshǎo 多少	*how much*

zěnme (yàng) 怎么（样）	*how*
wèishénme 为什么	*why*

Note: Question words do not move to the front of the sentence as they do in English. The order is that of so-called "echo questions," e.g. Tā shì shéi? 他／她是谁？ *Who is he/she? (lit., He/she is who?)*.

18. USE OF THE PREPOSITION ZÀI 在 AND OTHER LOCATION WORDS

The preposition zài 在 (*at, in, on*) is used to specify location. No form of *to be* is necessary in Chinese.

Wǒ zài xuéxiào (lǐ). 我在学校（里）。	*I am in school.*
Tā zài Měiguó. 他在美国。	*He is in the U.S.*

qiánbiān 前边	*in front of*
hòubiān 后边	*behind*
shàngbiān 上边	*above*
xiàbiān 下边	*under*
zuǒbiān 左边	*the left*
yòubiān 右边	*the right*
pángbiān 旁边	*beside*
zhōngjiān 中间	*between*
lǐ(biān) 里（边）	*inside/in*
wàibiān 外边	*outside*

zài 在 + location word + place or object name

Wǒ de shū zài zhuōzi de xiàbiān. 我的书在桌子的下边。	*My book is under the table.*

Note: The positioning of zhōngjiān 中间 is different: "A hé B de zhōngjiān A 和 B 的 中间," where A and B are separate place names or words.

19. *THERE IS/ARE*: YǑU 有 AND SHÌ 是

place word + location word + yǒu 有 + subject

Xuéxiào (lǐ) yǒu hěnduō xuésheng. 学校（里）有很多学生。	There are a lot of students in the school. (lit., School inside there are lots of students.)
Gōngyuán lǐ yǒu yī tiáo gǒu. 公园里有一条狗。	There is a dog in the park. (lit., Park inside there is a dog.)

place word + location word + shì 是 + place word

Gōngyuán de hòubiān shì xuéxiào. 公园的后边是学校。	There is a school behind the park. (lit., The back of the park is school.)

Note: Shì 是 can only be used to assert the existence of singular nouns.

20. HERE IS A LIST OF THE ONE HUNDRED MOST ESSENTIAL CHINESE CHARACTERS:

CHARACTER	PRONUNCIATION	MEANING
一	yī	one
二	èr	two
三	sān	three
四	sì	four
五	wǔ	five
六	liù	six
七	qī	seven
八	bā	eight
九	jiǔ	nine
十	shí	ten
百	bǎi	hundred
千	qiān	thousand
万	wàn	ten thousand
大	dà	big
中	zhōng	middle
小	xiǎo	small
车	chē	car
电	diàn	electricity
云	yún	cloud
雨	yǔ	rain
火	huǒ	fire
水	shuǐ	water
山	shān	mountain
上	shàng	on, above
下	xià	under
左	zuǒ	left

CHARACTER	PRONUNCIATION	MEANING
右	yòu	right
前	qián	in front of
后	hòu	behind
书	shū	book
菜	cài	dish, vegetable
鸡	jī	chicken
鸭	yā	duck
牛	niú	cow
羊	yáng	sheep
猪	zhū	pig
鱼	yú	fish
酒	jiǔ	wine
笔	bǐ	pen
字	zì	character
是	shì	to be
几	jǐ	several
美	měi	beautiful
国	guó	country
高	gāo	tall, high
低	dī	low
不	bù	not
没	méi	not to have
有	yǒu	to have, there is/there are
也	yě	also
了	le	(verb suffix)
东	dōng	east
南	nán	south
西	xī	west

CHARACTER	PRONUNCIATION	MEANING
北	běi	*north*
人	rén	*people*
今	jīn	*at present*
我	wǒ	*I, me*
你	nǐ	*you*
他	tā	*he*
她	tā	*she*
来	lái	*come*
去	qù	*go*
们	men	*(plural particle)*
做	zuò	*do*
元	yuán	*dollar*
两	liǎng	*two*
再	zài	*again*
见	jiàn	*see*
刀	dāo	*knife*
分	fēn	*separate, minute, cent*
到	dào	*until, reach*
力	lì	*strength*
加	jiā	*plus*
又	yòu	*also*
口	kǒu	*mouth*
门	mén	*door*
叫	jiào	*call*
名	míng	*first name*
和	hé	*and*
茶	chá	*tea*
在	zài	*in, on, at*

CHARACTER	PRONUNCIATION	MEANING
坐	zuò	*sit*
报	bào	*report, newspaper*
外	wài	*outside*
内	nèi	*inside*
天	tiān	*sky*
太	tài	*too (excessive), very*
好	hǎo	*good, well*
姓	xìng	*last name*
学	xué	*learn*
文	wén	*written language*
家	jiā	*home, family*
写	xiě	*write*
对	duì	*correct*
老	lǎo	*old*
年	nián	*year*
月	yuè	*month, moon*
日	rì	*day, sun*
从	cóng	*from*

21. IMPORTANT SIGNS IN CHINESE CHARACTERS:

CHARACTER	MEANING
男	*Men*
女	*Women*
卫生间 *or* 厕所 *or* 洗手间	*Lavatory, Toilet, Restroom*
有人	*Occupied (lit., there is person)*
无人	*Vacant (lit., there is no person)*
不准抽烟	*No Smoking*
不准进入	*No Admittance*

CHARACTER	MEANING
敲	*Knock*
铃	*Ring, Bell*
私人	*Private*
查询	*Inquire Within*
停! / 止步!	*Stop!*
去!	*Go!*
小心!	*Look out!*
危险!	*Danger!*
慢走	*Go slowly!*
绕道	*Detour*
警告	*Caution*
保持右走	*Keep to the Right*
桥	*Bridge*
不准停车	*No Parking*
衣帽间	*Check Room*
兑换	*Money Exchange*
资料	*Information*
等候室	*Waiting Room*
不要伸出窗外	*Don't Lean Out (of the Window)*
飞机场	*Airport*
铁路	*Railroad*
快车	*Express (lit., fast car)*
慢车	*Local (lit., slow car)*
站	*Stop (bus, train, etc.)*
不可张贴	*Post No Bills*
修理中	*Under Repair*
入口	*Entrance*
出口	*Exit*

CHARACTER	MEANING
配家具房子	*Furnished Rooms*
房子	*House*
油漆未干	*Wet Paint*
十字路口	*Crossroads*
肉店	*Butcher*
饼店	*Bakery*
牛奶	*Milk*
裁缝店	*Tailor Shop*
鞋店	*Shoe Store*
理发店	*Barber Shop*
菜市场 / 市场	*Grocer, Market*
药房 / 药店	*Pharmacy, Drugstore*
糖果店	*Confectioner, Candy Store*
文具店	*Stationery Store*
信箱	*Mail Box*
酒吧	*Bar, Tavern*
公安局	*Police Station*
酒	*Wines*
油站	*Gas Station*
书店	*Book Store*
市政府	*City Hall*
点心 / 小吃	*Refreshments, Snacks*
(冷) 水	*(Cold) Water*
(热) 水	*(Hot) Water*

Glossary

English - Chinese

A

a few/a little yī diǎndiǎn 一点点
a little more of ... zài lái yìdiǎn ... 再来一点 ...
a long time hěn jiǔ 很久
a lot hěn duō 很多
a while yī huìr 一会儿
abdominal pain (to have) dùzi tòng 肚子痛
able (to be) kěyǐ 可以 (in terms of permission),
  néng(gòu) 能(够) (in terms of proficiency)
about dàgài 大概, dàyuē 大约
academic performance chéngjì 成绩
accounting kuàijì 会计
  accountant kuàijìshī 会计师
across the street duìmiàn 对面
address dìzhǐ 地址
adjectival particle de 的
adverbial particle de 得
after zhīhòu 之后
after that ránhòu 然后
afternoon xiàwǔ 下午
afterwards ránhòu 然后
again zài 再
ago yǐqián 以前
airport jīchǎng 机场
  airplane fēijī 飞机, fēijī chǎng 飞机场
alcoholic drink jiǔ 酒
all dōu 都
all gone guāng 光
allow (to) ràng 让
  allowed (to be) kěyǐ 可以
almost chàbùduō 差不多
  almost time to do something (lit. quickly ...
    as of now) Kuài ... le. 快 ... 了。
alright hǎo ba 好吧
also yě 也, háiyǒu 还有
always zǒngshì 总是
America Měiguó 美国
  American (people) Měiguórén 美国人
and hé 和
and (for connecting two adjectives or
  adverbs) yòu ... yòu ... 又 ... 又 ...
another zài lái ... 再来 ...
anyone shénme rén yě, shéi yě 什么人也, 谁也
anything shénme dōngxi yě 什么东西也
anywhere nǎr, nǎli yě 哪儿, 哪里也

apartment gōngyù 公寓
appear to be kàn qǐlái 看起来
apple píngguǒ 苹果
apply (to) shēnqǐng 申请
approximately dàgài 大概
April sì yuè 四月
around zuǒyòu 左右
as ... adjective/adverb as ... (used for people and
  things nearby) yǒu ... zhème 有 ... 这么
  as ... adjective/adverb as ... (used for people and
    things far away) yǒu ... nàme 有 ... 那么
ask (to) wèn 问
  ask directions (to) (lit., to ask the road) wènlù
    问路
at zài 在
attend (a) class (to) shàngkè 上课
attend university (to) shàng dàxué 上大学
audit a class (to) pángtīng 旁听
August bā yuè 八月
aunt
  aunt (father's older brother's wife) bómǔ 伯母
  aunt (father's sister) gūgu 姑姑
  aunt (father's younger brother's wife) shěnshen
    婶婶
  aunt (mother's brother's wife) jiùmǔ/jiùmā
    舅母/舅妈
  aunt (mother's sister) yímǔ/yímā 姨母/姨妈
Australia Àozhōu 澳洲
  Australian Àozhōurén 澳洲人
autumn qiūtiān 秋天

B

back (body) bèibù 背部
bad huài 坏
badminton yǔmáoqiú 羽毛球
bag bāo 包
ball qiú 球
banana xiāngjiāo 香蕉
bandage to a wound (to) bāozā shāngkǒu
  包扎伤口
baseball bàngqiú 棒球
basketball lánqiú 篮球
bathroom wèishēngjiān 卫生间
be (to) shì 是
  be (located) at (to) zài 在
beautiful piàoliang 漂亮
because yīnwèi 因为
bed chuáng 床

bedroom wòfáng 卧房
beef niúròu 牛肉
beer píjiǔ 啤酒
before zhīqián 之前
behind hòubiān 后边
belly dùzi 肚子
belt pídài 皮带
between zhōngjiān 中间
  between ... and ... zài ... hé ... zhōngjiān
  在 ... 和 ... 中间
bicycle zìxíngchē 自行车
big dà 大
biology shēngwù 生物
birthday shēngrì 生日
bitter kǔ 苦
black hēi 黑
  black pepper hēi hújiāo 黑胡椒
bleed (to) liúxiě 流血
block lùkǒu 路口
blow (to) chuī 吹
blue lán 蓝
book shū 书
  bookstore shūdiàn 书店
  bookshelf shūjià 书架
boots xuēzi 靴子
boss lǎobǎn 老板
bottle píng 瓶
box hé 盒
boy nánháir 男孩儿, nánhái 男孩
bowl wǎn 碗
bread miànbāo 面包
breakfast zǎocān 早餐
bridge qiáo 桥
bring (to) gěi 给
  bring me ... Gěi wǒ ... 给我
Britain Yīngguó 英国
  British (people) Yīngguórén 英国人
brother (older) gēge 哥哥
  brother (younger) dìdi 弟弟
brown zōngsè 棕色
building dàlóu 大楼
bunch (as in cluster) chuàn 串
bus gōngchē 公车
  bus stop gōngchē zhàn 公车站
butter huángyóu 黄油
buy (to) mǎi 买

C

cabbage bāoxīncài 包心菜
cafeteria shítáng 食堂
cake dàngāo 蛋糕
calf xiǎotuǐ 小腿
call (to) jiào 叫
  called (to be) (full name) jiào 叫
  called (to be) (surname) xìng 姓
campus xiàoyuán 校园
can (noun) guàn 罐
Canada Jiānádà 加拿大
Cantonese Guǎngdōngrén 广东人
car chē, qìchē 车, 汽车
careful (to be) xiǎoxīn 小心
carp lǐyú 鲤鱼
carrot húluóbo 胡萝卜
carton hé 盒
cash xiànjīn 现金
cat māo 猫
  catch a cold (to) zháoliáng 着凉
CD jīguāng chàngpiàn 激光唱片
celery qíncài 芹菜
cereal màipiàn 麦片
chair yǐzi 椅子
change (monetary) língqián 零钱
change trains/subways/buses (to) huàn chē 换车
check (payment) zhīpiào 支票
  Check please! Qǐng nǐ jiézhàng! 请你结帐!
check (to) jiǎnchá 检查
  check (someone's) pulse (to) bǎmài 把脉
cheek liǎnjiá 脸颊
chemistry huàxué 化学
chest xiōngbù 胸部
  chest pain (to have) xiōngbù tòng 胸部痛
chicken jī 鸡
  chicken meat (boneless) jīròu 鸡肉
China Zhōngguó 中国
  Chinese (language) Zhōngwén 中文
  Chinese (people) Zhōngguórén 中国人
  Chinese cuisine Zhōngcài 中菜
chocolate qiǎokèlì 巧克力
chopsticks kuàizi 筷子
church jiàotáng 教堂
cinema diànyǐngyuàn 电影院
city chéngshì 城市
class kè 课

classmate tóngxué 同学

classroom jiàoshì 教室

classical music gǔdiǎn yīnyuè 古典音乐

clean gānjìng 干净

clean (to) qīnglǐ 清理

clock shízhōng 时钟

close (to) guān 关

clothes, clothing yīfu 衣服

clothing store fúzhuāng diàn 服装店

coat wàitào 外套

coffee kāfēi 咖啡

cold lěng 冷

cold (sickness) gǎnmào 感冒

colleague tóngshì 同事

color sè 色, yánsè 颜色

come (to) lái 来

come over (to) guòlái 过来

come in jìnlái 进来

company gōngsī 公司

comparatively bǐjiào 比较

computer diànnǎo 电脑

concentrate (to) jízhōng jīngshén 集中精神

Congratulations! Gōngxǐ nǐ! 恭喜你!

cook (to) shāocài 烧菜, shāofàn 烧饭, zuòfàn 做饭

cooked rice fàn 饭

cooking pēngrèn 烹饪

corner lùkǒu 路口

cost of living shēnghuófèi 生活费

cough késou 咳嗽

Could you ... ? (lit., bother you) máfan nǐ 麻烦你

Could I trouble you for ... Máfan nǐ gěi wǒmen ... 麻烦你给我们 ...

cousin

cousin (father's brother's daughter, older than you) tángjiě 堂姐

cousin (father's brother's daughter, younger than you) tángmèi 堂妹

cousin (father's brother's son, older than you) tánggē 堂哥

cousin (father's brother's son, younger than you) tángdì 堂弟

cross the street (to) guò mǎlù 过马路

crowded yōngjǐ 拥挤

cucumber huángguā 黄瓜

culottes qúnkù 裙裤

cup bēizi 杯子

currency unit, equivalent to the dollar unit yuán 元

colloquial word for yuán kuài 块

one one-hundredth of a yuán, equivalent to the cent fēn 分

one tenth of a yuán, equivalent to the dime jiǎo 角

colloquial word for jiǎo máo 毛

cycling qí zìxíngchē 骑自行车

D

dance (to) tiàowǔ 跳舞

dark shēn 深

daughter nǚ'ér 女儿

day tiān 天

deadline zuìhòu qīxiàn 最后期限

December shí'èr yuè 十二月

degree (temperature) dù 度

delicious hǎochī 好吃

department (college level) xì 系

department store bǎihuò gōngsī 百货公司

dessert tiándiǎn 甜点

diarrhea (to have) lā dùzi 拉肚子

dictionary zìdiǎn 字典

different bùtóng 不同

difficult nán 难

dim sum diǎnxīn 点心

dining room fàntīng 饭厅

dinner wǎncān 晚餐

dirty zāng 脏

discount (to give a) dǎzhé 打折

discuss (to) tántan 谈谈

dish of food cài 菜

dislike (to) bù xǐhuan 不喜欢

do (to) zuò 做

doctor yīshēng 医生

document wénjiàn 文件

dog gǒu 狗

Don't worry. Méi shì. 没事。

dormitory sùshè 宿舍

dress liányīqún 连衣裙

drink (to) hē 喝

drive (a car) (to) kāichē 开车

duck yā 鸭

E

each měi 每

ear ěrduo 耳朵

east dōng 东

eat (to) chī 吃
economize (to) shěng 省
egg(s) jīdàn 鸡蛋
eight bā 八
either ... or ... huòzhě 或者
elbow zhǒu 肘
electronics store (lit., home appliances
    store) jiāyòng diànqì diàn 家用电器店
elephant xiàng 象
eleven shíyī 十一
employee gùyuán 雇员
engineering gōngchéng 工程
    engineer gōngchéngshī 工程师
English (language) Yīngwén 英文
enlightened kāimíng 开明
even more gèng 更
evening wǎn 晚, wǎnshang 晚上
every měi 每
    every day měi tiān 每天
    everyone měi ge rén 每个人
    everything yīqiè 一切
examination kǎoshì 考试
examine (to) jiǎnchá 检查
exchange (to) huàn 换
Excuse me. Láojià. 劳驾。
Excuse me. (apologizing) Duìbùqǐ. 对不起。
    (asking for a favor), guì 贵 expensive
extracurricular activities kèwài huódòng
    课外活动
eye yǎnjing 眼睛

F

face liǎn 脸
familiar with (to be) shúxī 熟悉
family jiā 家
far yuǎn 远
fashionable shímáo 时髦
fast kuài 快
father fùqin 父亲
    dad bàba 爸爸
fax machine chuánzhēnjī 传真机
fear (to) pà 怕
February èr yuè 二月
feel (to) gǎndào 感到
    feel dizzy (to) tóuyūn 头晕
    feel nauseous (to) ěxin 恶心
    feel unwell(to) bù shūfu 不舒服
female nǚ 女

fever (to have a) fāshāo 发烧
fewer than (lit. not enough) bù gòu 不够
file dǎng'àn 档案, wénjiàn 文件
    filing cabinet dǎng'àn guì 档案柜
film diànyǐng 电影
finally zhōngyú 终于
find (to) zhǎo 找
fine hǎo 好
finger shǒuzhǐ 手指
    fingernail zhǐjia 指甲
finish class (to) fàngxué 放学
first xiān 先
fish yú 鱼
    fishing diàoyú 钓鱼
five wǔ 五
food fàn 饭, shíwù 食物
    food market càishìchǎng 菜市场
foot jiǎo 脚
football (American) gǎnlǎnqiú 橄榄球
for example bǐrú 比如
forehead étóu 额头
foreign wàiguó 外国
    foreign language wàiyǔ 外语
forget (to) wàng 忘
fork chāzi 叉子
forty sìshí 四十
four sì 四
France Fǎguó 法国
    French (people) Fǎguórén 法国人
    French (language) Fǎwén 法文
frequently jīngcháng 经常
Friday xīngqī wǔ 星期五
friend péngyou 朋友
from cóng 从
    from ... to ... cóng ... dào ... 从 ... 到 ...
fruit shuǐguǒ 水果

G

garlic suàntóu 蒜头
Germany Déguó 德国
    German (people) Déguórén 德国人
    German (language) Déwén 德文
get off (to) (a vehicle) xià chē 下车
get on (to) (a vehicle) shàng chē 上车
get out chùqù 出去
girl nǚháir 女孩儿, nǚhái 女孩, nǚháizi 女孩子
give (to) gěi 给
    Give me another ... Zài gěi wǒ ... 再给我 ...

Give me ... Gěi wǒ ... 给我

give/get an injection (to) dǎ zhēn 打针

glass bēizi 杯子

　glass (measure word) bēi 杯

go (to) qù 去

　go to the hospital (to) qù yīyuàn 去医院

　go abroad (to) chūguó 出国

　Go ahead. Hǎo ba. 好吧。

　go ahead (to) wǎng qián, zǒu ba 往前, 走吧

　go online (to) shàngwǎng 上网

　go straight ahead (to) yīzhí wǎng qián zǒu
　　一直往前走

　go to a clinic (to) qù zhěnsuǒ 去诊所

　go to a movie/the movies (to) kàn diànyǐng
　　看电影

　go to a stadium (to) qù tǐyùguǎn 去体育馆

　go to class (to), to start class shàngkè 上课

　go to school (to), to attend school shàngxué
　　上学

　go to the beach (to) qù hǎitān 去海滩

　go to work (to), be at work (to) shàngbān 上班

gold jīnsè 金色

good hǎo 好

goodbye zàijiàn. 再见。

graduate (to) bìyè 毕业

　graduate student yánjiūshēng 研究生

　graduate school yánjiūyuàn, yánjiūsuǒ 研究院,
　　研究所

grandfather

　grandfather (maternal side) wàigōng 外公

　grandfather (paternal side) yéye 爷爷

grandmother

　grandmother (maternal side) wàipó 外婆

　grandmother (paternal side) nǎinai 奶奶

grape pútao 葡萄

grasp (to) bǎ 把

green lǜ 绿, lǜsè 绿色

grey huīsè 灰色

H

half bàn 半

ham huǒtuǐ 火腿

hand shǒu 手

happy kuàilè 快乐

hat màozi 帽子

have (to) yǒu 有

　Do (you) have ... ? ... yǒu méiyǒu ... ?
　　... 有没有 ... ?

Do you have ... ? Nǐmen yǒu ... ma?
　你们有 ... 吗?

　don't/doesn't have méiyǒu 没有

　have a chat (to) tántan 谈谈

　Have a seat. Qǐng zuò. 请坐。

　have fun (to) wán de kāixīn 玩得开心

　have to (to) bìxū 必须

he tā 他

headache (to have a) tóu tòng 头痛

hear (to) tīngdào 听到

heel zúgēn 足跟

hello Nǐ hǎo. 你好。

help (to) bāngzhù 帮助

her (object pronoun) tā 她

her (possessive pronoun) tā de 她的

here zhèlǐ 这里

hers tā de 她的

hiking yuǎnzú 远足

him tā 他

his tā de 他的

history lìshǐ 历史

hit (to) dǎ 打

hobbies àihào 爱好

hockey qūgùnqiú 曲棍球

hold (to) ná 拿

holiday jiàqī 假期

home jiā 家

homework gōngkè 功课

Hongkongese Xiānggǎngrén 香港人

hospital yīyuàn 医院

hot là 辣, tàng 烫

hotel lǚguǎn 旅馆, lǚdiàn 旅店, jiǔdiàn 酒店

hour (amount of time) xiǎoshí 小时, zhōngtóu 钟头

　hour (o'clock) diǎn, diǎn zhōng 点, 点钟

house fángzi 房子

how zěnme yang? 怎么样, zěnyàng 怎样

　how far? yǒu duō yuǎn? 有多远?

　how long? duōjiǔ 多久

　how many? jǐ 几?

　How much?/ How many? duōshǎo 多少

　how to get to ... ? zěnme zǒu 怎么走

hungry è 饿

husband xiānsheng 先生

I

I wǒ 我

I don't want to ... Wǒ bù xiǎng ... 我不想 ...

I need ... Wǒ yào ... 我要 ...

I would like to have … Wǒ xiǎng yào … 我想要 …

I'm sorry Duìbùqǐ. 对不起。

I'm sorry. (lit., to find it embarrassing (to do something)) Bù hǎoyìsi. 不好意思。

ice cream bīngjílíng 冰激凌

if rúguǒ 如果

if … (then) rǔguǒ … jiù 如果 … 就

illness bìng 病

in lǐ 里, zài 在

in a hurry, in a rush cōngmáng 匆忙

in addition háiyǒu 还有

in front of qiánbiān 前边, ménkǒu 门口

in style shímáo 时髦

in this/that case … nà … 那 …

inexpensive piányi 便宜

inflammation fāyán 发炎

inside lǐbiān 里边

instant noodles fāngbiànmiàn 方便面

intelligent cōngmíng 聪明

interest xìngqù 兴趣

intersection lùkǒu 路口, shízì lùkǒu 十字路口

interview miànshì 面试

It's nothing. (Don't worry. No problem.) Méi shì. 没事。

it's only … zhǐshì 只是

Italy Yìdàlì 意大利

Italian (people) Yìdàlìrén 意大利人

Italian (language) Yìdàlìwén 意大利文

its tā de 它的

J

jacket jiákè 夹克

January yī yuè 一月

Japan Rìběn 日本

Japanese (people) Rìběnrén 日本人

Japanese (language) Rìwén 日文

job gōngzuò 工作

jogging huǎnbùpǎo 缓步跑, mànpǎo 慢跑

jot something down (to) jì xiàlái 记下来

juice guǒzhī 果汁

July qī yuè 七月

June liù yuè 六月

just now gāngcái 刚才

K

keep (to) liú 留

kick (to) tī 踢

kilogram gōngjīn 公斤

kilometers gōnglǐ 公里

kind (noun) zhǒng 种

kitchen chúfáng 厨房

knife dāo 刀

knitting biānzhī 编织

know a fact (to), know something (to) zhīdào 知道

know (to) (someone) rènshi 认识

know how to (to) huì 会

L

laboratory shíyànshì 实验室

laborer gōngrén 工人

large dà 大

large (size) dàhào 大号

last month shàng ge yuè 上个月

last week shàng ge lǐbài 上个礼拜

last year qùnián 去年

late night snack yèxiāo 夜宵, xiāoyè 宵夜

law fǎlǜ 法律

lawyer lǜshī 律师

learn (to) xué 学

leave zǒu 走

Leave. (polite) Zǒu ba. 走吧。

leave a message (to) liúyán 留言

leave one's own country (to) chūguó 出国

left zuǒ 左

left side (of) (the) zuǒbiān 左边

leg tuǐ 腿

less and less or more and more yuè lái yuè 越来越

let (to) ràng 让

let me ràng wǒ 让我

let … ràng … ba 让 … 吧

library túshūguǎn 图书馆

library card túshūzhèng 图书证

lie down (to) tǎng 躺

light qiǎn 浅

light green qiǎn lǜsè 浅绿色

like (to) xǐhuan 喜欢

lips zuǐchún 嘴唇

listen (to) tīng 听

live in (to) zhù zài 住在

lively, busy, bustling rènao 热闹

living room kètīng 客厅

lobster lóngxiā 龙虾

look (to) kàn 看

look for (to) zhǎo 找
love (to) ài 爱
lunch wǔcān 午餐

M

Mahjong Májiàng 麻将
major zhuānyè, zhǔxiū 专业, 主修
make (to) zuò 做
  make a date (to) yuē 约
  make a medical house call (a doctor) (to) chū zhěn 出诊
  make a phone call (to) dǎ diànhuà 打电话
  make an appointment (to) yuē 约, yùyuē 预约
male nán 男
man nánrén 男人
many, much hěn duō 很多
  many times hěn duō cì 很多次
March sān yuè 三月
market shìchǎng 市场
May wǔ yuè 五月
May I ... qǐng nǐ/nín 请你/您
  May I ask ... ? qǐng wèn 请问
  May I have... ? (lit., Could you give me ... ?)
    Nǐ kěyǐ gěi wǒ ... ma? 你可以给我 ... 吗?
maybe kěnéng 可能
me wǒ 我
meal fàn 饭
measure word for books, photo albums, magazines běn 本
measure word for cars, taxis, bicycles liǎng 两
measure word for plants kē 棵
measure word for bottled drinks píng 瓶
measure word for automobiles, bicycles, carts liàng 辆
measure word for garments worn over the lower half of the body, or for objects that are long and thin (scarves), also for animals (dogs, fish, bulls...) tiáo 条
measure word for garments worn over the upper part or full length of the body jiàn 件
measure word for knives bǎ 把
measure word for machines tái 台
measure word for meal dùn 顿
measure word for number of family members kǒu 口
measure word for objects that are pointed and thin, utensils, and some animals zhī 只
measure word for objects that are small and

round chuàn 串
measure word for objects that have a flat surface (tables, desks, chairs ...) zhāng 张
measure word for people, cities, groups, and nations gè 个
measure word for small plants and vegetables kē 颗
measure word for soup, rice (bowl) wǎn 碗
measure word for tables, desks, chairs zhāng 张
measure word for tile, tablets, other thin and flat objects piàn 片
measure word for water, coffee, tea, wine (cup, glass) bēi 杯
measure word of general unit for ordering food (dish, plate) pán 盘
meat ròu 肉
(medication) taken after a meal fàn hòu fú 饭后服
(medication) taken before a meal fàn qián fú 饭前服
medium (size) zhōnghào 中号
meet (to) rènshi 认识
meeting huìyì 会议
  have a meeting (to) kāihuì 开会
  in a meeting (to be) kāihuì 开会
menu càidān 菜单
meters mǐ 米
midnight bànyè 半夜
milk niúnǎi 牛奶
  milk tea nǎichá 奶茶
mine wǒ de 我的
minute fēn 分
  minute(s) fēnzhōng 分钟, fēn 分
Miss xiǎojie 小姐
Monday xīngqī yī 星期一
money qián 钱
more and more yuè lái yuè 越来越
moreover érqiě 而且
morning zǎoshang 早上
mother mǔqīn 母亲
  mom māma 妈妈
motorcycle mótuōchē 摩托车
mouth zuǐba 嘴巴, kǒu 口
movie diànyǐng 电影
  movie theater diànyǐngyuàn 电影院
Mr. xiānsheng 先生
Mrs. tàitai 太太

museum bówùguǎn 博物馆
mushrooms mógu 蘑菇
music yīnyuè 音乐
must bìxū 必须
mustard jièmo 芥末
my wǒ de 我的

N

Nanjingese Nánjīngrén 南京人
napa cabbage báicài 白菜
napkin cānjīn 餐巾
near jìn 近
  nearby fùjìn 附近
neck bózi 脖子
neighbor línjū 邻居
never cónglái méiyǒu... 从来没有...
new xīn 新
newspaper bàozhǐ 报纸
next week xià ge lǐbài 下个礼拜
next month xià ge yuè 下个月
next year míngnián 明年
next to pángbiān 旁边
night wǎnshang 晚上
nine jiǔ 九
nineteen shíjiǔ 十九
Ninety jiǔshí 九十
no, not bù 不
  negative particle used for commands bié 别,
    bùyào 不要
  no need to bùyòng 不用
  No problem. Méi shì. 没事。Méiyǒu wèntí.
    没有问题。
  Not bad. Bùcuò. 不错
noisy chǎo 吵
noodles miàntiáo 面条
noon zhōngwǔ 中午
north běi 北
nose bízi 鼻子
novel xiǎoshuō 小说
November shíyī yuè 十一月
now xiànzài 现在
nurse hùshi 护士

O

o'clock diǎn, diǎn zhōng 点, 点钟
October shí yuè 十月
of course dāngrán 当然
office bàngōngshì 办公室

official Chinese currency Rénmínbì 人民币
often jīngcháng 经常
ok hǎo ba 好吧
  ...is it alright? ...hǎo bù hǎo? ...好不好?
old (things) jiù 旧
on zài 在
  on (top of) shàngbiān 上边, shàng, 上
  on foot zǒulù 走路
  on the corner zài lùkǒu 在路口
  on/to the left zài zuǒbiān 在左边
  on the phone jiǎng diànhuà 讲电话
  on/to the right zài yòubiān 在右边
  on time zhǔnshí 准时
  on vacation fàngjià 放假
one yī 一
  one dozen yī dǎ 一打
  one hundred yībǎi 一百
  one million yībǎiwàn 一百万
  one more zài lái ... 再来 ...
  one thousand yīqiān 一千
onion yángcōng 洋葱
open (to) chǎng敞
  open (the mouth) (to) zhāngkāi 张开
  open-minded kāimíng 开明
or (suggesting a preference) háishì 还是
orange (color) júsè 橘色
orange (fruit) júzi 橘子
order (to) (food) diǎn 点
  order a dish (to) diǎn cài 点菜
ought to yīnggāi 应该
our wǒmen de 我们的
ours wǒmen de 我们的
out of style guòshí 过时
outside wàibiān 外边
over there zài nàli 在那里

P

painting túhuà 图画
pair shuāng 双
pants kùzi 裤子
paper zhǐ 纸
parent jiāzhǎng 家长
park gōngyuán 公园
particle for softening commands ba 吧
particle indicating completion of an
  action guò 过
particle indicating an ongoing action zài 在
particle indicating an ongoing state of

being zhe 着

particle indicating that an action has been completed le 了

particle used for comparison (than) bǐ 比

part-time job jiānzhí 兼职

pay (to) fù 付

pay by check (to) yòng zhīpiào fùqián 用支票付钱

pay by credit card (to) shuākǎ 刷卡

pay in cash (to) fù xiànjīn 付现金

Peking duck Běijīng (kǎo) yā 北京烤鸭

Pekingese Běijīngrén 北京人

pen bǐ 笔

pepper hújiāo 胡椒

perhaps kěnéng 可能

person, people rén 人

pharmacy yàofáng 药房

philosophy zhéxué 哲学

photograph zhàopiàn 照片

physics wùlǐ 物理

pink fěnhóngsè 粉红色

place lǐ 里

placed first (to be) pái dì yī míng 排第一名

plan (to) dǎsuan 打算

plaster cast (to have a) dǎ shígāo 打石膏

plate pánzi 盘子

play (ball games with hands, bridge or drums) (to) dǎ 打

play (piano) (to), to pluck tán 弹

play a game (to) wán yóuxì 玩游戏

play a sport (to) zuò yùndòng 做运动

play ball (to) dǎ qiú 打球

play drums (to) dǎ gǔ 打鼓

play piano (to) tán gāngqín 弹钢琴

play soccer (to) tī zúqiú 踢足球

play the flute (to) chuī dízi 吹笛子

play violin (to) lā xiǎotíqín 拉小提琴

please (used to make an invitation or ask a favor) qǐng 请

Please say that again. Qǐng zài shuō yī cì. 请再说一次。

Please sit. Qǐng zuò. 请坐。

please ... (lit., please you ...) qǐng nǐ/nín 请你/您

poetry shī 诗

police officer jǐngchá 警察

police station jǐngchá jú 警察局

polite kèqi 客气

popular liúxíng 流行

pop music liúxíng yīnyuè 流行音乐

pork zhūròu 猪肉

pork chop(s) zhūpái 猪排

twice-cooked pork huíguōròu 回锅肉

possessive particle de 的

post office yóujú 邮局

potatoe(s) mǎlíngshǔ 马铃薯, tǔdòu 土豆

pound bàng 磅

practice (to) liànxí 练习

prefix for ordinal numbers dì 第

prepare (to) zhǔnbèi 准备

prepare for a lesson (to) yùxí 预习

pretty piàoliang 漂亮

pretty good bùcuò 不错

principal xiàozhǎng 校长

printer dǎyìnjī 打印机, yìnbiǎojī 印表机

private tutoring sīrén bǔxí 私人补习

profession gōngzuò 工作

program, show jiémù 节目

pull (to) lā 拉

purple zǐsè 紫色

put (to) fàng 放

Q

quarter of an hour kè 刻

question particle ma 吗

quick kuài 快

quite tǐng 挺

R

radio shōuyīnjī 收音机

rainbow cǎihóng 彩虹

raincoat yǔyī 雨衣

read (to) kàn 看

read a map (to) kàn dìtú 看地图

read a book kàn shū 看书

red hóng 红, hóngsè 红色

red wine hóngjiǔ 红酒

reference book cānkǎoshū 参考书

refrigerator bīngxiāng 冰箱

relatively bǐjiào 比较

remind (to) tíxǐng 提醒

rest (to) xiūxi 休息

restaurant cānguǎn 餐馆, fànguǎn 饭馆

restroom cèsuǒ 厕所, xǐshǒujiān 洗手间

review (to) wēnxí 温习

review a lesson (to) fùxí 复习

ride (to) qí 骑
right yòu 右
  right side (of) (the) yòubiān 右边
ring jièzhi 戒指
road lù 路
roast kǎo 烤
  roast chicken kǎo jī 烤鸡
room fángjiān 房间
rose méiguì 玫瑰
Russian (language) Éwén 俄文

S

salad shālā 沙拉
salary xīnshuǐ 薪水
salty xián 咸
same yīyàng 一样
Saturday xīngqī liù 星期六
save (to) (as in to store up) chǔ 储, cún 存
say (to) shuō 说
scalding tàng 烫
scared of (to be) pà 怕
school xuéxiào 学校
season jìjié 季节
second(s) miǎo 秒
see (to) kànjiàn 看见, jiàn 见, kàn 看
  see a play (to) kàn xìjù 看戏剧
See you later! Děng huìr jiàn! 等会见!
  See you next time! Xià cì jiàn! 下次见!
  See you soon! Huítóu jiàn! 回头见!
self zìjǐ 自己
send a fax (to) fā chuánzhēn 发传真
September jiǔ yuè 九月
seven qī 七
several jǐ ge 几个
  several days jǐ tiān 几天
  several times jǐ cì 几次
Shanghaiese Shànghǎirén 上海人
she tā 她
ship chuán 船
shirt chènshān 衬衫
sister
  sister (older) jiějie 姐姐
  sister (younger) mèimei 妹妹
sore throat (to have a) sǎngzi tòng 嗓子痛
stomachache (to have a) wèi tòng 胃痛
shiver (to) fādǒu 发抖
shoes xiézi 鞋子
  shoestore xiédiàn 鞋店

shop shāngdiàn 商店
should yīnggāi 应该
shoulder jiānbǎng 肩膀
shrimp xiā 虾
shut (to) guān 关
sibling xiōngdìjiěmèi 兄弟姐妹
sick (to be) bìngle 病了
sidewalk rénxíngdào 人行道
silver yínsè 银色
sing (to) chànggē 唱歌
sit (to) zuò 坐
six liù 六
ski (to) huáxuě 滑雪
skirt qúnzi 裙子
skort qúnkù 裙裤
sleep (to) shuì 睡
  sleep (to) shuìjiào 睡, 睡觉
slice (measure word) piàn 片
slow, slowly màn 慢
small xiǎo 小, xiǎohào 小号
  small town xiǎo zhèn 小镇
sneakers yùndòngxié 运动鞋
soccer (football) zúqiú 足球
socks wàzi 袜子
soda sūdǎ shuǐ 苏打水
sofa shāfā 沙发
some yīxiē 一些
  someone yǒu rén 有人
  something (yī)diǎn dōngxi, (yī)xiē dōngxi
    (一) 点东西, (一) 些东西
  something to drink hē de 喝的
son érzi 儿子
soup tāng 汤
sour suān 酸
south nán 南
soy sauce jiàngyóu 酱油
Spain Xībānyá 西班牙
  Spanish (people) Xībānyárén 西班牙人
  Spanish (language) Xībānyáwén 西班牙文
spare ribs páigǔ 排骨
speak (to) shuō 说
spicy là 辣
spoon tāngchí 汤匙, sháozi 勺子
sport tǐyù 体育
spring chūntiān 春天
  spring rolls chūnjuǎn 春卷
staff yuángōng 员工, gōngzuò rényuán 工作人员
stand (to) zhàn 站

start (to) kāishǐ 开始
stay (to) dāi 待 (呆), liú 留
steak niúpái 牛排
steamed qīng zhēng 清蒸
   steamed fish qīng zhēng yú 清蒸鱼
still haí 还
stir-fried chǎo 炒
stir-fried dish chǎocài 炒菜
stitch up (to) (a wound) féngxiàn 缝线
store shāngdiàn 商店
   store clerk shòuhuòyuán 售货员
straight yīzhí 一直
street jiē 街
string beans sìjìdòu 四季豆
strong qiángzhuàng 强壮
student xuésheng 学生
study (to) xué 学
style kuǎnshì 款式
submit homework (to) jiāo gōngkè 交功课
subway dìtiě 地铁
   subway station dìtiě zhàn 地铁站
such as bǐrú 比如
sugar táng 糖
summer xiàtiān 夏天
Sunday xīngqī tiān 星期天
supper wǎncān 晚餐
supplement (to) (money) bāngbǔ 帮补
surname xìng 姓
sweater máoyī 毛衣
sweet tián 甜
swim (to) yóuyǒng 游泳

T

table zhuōzi 桌子
Taiji / Tai Chi Tàijíquán 太极拳
take (to) ná 拿
   take (to) (a form of transportation) zuò 坐, dā 搭
   take a business trip (to) chūchāi 出差
   take a cardiogram (to) zuò xīndiàntú 做心电图
   take medicine (to) chī yào 吃药
   take personal leave (to) qǐng (shì)jià 请⊠事⊠假
   take sick leave (to) qǐng bìngjià 请病假
   take (someone's) temperature (to) liáng tǐwēn 量体温
tall gāo 高
taste (to) cháng 尝
taxi chūzūchē 出租车
tea chá 茶

teach (to) jiāo 教
teacher lǎoshī 老师
telephone diànhuà 电话
   telephone booth diànhuàtíng 电话亭
television diànshì 电视
temperature (body) tǐwēn 体温
ten shí 十
ten thousand yīwàn 一万
tender nèn 嫩
tennis wǎngqiú 网球
test (to) kǎo 考
   test, to take an exam kǎoshì 考试
textbook kèběn 课本
Thank you. Xièxie. 谢谢。
that nà 那
the best zuì hǎo de 最好的
the most zuì 最
the year after next hòunián 后年
the year before last qiánnián 前年
theater xìyuàn 戏院
their/theirs tāmen de 他们的
them tāmen 他们
then ránhòu 然后
there nàli 那里
there is/there are yǒu 有
therefore suǒyǐ 所以
these zhèxiē 这些
they tāmen 他们
thigh dàtuǐ 大腿
think (to) xiǎng 想
thirteen shísān 十三
thirty sānshí 三十
this zhè 这
   this afternoon jīntiān xiàwǔ 今天下午
   this month zhège yuè 这个月
   this morning jīntiān zǎoshang 今天早上
   this way zhèbiān 这边
   this week zhège lǐbài 这个礼拜
   this year jīnnián 今年
those nàxiē 那些
three sān 三
throat sǎngzi 嗓子
Thursday xīng qī sì 星期四
ticket piào 票
tidy (to) qīnglǐ 清理
tie the score (to) dǎ chéng píngshǒu 打成平手
tight jǐn 紧
time (in broad terms) shíhou 时候

time (in hours and minutes) shíjiān 时间
time off fàngjià 放假
time(s) biàn 遍, cì 次
to, before (ten minutes to/before one
o'clock) chà (chà shí fēn yī diǎn), 差
(差十分一点)
today jīntiān 今天
together yīqǐ 一起
tomato fānqié 番茄
tomorrow míngtiān 明天
the day after tomorrow hòutiān 后天
tongue shétou 舌头
tonight jīntiān wǎnshang 今天晚上
too tài 太
tooth yáchǐ 牙齿
traditional Chinese dress qípáo 旗袍
traffic light hónglǜdēng 红绿灯
train station huǒchēzhàn 火车站
travel lǚxíng 旅行
trendy liúxíng 流行
trouble (to) máfan 麻烦
trunk bízi 鼻子
T-shirt T-xùshān/hànshān T-恤衫/汗衫
Tuesday xīngqī èr 星期二
turn
turn around the corner guǎi ge wān 拐个弯
turn left wǎng zuǒ zhuǎn 往左转
turn right wǎng yòu zhuǎn 往右转
twelve shí'èr 十二
twenty èrshí 二十
two èr 二
two (used to describe amount) liǎng 两

U

uncle
uncle (father's older brother) bóbo 伯伯
uncle (father's sister's husband) gūfu 姑夫
uncle (father's younger brother) shūshu 叔叔
uncle (mother's brother) jiùjiu 舅舅
uncle (mother's sister's husband) yífu 姨夫
under xiàbiān, xià 下边, 下
underpants nèikù 内裤
underpass rénxíng dìdào 人行地道
understand (to) míngbái 明白
university dàxué 大学
us wǒmen 我们
usually tōngcháng 通常

V

vacation jiàqī 假期
vanilla xiāngcǎo 香草
vegetables shūcài 蔬菜
vegetarian chīsù 吃素
very fēicháng 非常, tǐng 挺, hěn 很
volleyball páiqiú 排球
vomit (to) tùle 吐了

W

wait (to) děng 等
walk (to) zǒu 走
want (to) yào 要
Do you want …? Nǐ yào…ma? 你要 … 吗?
want (to), would like … xiǎng 想
wash (to) xǐ 洗
watch shǒubiǎo 手表
watch (to) kàn 看
watch TV (to) kàn diànshì 看电视
water shuǐ 水
we wǒmen 我们
wear (to) chuān 穿
Wednesday xīngqī sān 星期三
week xīngqī 星期
week lǐbài 礼拜
weekday (lit., workday) gōngzuòrì 工作日
weekend zhōumò 周末
well hǎo 好
well … nà 那
west xī 西
western cuisine xī cān 西餐
what shénme 什么
What nationality? Nǎ guórén? 哪国人?
what time shénme shíhou 什么时候
What time is it now? Xiànzài jǐdiǎn? 现在几点?
what time? jǐdiǎn 几点
what's more … érqiě 而且
when jǐdiǎn 几点, shénme shíhou 什么时候
where nǎli 哪里
Where (at)? Where is …? zài nǎli? 在哪里?
which nǎ 哪
which day nǎ tiān 哪天
which place nǎli 哪里
which station nǎge zhàn 哪个站
white bái, báisè 白, 白色
who, whom shéi 谁
whole body quánshēn 全身

why   wèishénme 为什么
wife   tàitai 太太
wlll   huì 会
wine   hóngjiǔ 红酒, jiǔ 酒
winter   dōngtiān 冬天
woman   nǚrén 女人
work   gōngzuò 工作
   work overtime (to)   jiābān 加班
   worker   gōngrén 工人
wrist   shǒuwàn 手腕
writing   xiězuò 写作

Y

year   nián 年
yellow   huáng 黄, huángsè 黄色
yesterday   zuótiān 昨天
   the day before yesterday   qiántiān 前天
yoga   yújiā 瑜伽
you   nǐ 你
you (plural)   nǐmen 你们
You're welcome.   Bù kèqi. 不客气。
young lady   xiǎojie 小姐
young, youthful   niánqīng 年轻
your (plural)   nǐmen de 你们的
your (singular)   nǐ de 你的
your (fml.)   nín de (fml.) 您的 (fml.)
yours (fml., plural)   nǐmen de 你们的

Z

zero   líng 零

Chinese - English

A

ài 爱   to love
àihào 爱好   hobbies
Àozhōu 澳洲   Australia
Àozhōurén 澳洲人   Australian

B

bā yuè 八月   August
bā 八   eight
ba 吧   particle for softening commands
bǎ 把   to grasp, measure word for knives
bàba 爸爸   dad
bái 白   white
báicài 白菜   napa cabbage
bǎihuò gōngsī 百货公司   department store
báisè 白色   white
bǎmài 把脉   to check (someone's) pulse
bàngōngshì 办公室   office
bàn 半   half
bàngqiú 棒球   baseball
bàng 磅   pound
bāngbǔ 帮补   to supplement (money)
bāngzhù 帮助   to help
bànyè 半夜   midnight
bāo 包   bag
bāoxīncài 包心菜   cabbage
bāozā shāngkǒu 包扎伤口   to bandage to a wound
bàozhǐ 报纸   newspaper
bēi 杯   measure word for water, coffee, tea, wine; cup, glass
běi 北   north
bèibù 背部   back
Běijīng (kǎo) yā 北京烤鸭   Peking duck
Běijīngrén 北京人   Pekingese
bēizi 杯子   cup, glass
běn 本   measure word for books, photo albums, magazines
bǐ 比   particle used for comparison (than)
bǐ 笔   pen
biàn 遍   times
biānzhī 编织   knitting
biǎodì 表弟   cousin (mother's sibling's or father's sister's son, younger than you)
biǎogē 表哥   cousin (mother's sibling's or father's

sister's son, older than you)

biǎojiě 表姐 cousin (mother's sibling's or father's sister's daughter, older than you)

biǎomèi 表妹 cousin (mother's sibling's or father's sister's daughter, younger than you)

bié 别 negative particle used for commands

bǐjiào 比较 relatively, comparatively

bìng 病 illness

bīngjílíng 冰激凌 ice cream

bìngle 病了 be sick

bīngxiāng 冰箱 refrigerator

bǐrú 比如 such as, for example

bìxū 必须 to have to, must

bìyè 毕业 to graduate

bízi 鼻子 nose, trunk

bóbo 伯伯 uncle (father's older brother)

bómǔ 伯母 aunt (father's older brother's wife)

bówùguǎn 博物馆 museum

bózi 脖子 neck

bù 不 no, not

bùcuò 不错 pretty good, not bad

bù gòu 不够 fewer than (lit. not enough)

Bù hǎoyìsi. 不好意思。 I'm sorry. (lit., to find it embarrassing (to do something))

Bù kèqi. 不客气。 You're welcome.

bù shūfu 不舒服 to feel unwell

bù xǐhuan 不喜欢 to dislike

bùtóng 不同 different

bùyào 不要 negative particle used for commands

bùyòng 不用 no need to

C

cài 菜 dish of food

càidān 菜单 menu

cǎihóng 彩虹 rainbow

càishìchǎng 菜市场 food market

cānguǎn 餐馆 restaurant

cānjīn 餐巾 napkin

cānkǎoshū 参考书 reference book

cèsuǒ 厕所 restroom

chá 茶 tea

chà (chà shí fēn yī diǎn) 差 (差十分一点) to, before (ten minutes to/before one o'clock)

chàbùduō 差不多 almost

cháng 尝 to taste

chǎng 敞 to open

chànggē 唱歌 to sing

chǎo 吵 noisy

chǎo 炒 stir-fried

chǎocài 炒菜 stir-fried dish

chāzi 叉子 fork

chē 车 car

chéngjì 成绩 academic performance

chéngshì 城市 city

chènshān 衬衫 shirt

chī yào 吃药 to take medicine

chī 吃 to eat

chīsù 吃素 vegetarian

chū zhěn 出诊 to make a medical house call (a doctor)

chǔ 储 to save

chuàn 串 measure word for objects that are small and round, bunch, cluster

chuān 穿 to wear

chuán 船 ship

chuáng 床 bed

chuánzhēnjī 传真机 fax machine

chūchāi 出差 to take a business trip

chúfáng 厨房 kitchen

chūguó 出国 to leave one's own country, to go abroad

chuī dízi 吹笛子 to play the flute

chuī 吹 to blow

chūnjuǎn 春卷 spring rolls

chūntiān 春天 spring

chūzūchē 出租车 taxi

cì 次 time(s)

cóng 从 from

cóng … dào … 从 … 到 … from … to …

cónglái méiyǒu 从来没有 never

cōngmáng 匆忙 in a hurry, in a rush

cōngmíng 聪明 intelligent

cún 存:: to store up

D

dǎ chéng píngshǒu 打成平手 to tie the score

dǎ diànhuà 打电话 to make a phone call

dǎ gǔ 打鼓 to play drums

dǎ qiú 打球 to play ball

dǎ shígāo 打石膏 to have a plaster cast

dǎ zhēn 打针 to give/get an injection

dà 大 large, big

dǎ 打 to hit, to play (ball games with hands, bridge, and drums)

dā 搭 take (a form of transportation)

dàgài 大概 approximately, about

dàhào 大号 large (size)

dāi 待 (呆) to stay

dàlóu 大楼 building

dàngāo 蛋糕 cake

dǎng'àn 档案 file

dǎng'àn guì 档案柜 filing cabinet

dāngrán 当然 of course

dāo 刀 knife

dǎsuan 打算 to plan

dàtuǐ 大腿 thigh

dǎyìnjī 打印机 printer

dàxué 大学 university

dàyuē 大约 about

dǎzhé 打折 to give a discount

de 得 adverbial particle

de 的 adjectival particle, possessive particle

Déguó 德国 Germany

Déguórén 德国人 German (people)

Děng huìr jiàn! 等会见! See you later!

děng 等 to wait

Déwén德文 German (language)

dì 第 prefix for ordinal numbers

diǎn cài 点菜 to order a dish

diǎn 点 to order (food); o'clock

diǎn zhōng点钟 o'clock, hour

diànhuà 电话 telephone

diànhuàtíng 电话亭 telephone booth

diànnǎo 电脑 computer

diànshì 电视 television

diǎnxīn 点心 dim sum

diànyǐng 电影 film, movie

diànyǐngyuàn 电影院 cinema, movie theater

diàoyú 钓鱼 fishing

dìdi 弟弟 younger brother

dìtiě 地铁 subway

dìtiě zhàn 地铁站 subway station

dìzhǐ 地址 address

dōng 东 east

dōngtiān 冬天 winter

dōu 都 all

dù 度 degree (temperature)

Duìbùqǐ. 对不起。 Excuse me. (apologizing)

duìmiàn 对面 across the street

dùn 顿 measure word for meal

duōjiǔ 多久 how long?

duōshǎo 多少 how much

dùzi tòng 肚子痛 to have abdominal pain

dùzi 肚子 belly

E

è 饿 hungry

èr yuè 二月 February

èr 二 two

ěrduo 耳朵 ear

érqiě 而且 moreover, what's more …

èrshí 二十 twenty

érzi 儿子 son

étóu 额头 forehead

Éwén俄文 Russian (language)

ěxin 恶心 to feel nauseous

F

fā chuánzhēn 发传真 to send a fax

fādǒu 发抖 to shiver

Fǎguó 法国 France

Fǎguórén 法国人 French (people)

fǎlǜ 法律 law

fàn hòu fú 饭后服 (medication) taken after a meal

fàn qián fú 饭前服 (medication) taken before a meal

fàn 饭 meal, food (lit., cooked rice)

fàndiàn 饭店 hotel

fàng 放 to put

fāngbiànmiàn 方便面 instant noodles

fàngjià 放假 on vacation, time off

fángjiān 房间 room

fànguǎn 饭馆 restaurant

fàngxué 放学 to finish class

fángzi 房子 house

fānqié 番茄 tomato

fàntīng 饭厅 dining room

fāshāo 发烧 to have a fever

Fǎwén法文 French (language)

fāyán 发炎 inflammation

fēicháng 非常 very

fēijī 飞机 airplane

fēijī chǎng 飞机场 airport

fēn 分 minute

fēn 分 one one-hundredth of a yuán, equivalent to the cent; minute(s)

féngxiàn 缝线 to stitch up (a wound)

fěnhóngsè 粉红色 pink

fēnzhōng 分钟 minute(s)

fù xiànjīn 付现金 to pay in cash

fù 付 to pay

fùjìn 附近 nearby

fùqin 父亲 father
fùxí 复习 to review a lesson
fúzhuāng diàn 服装店 clothing store

G

gǎndào 感到 to feel
gāngcái 刚才 just now
gānjìng 干净 clean
gǎnlǎnqiú 橄榄球 football (American)
gǎnmào 感冒 a cold
gāo 高 tall
gè 个 measure word for people, cities, groups, and nations
gēge 哥哥 older brother
Gěi wǒ … 给我 bring me … , give me …
gěi 给 to bring, to give
gèng 更 even more
Gōng xǐ nǐ! 恭喜你! Congratulations!
gōngchē 公车 bus
gōngchē zhàn 公车站 bus stop
gōngchéng shī 工程师 engineer
gōngchéng 工程 engineering
gōngjīn 公斤 kilogram
gōngkè 功课 homework
gōnglǐ 公里 kilometers
gōngrén 工人 laborer, worker
gōngsī 公司 company
gōngyù 公寓 apartment
gōngyuán 公园 park
gōngzuò rényuán 工作人员 staff
gōngzuò 工作 work, job, profession
gōngzuòrì 工作日 weekday (lit., workday)
gǒu 狗 dog
guǎi ge wān 拐个弯 turn around the corner
guān 关 shut, close
guàn 罐 can (noun)
guāng 光 all gone
Guǎngdōngrén 广东人 Cantonese
gǔdiǎn yīnyuè 古典音乐 classical music
gūfu 姑夫 uncle (father's sister's husband)
gūgu 姑姑 aunt (father's sister)
guì 贵 expensive
guò mǎlù 过马路 to cross the street
guò 过 particle indicating completion of an action
guòlái 过来 to come over
guòshí 过时 out of style
guǒzhī 果汁 juice
gùyuán 雇员 employee

H

haí 还 still
háishì 还是 or (suggesting a preference)
háiyǒu 还有 also, in addition
hànshān 汗衫 T-shirt
hǎo ba 好吧 ok, alright, go ahead
… hǎo bù hǎo? 好不好? … is it alright?
hǎo 好 good, fine, well
hǎochī 好吃 delicious
hē de 喝的 something to drink
hé 和 and
hē 喝 to drink
hé 盒 box, carton
hēi hújiāo 黑胡椒 black pepper
hēi 黑 black
hēisè 黑色 black
hěn duō cì 很多次 many times
hěn duō 很多 a lot, many, much
hěn jiǔ 很久 a long time
hěn, tǐng 很, 挺 very
hóng shāo zhūròu, hóng shāo ròu 红烧猪肉, 红烧肉 braised pork
hóng shāo 红烧 braised (in soy sauce)
hóng 红 red
hóngjiǔ 红酒 red wine
hónglùdēng 红绿灯 traffic light
hóngsè 红色 red
hòubiān 后边 behind
hòunián 后年 the year after next
hòutiān 后天 the day after tomorrow
huáxuě 滑雪 to ski
huài 坏 bad
huàn chē 换车 to change trains/subways/buses
huàn 换 to exchange
huǎnbùpǎo 缓步跑 jogging
huáng 黄 yellow
huángguā 黄瓜 cucumber
huángsè 黄色 yellow
huángyóu 黄油 butter
huàxué 化学 chemistry
huì 会 to know how to, will
huíguōròu 回锅肉 twice-cooked pork
huīsè 灰色 grey
Huítóu jiàn! 回头见! See you soon!
huìyì 会议 meeting
hújiāo 胡椒 pepper
húluóbo 胡萝卜 carrot

huǒchēzhàn 火车站 train station
huǒtuǐ 火腿 ham
huòzhě 或者 either ... or ...
hùshi 护士 nurse

J

jī 鸡 chicken
jǐ cì 几次 several times
jǐ ge 几个 several
jǐ tiān 几天 several days
jì xiàlái 记下来 to jot something down
jǐ 几 how many
jiā 家 family, home
jiābān 加班 to work overtime
jiákè 夹克 jacket
jiàn 件 measure word for garments worn over the upper part or full length of the body
jiàn 见 to see
Jiānádà 加拿大 Canada
jiānbǎng 肩膀 shoulder
jiǎnchá 检查 to examine, to check
jiǎng diànhuà 讲电话 on the phone
jiàngyóu 酱油 soy sauce
jiānzhí 兼职 part-time job
jiāo gōngkè 交功课 to submit homework
jiào 叫 to call, to be called
jiāo 教 to teach
jiǎo 脚 foot
jiǎo 角 one tenth of a yuán,
jiàoshì 教室 classroom
jiàotáng 教堂 church
jiàqī 假期 holiday, vacation
jiāyòng diànqì diàn 家用电器店 electronics store (lit., home appliances store)
jiāzhǎng 家长 parent
jīchǎng 机场 airport
jīdàn 鸡蛋 egg(s)
jǐdiǎn 几点 what time?, when?
jiē 街 street
jiémù 节目 program, show
jiějie 姐姐 older sister
jièmo 芥末 mustard
jièzhi 戒指 ring
jīguāng chàngpiàn 激光唱片 CD
jìjié 季节 season
jǐn 紧 tight
jìn 近 near
jǐngchá jú 警察局 police station

jǐngchá 警察 police officer
jīngcháng 经常 often, frequently
jìnlái 进来 come in
jīnnián 今年 this year
jīnsè 金色 gold
jīntiān wǎnshang 今天晚上 tonight
jīntiān xiàwǔ 今天下午 this afternoon
jīntiān zǎoshang 今天早上 this morning
jīntiān 今天 today
jīròu 鸡肉 chicken meat (boneless)
jiǔ yuè 九月 September
jiǔ 九 nine
jiù 旧 old (things)
jiǔ 酒 wine, alcoholic drink
jiùjiu 舅舅 uncle (mother's brother)
jiùmǔ/jiùmā 舅母, 舅妈 aunt (mother's brother's wife)
jiǔshí 九十 ninety
jízhōng jīngshén 集中精神 to concentrate
júsè 橘色 orange (color)
júzi 橘子 orange (fruit)

K

kāfēi 咖啡 coffee
kāichē 开车 to drive (a car)
kāihuì 开会 in a meeting, to have a meeting
kāimíng 开明 open-minded, enlightened
kāishǐ 开始 to start
kàn 看 to see, to look, to read
kàn diànyǐng 看电影 to go to a movie/the movies
kàn dìtú 看地图 to read a map
kàn qǐlái 看起来 appear(s) to be
kàn shū 看书 read a book
kàn xìjù 看戏剧 to see a play
kànjiàn 看见 to see
kǎo jī 烤鸡 roast chicken
kǎo 烤 roast
kǎo 考 to test
kǎoshì 考试 test, examination, to take an exam
kěnéng 可能 maybe, perhaps
kè 课 class
kè 刻 quarter of an hour
kē 棵 measure word for plants and grass
kē 颗 measure word for small plants and vegetables
kèběn 课本 textbook
kèqi 客气 polite
késou 咳嗽 cough

kètīng 客厅 living room

kèwài huódòng 课外活动 extracurricular activities

kěyǐ 可以 to be able (in terms of permission), to be allowed

kǒu 口 mouth; measure word for number of family members

kǔ 苦 bitter

Kuài … le 快　了 almost time to do something (lit. quickly … as of now)

kuài 块 colloquial word for yuán

kuài 快 fast, quick

kuàijìshī 会计师 accountant

kuàijì 会计 accounting

kuàilè 快乐 happy

kuàizi 筷子 chopsticks

kuǎnshì 款式 style

kùzi 裤子 pants

L

lā dùzi 拉肚子 to have diarrhea

lā xiǎotíqín 拉小提琴 to play violin

lā 拉 to pull

là 辣 hot, spicy

lái 来 to come

lánqiú 篮球 basketball

lán 蓝 blue

lánsè 蓝色 blue

lǎobǎn 老板 boss

Láojià. 劳驾。 Excuse me. (asking for a favor)

lǎoshī 老师 teacher

le 了 particle indicating that an action has been completed

lěng 冷 cold

lǐ 里 place, in

liǎn 脸 face

liáng tǐwēn 量体温 to take (someone's) temperature

liǎng 两 two (used to describe amount), measure word for cars, taxis, bicycles

liǎnjiá 脸颊 cheek

liànxí 练习 to practice

liányīqún 连衣裙 dress

lǐbài 礼拜 week

lǐbiān 里边 in, inside

lijiāoqiáo 立交桥 overpass

líng 零 zero

língqián 零钱 change (monetary)

línjū 邻居 neighbor

lìshǐ 历史 history

liù yuè 六月 June

liù 六 six

liú 留 to stay, to keep

liúxiě 流血 to bleed

liúxíng yīnyuè 流行音乐 pop music

liúxíng 流行 popular, trendy

liúyán 留言 to leave a message

lǐyú 鲤鱼 carp

lóngxiā 龙虾 lobster

lǜ 绿 green

lù 路 road

lǚguǎn 旅馆 hotel

lùkǒu 路口 corner, intersection, block

lǜsè 绿色 green

lǜshī 律师 lawyer

lǚxíng 旅行 travel

M

ma 吗 question particle

máfan 麻烦 to trouble

　máfan nǐ 麻烦你 Could you…? (lit., bother you)

　Máfan nǐ gěi wǒmen … 麻烦你给我们 …
　　Could I trouble you for …

mǎi 买 to buy

màipiàn 麦片 cereal

Májiàng 麻将 Mahjong

mǎlíngshǔ 马铃薯 potatoes

māma 妈妈 mom

màn 慢 slow, slowly

mànpǎo 慢跑 jogging

māo 猫 cat

máo 毛 equivalent to the dime; colloquial word for jiāo

máoyī 毛衣 sweater

màozi 帽子 hat

měi ge rén 每个人 everyone

Méi shì. 没事。 It's nothing., Don't worry., No problem.

měi tiān 每天 every day

měi 每 every, each

méiguì 玫瑰 rose

Měiguó 美国 America

Měiguórén 美国人 American (people)

mèimei 妹妹 younger sister

Méiyǒu wèntí. 没有问题。 No problem.

méiyǒu 没有 don't/doesn't have

ménkǒu 门口 in front of (lit. at the door)
mǐ 米 meters
miànbāo 面包 bread
miànshì 面试 interview
miàntiáo 面条 noodles
miǎo 秒 second(s)
míngbai 明白 to understand
míngnián 明年 next year
míngtiān 明天 tomorrow
mógu 蘑菇 mushrooms
mótuōchē 摩托车 motorcycle
mǔqīn 母亲 mother

N

nǎge zhàn 哪个站 which station
Nǎ guórén? 哪国人? What nationality?
nǎ tiān 哪天 which day
nàxiē 那些 those
nǎ 哪 which
ná 拿 to hold, to take
nà 那 that
nà … 那 … that, well …, in this/that case …
nǎichá 奶茶 milk tea
nǎinai 奶奶 grandmother (paternal side)
nàli 那里 there
nǎli 哪里 where, which place
nǎli yě 哪里也 anywhere
nán 南 south
nán 男 male
nán 难 difficult
nánhái 男孩 boy
nánháir 男孩儿 boy
Nánjīngrén 南京人 Nanjingese
nánrén 男人 man
nǎr yě 哪儿也 anywhere
nèikù 内裤 underpants
nèn 嫩 tender
néng(gòu) 能够 to be able (in terms of proficiency)
nǐ 你 you
nǐ de 你的 your, yours (singular)
nǐ hǎo 你好 hello
Nǐ hǎo ma? 你好吗? How are you?
Nǐ kěyǐ gěi wǒ … ma? 你可以给我 … 吗?
　　May I have… ? (lit., Could you give me … ?)
Nǐ ne? 你呢? And you?
Nǐ yào…ma? 你要 … 吗? Do you want … ?
nián 年 year
niánqīng 年轻 young, youthful

nǐmen de 你们的 your, yours (plural)
Nǐmen yǒu … ma? 你们有 … 吗? Do you have
　　… ?
nǐmen 你们 you (plural)
nín de 您的 your/yours (fml.)
niúnǎi 牛奶 milk
niúpái 牛排 steak
niúròu 牛肉 beef
nǚ 女 female
nǚ'ér 女儿 daughter
nǚháir 女孩儿 girl
nǚháizi 女孩子 girl
nǚhái 女孩 girl
nǚrén 女人 woman

P

pà 怕 to be scared of, to fear
pái dì yī míng 排第一名 to be placed first
páigǔ 排骨 spare ribs
páiqiú 排球 volleyball
pán 盘 measure word of general unit of ordering
　　food; dish, plate
pángbiān 旁边 next to
pángtīng 旁听 to audit a class
pánzi 盘子 plate
pēngrèn 烹饪 cooking
péngyou 朋友 friend
piào 票 ticket
piàn 片 measure word for tile, tablets, other thin
　　and flat objects; slice
piányi 便宜 inexpensive
piàoliang 漂亮 beautiful, pretty
pídài 皮带 belt
píjiǔ 啤酒 beer
píng 瓶 measure word for bottled drinks; bottle
píngguǒ 苹果 apple
pútao 葡萄 grape

Q

qī 七 seven
qī yuè 七月 July
qí zìxíngchē 骑自行车 cycling
qí 骑 to ride
qiǎn lǜsè 浅绿色 light green
qiǎn 浅 light
qián 钱 money
qiánbiān 前边 in front of
qiángzhuàng 强壮 strong

qiánnián 前年 the year before last
qiántiān 前天 the day before yesterday
qiáo 桥 bridge
qiǎokèlì 巧克力 chocolate
qìchē 汽车 car
qíncài 芹菜 celery
qǐng 请 please (used to make an invitation or ask a favor)
qǐng (shì)jià 请（事）假 to take personal leave
qǐng bìngjià 请病假 to take sick leave
Qǐng nǐ jiézhàng! 请你结帐! Check please!
qǐng nǐ/nín 请你/您 please … (lit., please you …), may I …
qǐng wèn 请问 May I ask … ?
Qǐng zài shuō yī cì. 请再说一次. Please say that again.
qīng zhēng yú 清蒸鱼 steamed fish
qīng zhēng 清蒸 steamed
Qǐng zuò. 请坐. Have a seat., Please sit.
qīnglǐ 清理 to clean, to tidy
qípáo 旗袍 traditional Chinese dress
qiú 球 ball
qiūtiān 秋天 autumn
qù 去 to go
qù hǎitān 去海滩 to go to the beach
qù tǐyùguǎn 去体育馆 to go to a stadium
qù yīyuàn 去医院 to go the hospital
qù zhěnsuǒ 去诊所 to go to a clinic
quánshēn 全身 whole body
qūgùnqiú 曲棍球 hockey
qùnián 去年 last year
qúnkù 裙裤 culottes, skort
qúnzi 裙子 skirt

R

ràng … ba 让 … 吧 let …
ràng 让 to allow, to let
ràng wǒ 让我 let me
ránhòu 然后 after that, afterwards, then
rén 人 person, people
rènào 热闹 lively, busy, bustling
Rénmínbì 人民币 official Chinese currency
rènshi 认识 to know (someone), to meet
rénxíng dìdào 人行地道 underpass
rénxíngdào 人行道 sidewalk
Rìběn 日本 Japan
Rìběnrén 日本人 Japanese (people)
Rìwén 日文 Japanese (language)
ròu 肉 meat

rǔguǒ … jiù 如果 … 就 if … (then)
rúguǒ 如果 if

S

sān yuè 三月 March
sān 三 three
sǎngzi tòng 嗓子痛 to have a sore throat
sǎngzi 嗓子 throat
sānshí 三十 thirty
sè 色 color
shāfā 沙发 sofa
shālā 沙拉 salad
shàngbān 上班 to go to work, to be at work
shàng chē 上车 to get on (a vehicle)
shàng dàxué 上大学 to attend university
shàng ge lǐbài 上个礼拜 last week
shàng ge yuè 上个月 last month
shàngxué 上学 to go to school, to attend school
shàngbiān, shàng 上边,上 on (top of)
shāngdiàn 商店 shop/store
Shànghǎirén 上海人 Shanghaiese
shàngkè 上课 to attend (a) class, to go to class
shàngwǎng 上网 to go online
shāocài 烧菜 to cook
shāofàn 烧饭 to cook
sháozi 勺子 spoon
shéi 谁 who, whom
shēn 深 dark (colors)
shěng 省 to economize
shēnghuófèi 生活费 cost of living
shēngrì 生日 birthday
shēngwù 生物 biology
shénme dōngxi yě 什么东西也 anything
shénme rén yě, shéi yě 什么人也, 谁也 anyone
shénme shíhou 什么时候 what time, when
shénme 什么 what
shēnqǐng 申请 to apply
shēnshen 婶婶 aunt (father's younger brother's wife)
shétou 舌头 tongue
shī 诗 poetry
shí'èr yuè 十二月 December
shíyī yuè 十一月 November
shí yuè 十月 October
shí 十 ten
shì 是 to be
shìchǎng 市场 market
shí'er 十二 twelve

Advanced Chinese

shíhou 时候 **time** (in broad terms)
shíjiān 时间 **time** (in hour and minutes)
shímáo 时髦 **fashionable, in style**
shíwù 食物 **food**
shíyànshì 实验室 **laboratory**
shíyī 十一 **eleven**
shízhōng 时钟 **clock**
shízì lùkǒu 十字路口 **intersection**
shòuhuòyuán 售货员 **store clerk**
shǒu 手 **hand**
shǒubiǎo 手表 **watch**
shǒuwàn 手腕 **wrist**
shōuyīnjī 收音机 **radio**
shǒuzhǐ 手指 **finger**
shū 书 **book**
shuākǎ 刷卡 **to pay by credit card**
shuāng 双 **pair**
shūcài 蔬菜 **vegetables**
shūdiàn 书店 **bookstore**
shuì 睡 **to sleep**
shuìjiào 睡，睡觉 **to sleep**
shuǐ 水 **water**
shuǐguǒ 水果 **fruit**
shūjià 书架 **bookshelf**
shuō 说 **to say, to speak**
shūshu 叔叔 **uncle** (father's younger brother)
shúxī 熟悉 **to be familiar with**
sì yuè 四月 **April**
sì 四 **four**
sìjìdòu 四季豆 **string beans**
sīrén bǔxí 私人补习 **private tutoring**
sìshí 四十 **forty**
suān 酸 **sour**
suàntóu 蒜头 **garlic**
sūdǎ shuǐ 苏打水 **soda**
suǒyǐ 所以 **therefore**

T

tā de 他的 **his**
tā de 她的 **her** (possessive pronoun), **hers**
tā 他 **he, him**
tā 她 **she, her**
tái 台 **measure word for machines**
tài 太 **too**
Tàijíquán 太极拳 **Taiji / Tai Chi**
tàitai 太太 **Mrs., wife**
tāmen de 他们的 **their, theirs**
tāmen 他们 **they, them**

tán gāngqín 弹钢琴 **to play piano**
tán 弹 **to play** (piano), **to pluck**
tāng 汤 **soup**
tàng 烫 **hot, scalding**
táng 糖 **sugar, candy**
tǎng 躺 **to lie down**
tāngchí 汤匙 **spoon**
tángdì 堂弟 **cousin** (father's brother's son, younger than you)
tánggē 堂哥 **cousin** (father's brother's son, older than you)
tángjiě 堂姐 **cousin** (father's brother's daughter, older than you)
tángmèi 堂妹 **cousin** (father's brother's daughter, younger than you)
tántan 谈谈 **to have a chat, to discuss**
tǐyù 体育 **sports**
tī zúqiú 踢足球 **to play soccer**
tī 踢 **to kick**
tiān 天 **day**
tián 甜 **sweet**
tiándiǎn 甜点 **dessert**
tiáo 条 **measure word for garments worn over the lower half of the body, or for the objects that are long and thin, also for animals** (dogs, fish, bulls...)
tiàowǔ 跳舞 **to dance**
tīng 听 **to listen**
tǐng 挺 **quite, very**
tīngdào 听到 **to hear**
tǐwēn 体温 **temperature** (body)
tíxǐng 提醒 **to remind**
tǐyù 体育 **sport**
tōngcháng 通常 **usually**
tóngshì 同事 **colleague**
tóngxué 同学 **classmate**
tóu tòng 头痛 **to have a headache**
tóuyūn 头晕 **to feel dizzy**
tǔdòu 土豆 **potato**
túhuà 图画 **painting**
tuǐ 腿 **leg**
tùle 吐了 **to vomit**
túshūguǎn 图书馆 **library**
túshūzhèng 图书证 **library card**
T-xùshān T-恤衫 **T-shirt**

W

wàibiān 外边 **outside**
wàigōng 外公 **grandfather** (maternal side)

wàiguó 外国 foreign

wàipó 外婆 grandmother (maternal side)

wàitào 外套 coat

wàiyǔ 外语 foreign language

wán de kāixīn 玩得开心 to have fun

wán yóuxì 玩游戏 to play a game

wǎn 碗 measure word for soup, rice; bowl

wǎn 晚 evening

wǎncān 晚餐 dinner, supper

wǎng qián 往前 to go ahead

wǎng yòu zhuǎn 往右转 turn right

wǎng zuǒ zhuǎn 往左传 turn left

wàng 忘 to forget

wǎngqiú 网球 tennis

wǎnshang 晚上 evening, night

wàzi 袜子 socks

wèi tòng 胃痛 to have a stomachache

wèishēngjiān 卫生间 bathroom

wèishénme 为什么 why

wèn 问 to ask

wénjiàn 文件 document, file

wènlù 问路 to ask directions (lit., to ask the road)

wēnxí 温习 to review

wǒ bù xiǎng … 我不想 … I don't want to …

wǒ de 我的 my, mine

Wǒ xiǎng yào … 我想要 … I would like to have …

Wǒ yào … 我要 … I need …

wǒ 我 I, me

wòfáng 卧房 bedroom

wǒmen de 我们的 our, ours

wǒmen 我们 we, us

wǔ yuè 五月 May

wǔ 五 five

wǔcān 午餐 lunch

wùlǐ 物理 physics

X

xì 系 department (college level)

xī càn 西餐 western cuisine

xǐ 洗 to wash

xī 西 west

xiā 虾 shrimp

xià chē 下车 to get off (a vehicle)

Xià cì jiàn! 下次见! See you next time!

xià ge lǐbài 下个礼拜 next week

xià ge yuè 下个月 next month

xiàbiān, xià 下边, 下 under

xiān 先 first

xián 咸 salty

xiǎng 想 to want, think, would like …

xiàng 象 elephant

xiāngcǎo 香草 vanilla

Xiānggǎngrén 香港人 Hongkongese

xiāngjiāo 香蕉 banana

xiànjīn 现金 cash

xiānsheng 先生 Mr., husband

Xiànzài jǐdiǎn? 现在几点? What time is it now?

xiànzài 现在 now

xiǎo zhèn 小镇 small town

xiǎo 小 small

xiǎojie 小姐 Miss., young lady

xiǎoshí 小时 hour (amount of time)

xiǎoshuō 小说 novel

xiǎotuǐ 小腿 calf

xiǎoxīn 小心 to be careful

xiāoyè 宵夜 late night snack

xiàoyuán 校园 campus

xiàozhǎng 校长 principal

xiàtiān 夏天 summer

xiàwǔ 下午 afternoon

Xībānyá 西班牙 Spain

Xībānyárén 西班牙人 Spanish (people)

Xībānyáwén 西班牙文 Spanish (language)

Xièxie. 谢谢。 Thank you.

xiédiàn 鞋店 shoe store

xiézi 鞋子 shoes

xiězuò 写作 writing

xǐhuan 喜欢 to like

xīn 新 new

xīngqī èr 星期二 Tuesday

xīngqī liù 星期六 Saturday

xīngqī sān 星期三 Wednesday

xīngqī sì 星期四 Thursday

xīngqī tiān 星期天 Sunday

xīngqī wǔ 星期五 Friday

xīngqī yī 星期一 Monday

xīngqī 星期 week

xìng 姓 surname, to be called

xìngqù 兴趣 interest

xīnshuǐ 薪水 salary

xiōngbù tòng 胸部痛 to have chest pain

xiōngbù 胸部 chest

xiōngdìjiěmèi 兄弟姐妹 sibling

xǐshǒujiān 洗手间 restroom

xiūxi 休息 to rest

xìyuàn 戏院 theater
xué 学 to study, to learn
xuésheng 学生 student
xuéxiào 学校 school
xuēzi 靴子 boots

Y

yā 鸭 duck
yáchǐ 牙齿 tooth
yángcōng 洋葱 onion
yǎnjing 眼睛 eye
yánjiūshēng 研究生 graduate student
yánsè 颜色 color
yánjiūyuàn, yánjiūsuǒ 研究院, 研究所 graduate school
yàofáng 药房 pharmacy
yào 要 to want
yě 也 also
yèxiāo 夜宵 late night snack
yéye 爷爷 grandfather (paternal side)
yībǎiwàn 一百万 one million
yībǎi 一百 one hundred
yī bēi jiǔ 一杯酒 a glass of wine
yī dǎ 一打 one dozen
yī diǎndiǎn 一点点 a few/a little
yī huìr 一会儿 a while
yīqiān 一千 one thousand
yīwàn 一万 ten thousand
yī yuè 一月 January
yī 一 one
Yìdàlì 意大利 Italy
Yìdàlìrén 意大利人 Italian (people)
Yìdàlìwén 意大利文 Italian (language)
yífu 姨夫 uncle (mother's sister's husband)
yīfu 衣服 clothes, clothing
yímǔ/yímā 姨母/姨妈 aunt (mother's sister)
yìnbiǎojī 印表机 printer
yīnggāi 应该 should, ought to
Yīngguó 英国 Britain
Yīngguórén 英国人 British (people)
Yīngwén 英文 English (language)
yínháng 银行 bank
yínsè 银色 silver
yīnwèi 因为 because
yīnyuè 音乐 music
yīqǐ 一起 together
yǐqián 以前 ago
yīqiè 一切 everything

yīshēng 医生 doctor
yīxiē 一些 some
yīyàng 一样 same
yīyuàn 医院 hospital
yīzhí wǎng qián zǒu 一直往前走 go straight ahead
yīzhí 一直 straight
yǐzi 椅子 chair
yòng zhīpiào fùqián 用支票付钱 to pay by check
yōngjǐ 拥挤 crowded
yǒu duō yuǎn? 有多远? how far?
yǒu rén 有人 someone
yóuyǒng 游泳 to swim
yòu 右 right
yǒu 有 to have, there is/are
yòu … yòu … 又 … 又 … and (for connecting two adjectives or adverbs)
yǒu … nàme 有 … 那么 as … adjective/adverb as … (used for people and things far away)
yǒu … zhème 有 … 这么 as … adjective/adverb as … (used for people and things nearby)
… yǒu méiyǒu … ? … 有没有 … ? Do (you) have … ?
yòubiān 右边 the right side of
yóujú 邮局 post office
yú 鱼 fish
yuán 元 currency unit, equivalent to the dollar unit
yuǎn 远 far
yuángōng 员工 staff
yuǎnzú 远足 hiking
yuè lái yuè 越来越 more and more, less and less
yuè 月 month
yuē 约 to make an appointment, to make a date
yújiā 瑜伽 yoga
yǔmáoqiú 羽毛球 badminton
yùndòngxié 运动鞋 sneakers
yùxí 预习 to prepare for a lesson
yǔyī 雨衣 raincoat
yùyuē 预约 to make an appointment

Z

zài … hé … zhōngjiān 在 … 和 … 中间 between … and …
Zài gěi wǒ … 再给我 … Give me another …
zài jiā 在家 at home
Zàijiàn. 再见。 Goodbye.
zài lái … 再来 … one more, another
zài lái yīdiǎn … 再来一点 … a little more of …

zài lùkǒu 在路口 on the corner
zài nàli 在那里 over there
zài nǎli? 在哪里? (At) where? Where is … ?
zài nǎli? 在哪里? Where is … ?
zài 再 again
zài 在 at, in, on; particle indicating an ongoing
   action, to be (located) at
zāng 脏 dirty
zǎocān 早餐 breakfast
zǎoshang 早上 morning
zěnme yàng? 怎么样 how … ?
zěnme zǒu 怎么走 how to get to … ?
zěnyàng 怎样 what, how
zhàn 站 to stand
zhāng 张 measure word for objects that have a
   flat surface (tables, desks, chairs…)
zhāngkāi 张开 to open (the mouth)
zhǎo 找 to look for, to find
zháoliáng 着凉 to catch a cold
zhàopiàn 照片 photograph
zhàoxiàngjī 照相机 camera
zhèbiān 这边 this way
zhège lǐbài 这个礼拜 this week
zhège yuè 这个月 this month
zhèxiē 这些 these
zhe 着 particle indicating an ongoing state of being
zhè 这 this
zhèlǐ 这里 here
zhéxué 哲学 philosophy
zhī 只 measure word for objects that are pointed
   and thin, utensils, and some animals
zhǐ 纸 paper
zhīdào 知道 to know a fact, to know something
zhīhòu 之后 after
zhǐjia 指甲 fingernail
zhīpiào 支票 check (payment)
zhīqián 之前 before
zhǐshì 只是 it's only …
zhǒng 种 kind (noun)
Zhōngcài 中菜 Chinese cuisine
Zhōngguó 中国 China
Zhōngguórén 中国人 Chinese (people)
zhōnghào 中号 medium (size)
zhōngjiān 中间 between
zhōngtóu 钟头 hour (amount of time)
Zhōngwén 中文 Chinese (language)
zhōngwǔ 中午 noon
zhōngyú 终于 finally

zhǒu 肘 elbow
zhōumò 周末 weekend
zhù zài 住在 to live in
zhuānyè, zhǔxiū 专业, 主修 major
zhǔnbèi 准备 to prepare
zhǔnshí 准时 on time
zhuōzi 桌子 table
zhūpái 猪排 pork chop(s)
zhūròu 猪肉 pork
zìdiǎn 字典 dictionary
zìjǐ 自己 self
zǐsè 紫色 purple
zìxíngchē 自行车 bicycle
zōngsè 棕色 brown
zǒngshì 总是 always
Zǒu ba. 走吧。 Leave. (polite)
zǒulù 走路 on foot
zǒu 走 to leave, to walk
zǒu 走 to leave, to get out
zúgēn 足跟 heel
zuì hāo de 最好的 the best
zuì 最 the most
zuǐba 嘴巴 mouth
zuǐchún 嘴唇 lips
zuìhòu qīxiàn 最后期限 deadline
zuò xīndiàntú 做心电图 to take a cardiogram
zuò yùndòng 做运动 to play a sport
zuò 做 to do, to make
zuò 坐 sit, to take (a form of transportation)
zuǒ 左 left
zuǒbiān 左边 the left side of
zuòfàn 做饭 to cook
zuótiān 昨天 yesterday
zuǒyòu 左右 around
zúqiú 足球 soccer (football)